Praise for *Just Jones*

"*Just Jones* is lightning in a bottle—pure genius on paper. If you can imagine a hilarious mystery filled with useful wisdom that is fresh and new, you've just conjured up this book. Andy Andrews is our generation's Mark Twain. *Just Jones* is the latest proof."

—DAVE RAMSEY
NATIONAL BESTSELLING AUTHOR

"*Just Jones* is a rare accomplishment—a mystery that is at times touching but often so funny that I laughed out loud. When one wraps an awesome story around wisdom with the power to change lives . . . well, how many great books can you name like that? *Just Jones* is a masterpiece."

—MICHAEL HYATT
NEW YORK TIMES BESTSELLING AUTHOR

"'A jail is also a near-perfect starting gate.' And with this bit of wisdom, Jones, whom we have come to know as the *noticer*, leads us into another can't-stop-reading story. Or is it a biography of the reader? Andy Andrews is the master of telling tales that end up being all about us. His newest weaving, *Just Jones*, is no exception. I dare you to read it! Then order a dozen copies to send to people who are longing for someone to tell them a story about themselves *as they could be*."

—GLORIA GAITHER
WRITER, LYRICIST

"Andy's work has profoundly impacted me, and his newest release, *Just Jones*, reminds us that just because something hasn't yet been done, doesn't mean that it can't be accomplished. After reading this book, you will not only be more convinced than ever that the only limitations on your life are the ones you put on yourself but also realize that now is the time to stop making excuses, start making a difference, and begin fully living your life."

—JOHN O'LEARY
#1 NATIONAL BESTSELLING AUTHOR, PODCAST HOST, AND SPEAKER

"This latest soon-to-be-classic from Andy Andrews continues to challenge us to think about life and our current situations from different and unique perspectives. And always with the focus of helping us evolve, grow, and prosper. In addition, the story that surrounds and propels all this valuable information is one of the best (and most fun) you'll ever read."

—STEVE JACOBSON
CEO FAIRWAY MORTGAGE

Other Books by Andy Andrews

NOVELS

Return to Sawyerton Springs
The Heart Mender
The Lost Choice
The Noticer
The Noticer Returns
The Traveler's Gift
The Traveler's Summit

NONFICTION

How Do You Kill 11 Million People?
The Bottom of the Pool
The Butterfly Effect
The Little Things
The Seven Decisions
The Traveler's Gift Journal

YOUNG ADULT

The Young Traveler's Gift

CHILDREN'S AND GIFT

Baseball, Boys, and Bad Words
Henry Hodges Needs a Friend
The Kid Who Changed the World
The Perfect Moment
Socks for Christmas

Just
JONES

Sometimes a thing is impossible . . .
until it is actually done

ANDY
ANDREWS

W PUBLISHING GROUP

AN IMPRINT OF THOMAS NELSON

Published in Nashville, Tennessee, by W Publishing Group, an imprint of Thomas Nelson.

Thomas Nelson titles may be purchased in bulk for educational, business, fundraising, or sales promotional use. For information, please e-mail SpecialMarkets@ThomasNelson.com.

Any internet addresses, phone numbers, or company or product information printed in this book are offered as a resource and are not intended in any way to be or to imply an endorsement by Thomas Nelson, nor does Thomas Nelson vouch for the existence, content, or services of these sites, phone numbers, companies, or products beyond the life of this book.

ISBN 978-0-7852-2657-4 (eBook)

Library of Congress Control Number: 2020940130

ISBN 978-0-7852-2656-7 (HC)

Printed in the United States of America

20 21 22 23 24   LSC   10 9 8 7 6 5 4 3 2 1

Dedicated to my sons, Austin and Adam:
I could not be more proud of the men you continue to become.

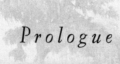

Prologue

The Land Between Two Rivers at the Time of Emergence

Adapted from the Historical Record of the Muscogee (Creek) Nation

It was the first story to be told. In the beginning, Hesaketvmese created sky and dirt and water. Soon He made the eagle to guard the sky, corn to spring from the dirt, and fish to keep the bugs out of the water. Seeing that it was all good, Hesaketvmese then made His children.

In the moment of first breath, Hesaketvmese swept His left hand across the land and spread a giant cloud of fog around His children. They could not see each other and were quickly separated. Groups began to form as they located first one, then another in the mist—but as they tried to find their way, each group moved farther from the others.

When the fog finally began to blow away, the people who were first able to see called themselves the Wind Clan. As the fog cleared from all the land, clans took their names from the first things they saw and so became the Bear, Deer, Turkey, Alligator, Raccoon, and Bird Clans.

By this time, just as Hesaketvmese had intended, His children had scattered to the four directions. Some went to the rising sun; some wandered the other way and made their homes where the sun hides itself in the darkness. Many journeyed into the cold wind until they had to build shelter, while most of the rest walked until coming to the big water. There, it is said that Hesaketvmese fed them with food from inside wet stones.

Of all Hesaketvmese's children, only the Wind Clan chose to stay where He had made them—in the land between two rivers.

Hesaketvmese had worked hard to forge His people and make a beautiful home for them. As He saw that it was good, the Master of Breath swept His right hand in a circle and built a place of rest for Himself. Surrounded by a vast beaver ruin and across a great swamp ran a long, narrow lake that connected two mighty rivers—the Alibamu and the Chikashsha. There, on a high bluff overlooking the ancient lake, Hesaketvmese created what all would call the "Place of Coverings."

He placed twelve oak trees in a wide circle. When He had arranged them perfectly, Hesaketvmese created the greatest tree of them all and placed it in the center. Hesaketvmese told these oaks to keep their green leaves through all seasons and decreed that the one He had placed in the center would grow to the top of the sky.

With His fingers, Hesaketvmese tangled the branches of the mighty oak trees He had placed in a circle and bound them to the branches of His special tree. This created a covering to provide shelter and prevent His children from climbing to His home before it was time for their spirits to join Him there. The trees threw shade upon the ground, and the earth underneath their covering was clean and cool.

Sweet acorns fell there in such numbers that they piled upon themselves and had to be pushed aside before one could walk through

2

or sit down to rest. None lasted for long, however, because the acorns were eaten by every animal in the forest. And when the animals feasted there, all did so peacefully and with consideration for each other because they knew this was what Hesaketvmese expected of them.

The Master of Breath had made it known that all clans were welcome there at any time, but there was a specific law that was to be observed without exception. When under the Coverings of Hesaketvmese, all present were to be kindhearted and patient. Each clan was to seek deep understanding of the others. All were to use words of joy and gratefulness and praise.

When plans were made about how the clans would work together and how the people would prepare for winter, chiefs and members of fire councils came together under the center tree. Hesaketvmese would also be there to watch and listen closely to everything that was done or said. Everyone felt the master's presence, and so everyone carefully considered each word before speaking aloud.

This was how things were done in the days when the earth was young and people were kind one to another. But there came a time when Setvne, the evil one Hesaketvmese cast into the swamp (and allowed to rule under its foul waters) began to cause trouble. Where harmony had once existed between brothers, Setvne created discord. Where families had only known trust, the evil one stirred suspicion. And though generosity had been their way, Setvne introduced the clans to jealousy.

One day, during this season of discontent, a loud burst of sound was heard across the land. As the clans gathered at the Coverings, they looked to the biggest oak—the tree in the center—and saw that its body had split. The crack was only the size of a warrior's finger, but it was deep, and it slowly widened as everyone watched in alarm.

Accusations began to fly, and arguments intensified, but before blood was taken, the voice of Hesaketvmese, as if carried by thunder, sounded within them all. "Stop this fighting," they heard. "I did not create your hearts for trouble."

There was a cry then from many of the people, for all knew Hesaketvmese's chosen tree was being rent in two because of his displeasure with them.

At that very moment, the old people tell us, a warrior named Cesvs stepped forward with a longbow of golden oak and strung it quickly. Holding a single arrow up and into the sunlight, all eyes were drawn to the arrow's stone. Sharpened to a keen edge, its shape was a study in perfection, each side tapering to a thorn's point at its tip. But most incredible was the astonishing color of the arrow's stone. Almost aglow in the sunlight, the arrow's head was whiter than snow.

Of the broadening crack, the warrior said, "Though the grain of the tree springs from the same root, its wood has now decided to disagree. By going in different directions, neither side is as strong as they once were together."

Some were nodding, and all were quiet. "Not only have the two sides chosen a course that will make them ever weaker," Cesvs continued to explain, "but they have now opened themselves to a future in which they will become weaker still.

"Without protection, this crack is an entryway for crawling things to journey into the tree's heart. If that pathway is not blocked, the heart will be captured, the enemy will then be free to consume it from within, and the tree will die."

"Can anything be done?" a warrior asked. "Is there anything we can do?" another woman offered.

For a moment he said nothing, and tears began to flow from the people, for they were very sorry for what they had caused. And they were ashamed.

Finally the warrior spoke. "I have come to bind you together—to make all things new." With those words, he walked from the center tree and did not stop until he had taken as many strides as there are fingers on the hands of twenty-five warriors.

Reaching one of the twelve trees, he turned, planted his feet, drew his bow, and let the arrow fly. The white arrowhead buried itself firmly into the crack of the chosen tree.

There were exclamations followed by stunned silence as the warrior returned. Carefully, he reached for the arrow's shaft and twisted it, easing it out of the crack *without* the arrowhead.

"The arrow stone," he said, "has gone into the deepest part of the tree's wound. There, each side of the stone will begin binding together the two sides that should have never been apart.

"This tree is now a symbol of peace. It will continue to grow, but only you will decide whether or not the healing wisdom begun this day will continue to bind your own wounds of foolishness."

The old people say that when Cesvs spoke his final words, he placed the bow over his shoulders and began to climb up the very tree he had just saved. He climbed until they could no longer see or hear him, and all present knew he had returned to his father, Hesaketvmese.

From that day forward all the great chiefs would travel to the Coverings on solstice–the day the sun stands still. There, they would light a council fire and speak in honor of the warrior who brought peace to their people. The gathering was always ended with a ceremonial binding of the wound.

As the blaze turned to embers, a single arrow stone–the most beautiful and valuable of all they carried among them–was selected. Together, the great chiefs would press the symbol of their commitment to Hesaketvmese–and to each other–into the ancient wound of the massive tree they called the Peacemaker Oak.

One

Keely Higgins was bent at the waist, lightly touching her dark hair with the tips of her fingers. "Why did I even wake up?" she groaned. "My head is about to explode."

The old man sitting next to her on the metal bench crossed his arms and frowned. "Is it a sinus thing?" he asked. "Or an 'I had too much to drink' kind of headache? Could be from tension. Tension'll cause 'em. You know, that kind that comes from your shoulders, up the back of your neck, and over your head? Those are from tension. So if it's from tension, I'm sure it's a bad one."

Keely sat up and turned stiffly to face the old man. Staring at him through cloudy eyes, she paused for a moment. Then, taking a deep breath to demonstrate her patience with his questions, she answered. "I've had a cold for three weeks. Yes, I drank too much last night. And I've been told that stressful environments create tension. Might this be considered a stressful environment?"

The old man grinned.

"My point," she continued, "though I am not sure why I feel compelled to make one for *you*, is that—now that I think about it—my headache is probably the tragic consequence of combining all three.

My nose *is* stopped up, I *am* hung over, and I'm in jail. So, yes. All three. Sinus, alcohol, and tension. But thanks for asking."

With that, Keely considered the conversation finished. Lifting her feet to the bench, the young woman wrapped her arms around her knees and positioned her face in such a way as to be shielded from any further interruption.

The two were surrounded by bars, seated on the far side of an area approximately fifteen by forty feet. The absence of beds and the substantial size of the locked space suggested a temporary function. A double row of benches was fastened firmly to the cement floor with one situated along the back wall, which was also solid concrete. The "seating" was illuminated, but not so sharply as the brightly lit area near the locked door.

"It is rather exciting to be here." The old man's comment broke the brief silence. Keely turned her head, peering up from her self-made cocoon with one eye and saw his arms were still crossed and that he had leaned back against the wall. He appeared to be quite relaxed, almost happy, she thought. Certainly, he was at ease. As she watched, he turned this way and that, looking around as if this were one of the most interesting places he'd ever seen, before saying, "Yes . . . a jail cell can be a remarkable tool."

"Ahh . . . yeah. It's remarkably horrible," Keely said. "And exciting? I don't even know what you . . . A tool? What does that . . . ? Oh, my head. Never mind." She went back into her cocoon, her aching head cradled in her hands.

Standing, the old man stretched and yawned loudly.

A muffled, "Shh," came from Keely's huddled figure.

The old man's eyebrows lifted in an expression of pure innocence. "I'm sorry," he said, although he was not. "I didn't catch what you just said," he finished, although he absolutely had.

Keely's words were still muffled, but her response was delivered with much more energy. "God!" she wailed. "Can you please shut up for a minute?"

"Certainly," he said a bit frostily. "If you're going to put it that way, of course I can." With that pronouncement, the old man turned away from Keely while crossing his arms and tightly clamping his right hand over his mouth. For several seconds, he rocked back and forth. Had anyone been watching, they might have been confused, for it would have been apparent that old gentleman was laughing uproariously. But to himself. And without making a sound.

He wore blue jeans and a white T-shirt with leather flip-flops. His longish, snow-white hair framed a deeply tanned face and the most startling eyes Keely had ever seen. In fact, they were the first thing she'd noticed after being placed in the cell. The old man's eyes were blue, but it was a lighter—no, a brighter—shade of blue than she had ever seen.

It was as if his eyes had been encased in crystal. There was a clarity to them Keely was unable to define. She had heard of eyes that sparkled, but always considered that specific description a way of referring to excitement reflected in a person's face. But this old man? His eyes really did sparkle.

He had already been in the cell when Keely was locked in during the early morning hours. When the door had shut behind her, the officer quickly departed. Keely simply stood by the door with tears streaming down her face. Vomit had soaked the front of her blouse and a swelling red knot was evident on her forehead. She had been angry, afraid, and drunk.

Now, her head pounded ferociously, but she was beginning to recall those first moments in the cell. The old man had stood when she walked in, Keely remembered. And he had said something. What was it? Oh yes . . . he had bowed slightly and said, "Welcome. Come in and rest. I've been waiting and am glad you're here."

Weird. Had he really said that, or did she imagine it? Her recollection was murky at best.

Nevertheless, what the old man said penetrated the fog in her brain and brought her back to the present. "You know," Keely said as she lifted her head with a sigh, "I'm sure I'll regret asking, but why is a jail cell a 'remarkable tool'?"

The old man grinned. "When a life is spinning out of control, few things bring reality into utter focus as effectively as a jail cell. Oftentimes, it is a *lack* of *proper* focus that allows a life to spin out of control in the first place."

"Proper focus?" Keely asked with a hint of suspicion. "What do you mean 'proper'?" The young woman did not lose the old man's gaze as she straightened and leaned against the back wall.

He sat down beside her and considered his answer for a moment before speaking. "Lots of people believe they lack focus," he said, "when 'focus' is not what's missing at all. For instance, at least part of why you find yourself in jail at this moment proves how effectively you were able to focus last night. Unfortunately, you focused on vodka tonics." The old man patted her on the hand.

"Many people say they can't focus because they worry all the time." He chuckled. "You see, focus isn't their problem. Because worry *is* focus. It's focus on the wrong thing. When we worry, we lack *proper* focus."

Keely stared at the old man for a moment through half-open eyes. "Who are you?" she said.

"Jones," he said and smiled. Then, nudging her playfully with his shoulder, he added, "Not Mr. Jones. Just Jones." She didn't return the smile but watched as he stood and stepped to the brightly lit area near the cell door. "A jail is also a near-perfect starting gate," he said absently as he ran his hand along the steel bars and poked his finger into a welded joint.

Keely's eyes narrowed. She wanted the old man to shut up. Why wouldn't he just be quiet and let her go back to sleep? She knew that the only way to shut him up was to be unresponsive and so decided that she would not say another word. Almost immediately, however, Keely blurted out another question. "Why a starting gate?" she heard herself say.

When Keely asked her question, she frowned as if she had eaten something distasteful. For some reason, the old man thought that was funny and laughed, motioning for her to stand and join him at the door. "C'mere, young lady," he said. "Move into the light." He was only a short distance away but held his hand out toward her.

Keely did not want to stand or even shift position but felt oddly compelled to do as this man, Jones, asked. Reluctantly, she stood and almost immediately sat back down and leaned against the concrete wall. With her eyes closed, Keely groaned. "Can't do it," she said. "I feel like I'm going to throw up."

It was a moment or two before Keely realized that the old man had not responded. Opening her eyes, she was taken aback to see him in the same position—right hand still reaching forward—and in the same place as he had been when she'd attempted to stand. There was one difference, she noted. Jones was no longer smiling.

Neither was he frowning, the young woman decided. Instead, the expression on his face was one of concern. Or urgency. Or longing, Keely thought. In any case, she strongly sensed the old man's determination. Choosing not to think about it any longer, Keely closed her eyes again.

"Hey!"

Keely jumped, startled. The old man had practically yelled at her and if she hadn't felt so badly, she'd have yelled right back. But a low snarl was the best she could muster. "What?"

"Don't quit now," he said. "Come on. Try again."

Keely was about to end the conversation with a rude yet crisply articulated comment, but as she gathered breath for the effort, the old man tilted toward her at an impossible angle. Forgetting what she was about to say, Keely blinked hard and looked closely. His right hand remained outstretched, but with his left, Jones had gripped a bar of the cell. He was leaning as far as the span of his arms would allow. The old man wiggled his fingers toward her and said again, "Come on."

To Keely, it was a ridiculous visual. Here she was—in a jail cell—and this old guy was reaching out for her like she was in the water. Sinking . . . or needing help. Or something.

"I am drowning, aren't I?"

"Yes," Jones said simply. "Yes, you are."

Two

Zero. It was a word that perfectly described the amount of sense this phone call was making to me. It was the middle of the night and I was not yet fully awake.

"What?" I managed to croak, requesting the information be repeated. I wasn't certain I had heard correctly.

"Who?" Again, I asked the caller to restate the information.

"Why?" This, I asked several times. True, I was in a fog, but the news she was attempting to deliver was almost incomprehensible.

"When?" Not that I cared. At this point, I was stalling for time, struggling to think clearly, but it wasn't working. This made no sense. Or as I stated earlier, zero sense. Was this someone's idea of a joke?

I turned the clock on the bedside table toward me. It read 3:27, a time that is either late at night or early in the morning, depending upon who you are. For me, it was both. As a writer and a speaker, I often rise early to peck away on my computer keyboard in the predawn silence. On the other hand, flight delays or long drives occasionally cause me to crawl into bed about this time. And upon those occasions, I consider it "late."

Crossing the room, I quickly pulled on the blue jeans I'd left draped across a chair and headed to the closet for a shirt.

"Are you going to your office?" Polly said sleepily. "And did the phone ring?"

"No to the first question," I replied in the darkness. "Yes to the second. And as an aside, good grief, I wish I could sleep like that." Despite the circumstances, I smiled and shook my head, acknowledging to myself once again how vastly different my wife and I were in so many ways. This way had practically become a family joke: A hurricane couldn't wake her up. Me? Drop a feather on the floor and I'm out of bed, dressed, and ready to go.

"If you aren't headed to your office, why are you getting dressed?" She shook off the sleep and sat up to turn on the lamp. "And who called at"–Polly leaned over to look at the clock–"3:29 in the morning?"

Now fully clothed, I approached her side of the bed and turned off the lamp. "Well," I began, "it's one of those 'good news/bad news' kind of things."

"Okay . . . ," she said, waiting.

I kissed her on the head. "The good news is that Jones is back. The bad news, however"–I took a deep breath and sighed–"is that apparently, the old man is in jail."

There was a faint orange glow in the eastern sky. I was driving into the sunrise and just past the halfway point between my home in Orange Beach, Alabama, and Clanson, Florida. Unable to quickly find it on a map as I'd hurried from the house ninety minutes before, I was nonetheless unconcerned about finding the small town.

Even without help from my trusty "Map of the Southeastern United States," I'd left my driveway with no doubts about the trip.

Such are the miracles of GPS. Not only does the Global Positioning System provide turn-by-turn instructions about all aspects of a drive, the technology apparently bestows confidence upon the driver as well. And for someone like me—one of society's directionally challenged—that's a big deal.

As color began to fill the horizon, I glanced at the screen in the dashboard. The straight path route I had chosen, I realized, was taking me north of what some referred to as "Cracker Kingdom." The name is spoken with admiration, a nod to the original Florida Crackers who first populated the area as pioneer settlers. Searching for a new life, they began to arrive after Spain traded Florida to Great Britain in 1763. Legend has it that the name "Cracker" was given to these people as a reference to the cracking of the long, rawhide whips they used to round up wild cattle.

The area, though, marked by the occasional small town, is still mostly untamed wilderness. A combination of palmed prairie and hardwood swamp, Cracker Kingdom's desolate roads can make for an unusual adventure. Driving through the area after dark, one is reminded of scary stories from childhood—tales so vivid that decades later, in a place like this, healthy imaginations can run wild.

Even today, every now and then, someone will swear to having encountered a hatchet-wielding escapee from the insane asylum from whom they barely got away after they slowed their car to pick up a hitchhiker, who turned out to be a ghost girl in a prom dress with a golden arm.

In the daylight, however, this unspoiled stretch of Florida has some of the most beautiful scenery in the state. Perhaps, I've often thought, the real reason it remains so unspoiled is because its two-lane roads are rarely used by visitors en route to the Gulf of Mexico.

With its moss-draped trees and alligator-infested backwaters, this forgotten treasure seems practically invisible to outsiders. Instead, they seem to prefer the traffic of several unbending four-lanes that run north and south connecting Interstate 10 and whatever beach they have selected for vacation. These highways were clear-cut through the landscape years ago and have since been cemented into place by vast walls of convenience stores and fast-food joints. In any case, for whatever reason, most tourists drive the straightest shot they can find.

As the top edge of the sun became visible, my musings turned to the reason for this drive. I was unsettled, having no idea why the old man had been jailed, and couldn't imagine what he might have done to deserve it, but I would get him out. Or be there when he got out. Or something.

Jones had inserted himself into my life decades ago. To say that I was at "loose ends" during that time would be understating the situation by a large degree. I had been nineteen when my mother, after a long bout with cancer, had finally succumbed. Shortly after, my grief-stricken father, in an otherwise survivable automobile accident, had managed to follow her into the afterlife by not wearing a seat belt.

Suffice it to say, I was no financial genius at the age of nineteen. It did not take me much more than a year to run through the $2,500 my parents' life insurance policies paid out upon their deaths. My father had been a minister, my mother a homemaker, so there were no houses or cars. No land or jewelry. No stock certificates or baseball card collections or jars of cash buried under cabbages in a garden. No, the life insurance was my entire inheritance.

Since I already owned an old car, I bought a trailer with the money. "Mobile home" is far too fancy a description for the ancient, wobbly box of very thin sheet metal with holes in the floor I acquired. Still, however, I couldn't afford it. Inconveniences like electric bills and paying for food began to get in the way.

First, I sold the car and got a small, used motorcycle. Within a year, I had to sell my trailer, but I wasn't really concerned. Having gotten $1,500 for it, I was practically rich. After all, I still had my motorcycle. Oh, and I bought a tent.

My thinking at the time was: *Hey, I'm single, I have transportation, a roof over my head, and cash in my pocket. What more does a guy in his early twenties really need?*

What more? Apparently nothing because several months later that's exactly what I had: nothing. So I moved to the beach. To be clear, I did not move to a house on the beach. I moved to the beach. I lived *on* the beach. In the sand.

I knew I was alone, but it didn't take too long for me to become sad and angry as well.

Today, as strange as it may seem to the tourists—the convention-goers and the vast flocks of Michigan or Wisconsin "snowbirds" who visit year-round—back then, Orange Beach, Alabama, was not a "year-round" place. It is probably inconceivable to most that during the 1970s and early '80s, the tiny resort communities along the panhandle of Florida and the Alabama Gulf Coast became ghost towns in winter.

Restaurants closed, and shops were boarded up. Almost everyone in Orange Beach and our sister city, Gulf Shores, hunkered down, counted the change left in tip jars, and hoped the money they had made from March to mid-October would carry them through until the following spring. Me? I had no tip money. But I ate a lot of fish.

When the old man stepped into my life, a couple more years had passed, and I was sleeping most nights under the Gulf State Park Pier. Today, I still live in the area—Orange Beach, Alabama—and the pier is still here, now the longest anywhere on the Gulf of Mexico. Of course, hurricanes have required it be given an update or two since that time.

One of the more interesting facelifts to me is the newfangled strip-slat decking. All wood, the idea is that in the event of a hurricane's high winds and water, the slats will blow away, leaving the concrete structure of the massive pier intact.

Back when I had quietly requisitioned the pier as my home, the whole thing was a cement company's dream. There was no wood. Even the decking was comprised of enormous slabs of concrete set end to end on colossal pilings. As people walked excitedly out onto this beautiful landmark—an above-water reef that stretched far into the Gulf—they all had their heads up and their eyes glued to those already fishing.

For almost two years, Jones was the only person who'd figured out that I had a tiny home under that pier. Just beyond the parking lot, below the first concrete slab, right where it began to angle up, I burrowed under a concrete girder. Behind the massive crosspiece was where my hiding place was created. All the work was done with my hands and a small shovel and in truth, I'd have been easy to find . . . if anyone had known where to look.

Through the years, I've been asked many times how I was able to turn my life around. Usually someone will put it like this: "How did you escape from under the pier?" It's a funny question to me, as if they assume I was trapped under there and almost never saw daylight again!

On the other hand, I see their point. In a way, I *was* trapped, because how I lived at that time became who I thought myself to be . . . scruffy and unkempt, without much hope or direction, and with anger quietly bubbling under the surface of my soul. Then Jones showed up, and I began to see a little daylight in my life.

Curiously, Jones never *told* me what to do. He only asked questions and made observations. Yet, it was with these tools—one a chisel, the other a hammer—that the old man dramatically expanded my thought process.

Remember, this was the guy who told me, "You can't believe everything you think."

At the time, the concept rattled my brain, but—as odd as it seemed—that one statement pointed my life in a particular direction. It eased me onto a pathway that would have me on a constant search for new answers—better solutions—ones that lay beyond what many experts had already accepted about "how it was done" or "the best way to do it."

The truth I finally understood in the statement, "You can't believe everything you think," eventually led me to a mission of helping other people move into the light, just as Jones had done for me.

By the way, I didn't just come up with that "move into the light" phrase. That, too, is a direct quote from Jones. Actually, it was one of the things he said to me when we first met. Maybe it's because there really were sodium vapor bulbs illuminating the sand just outside my "home," but, honestly, it was a long time before I connected those words with the darkness that I had been living in and his part in saving me from it.

He was a crafty old guy—funny sometimes, too—but I can't say he was particularly tactful. Once, I came at him with some statistics in order to argue the point of a story he had told the day before. When I finished my prepared volley, the old man laughed and told me I had done well for someone who had collected the argument's research in less than ten minutes. "Numbers alone can tell a story without context," he said. "Decisions made without context rarely reach their potential."

Listening closely, I became aware that perhaps my "debate" victory had not been as decisive as I'd thought. Jones continued, "Reading . . . listening . . . being quiet occasionally—quiet enough to deeply consider what you are learning—these are ways one can wring context from what had previously been mere fact. Commit to these activities, and you'll possess an advantage that will make itself known in every area of your life."

He paused. When his eyes narrowed a bit and a mischievous grin crept across his face, I knew what was coming. Everything the old man had said so far could have been listed in Column A: "Jones with a Chisel." Now, I figured, I was about to experience "Jones with a Hammer." Sure enough, he pounded home his point with this gem: "Facts and data are usually the default position for people who are not working on themselves."

Wow. Okay. I got it.

Here's another example of Jones using his considerable wit to cover a direct message he wished to convey. During the time I was living under the pier, I had been washing boats with two other guys in a marina. We were working on a huge sportfishing yacht when they suddenly offered me the princely sum of five whole dollars to jump from the boat's tuna tower—a lookout position forty-two feet above the water.

To win the prize money, however, my leap would have to be over the dock and into the next boat slip fifteen feet away. Without hesitation, I climbed the tower . . . and jumped. As might be expected, I managed the forty-two vertical feet quite easily. Once airborne, however, I sensed the fifteen *horizontal* feet might contain a higher level of difficulty.

Though I was freefalling at the time, my calculation proved to be correct, and I was reminded once more of the adage "Close only counts in horseshoes and hand grenades." I was about an inch shy of clearing the dock completely. Unfortunately, that inch connected with my left forearm. Nothing was broken, but the scrape was impressive.

Also impressive was the sensitive concern about my well-being offered immediately by my "friends" who—before I even made it to the surface—were loudly announcing that they were not going to pay because I had failed the attempt. Nice.

That evening, I was walking the beach with Jones and moaning about my bad fortune. "Why in the world did I do that?" I asked myself aloud.

Though I had not meant the question for him, the old man chuckled and answered immediately, saying, "I think you let your 'want to' get overwhelmed by your 'should I?'"

I laughed and shrugged it off. "Oh well," I said. "Everything happens for a reason, right?"

With the same chuckle as before, he responded, "Oh sure. But sometimes that reason is because you weren't thinking clearly and did something stupid." My eyebrows went up, and he added, "Keep your head fixed on principles that will guide your life. Otherwise, your mind and body will drift, and you won't know it until it's too late. Consider the things you'd like to accomplish in the future and how tragic it would be to end up an inch shy on all of them."

Glancing at the GPS in my Ford truck, I saw that I was less than ten minutes away from my destination, and Jones weighed more heavily on my mind than ever before. By the dozens, it seemed, fleeting thoughts and episodes from the past were flitting through my consciousness, each remembrance separate and contained, every scene individually complete in my mind's eye. In reality, I suppose, it all happens in an instant unless we dial into a particular event. I thought again of that much younger version of myself and an admonition I'd received at that time from the old man.

Earlier I mentioned being scruffy and unkempt. Well, I was. As Jones would say, "Not a judgment. Just an observation."

It was 11 a.m. on a weekday and time to clean fish for Nancy, the owner of Sea N Suds. I was about to walk up the beach and had on blue jean cut-off shorts and a T-shirt that was particularly wrinkled. Neither, I am certain, had it been recently washed. Jones was sitting in the shade of a nearby palm when I emerged from underneath the pier. I told him where I was headed.

"Just a suggestion," he said, "but you might want to grab another shirt. That'n has seen better days."

I stared at him and responded, "I'm just cleaning fish. The fish don't care how I dress."

The old man laughed and remarked, "Well, you got me there. That is entirely true. But the *truth* of the thing is a different matter." He paused to see if I was listening. I was, and he took the opportunity to give me an incredibly valuable example of proper thinking.

"You are surely right," he began. "The fish don't care nothing about the way you dress. Those fish don't care how you act when you're at Sea N Suds or what you do when you ain't even close to the place. However . . . you are working for Nancy—a lady whose livelihood depends upon how the customers of her restaurant perceive her employees, what they do and how they act.

"Patrons of a restaurant who see food prepared by someone who's not at least as clean as they'd like their food to be . . . well, they tend to find another place to eat. When they leave and don't come back, that affects the livelihood of the restaurant's owner. That livelihood—the money your boss makes from that restaurant—is what pays you. Without a successful business owner, you are out of work.

"As an employee—the fish cleaner—you are one of the first people your boss's customers see. If the fish cleaner is messy and not particular about how he dresses or even if his clothes are washed, the customers are likely to think, 'Maybe those fish aren't too clean either.'

"Fish that aren't entirely clean can make a person sick. Folks know this and wisely stay away from any fish they suspect might not be cleaned properly. If your boss's customers decide they'd rather not risk eating fish that might not've been cleaned properly, your boss's livelihood is diminished. And when she doesn't have the money to pay a fish cleaner, she cleans the fish herself. Which means . . ."

Jones let that last part hang there until I filled in the rest of the thought. "Which means," I said, "that I'm out of work."

He smiled and winked. I turned and motioned for him to follow me back to the pier, which he did. Looking both ways, we ducked underneath, and soon I was into the plastic storage container I used for clean clothes.

While I was changing shirts and combing my hair, he left me with this: "Noting a person's messy appearance at work is just an observation, not a judgment. But observations over time—added together and weighed carefully in context—do lead to judgment. It's usually the quiet and unspoken kind, but it is still judgment. And in today's world, this kind of judgment becomes the difference in yes and no, hired or rejected, laid off or retained, promoted or passed over.

"And most folks don't have a clue as to what happened, one way or another."

As I smiled at the memory of how Jones had been so "on the mark" back then, I thought about how long it had been since I'd seen him. Six years? Seven? I wasn't certain, but knowing it wouldn't be long now, I turned into the parking lot of the Clanson Detention Center.

Three

Gripping the bar, Jones leaned forward and held his free hand out, toward Keely. "Come on," he urged. "Move into the light."

"No," she said with all the energy she could pack into two letters. She was doing her best to communicate just how idiotic she thought the old man was.

With one arm straightened from the cage bar, Jones tilted even more and reached for Keely with his other arm. Palm open, fingers waggling an invitation. If not for knowing where she was and what was *really* going on, for a second there, Keely thought, the old man looked like an Olympian executing a swan dive.

"I am fine." Those three words were hurled with the weight of a soaked blanket tossed outdoors on an arctic night. They were meant to halt the progress of an approach, to forestall any imagined advance.

"I can see well enough from here."

Perhaps the day might come when an older, wiser version of Keely Higgins might feel ready to look back, examine, and appraise this particular moment. Maybe the older version of her will decide to flip the "on" button in her imagination and order up the scene.

If so, what she will experience could be described as a "mind movie." Of course, being the only patron in that theater, Keely's mental projector will be capable of fast-forwarding the motion, moving it backward, and slowing it down to barely a crawl. From this unique vantage point, she will be able to watch again and again, probably in fascination, as a younger, much thinner version of herself speaks dismissively to an elderly man.

"I can see well enough from here," Keely will see and hear herself say as if the old man were a useless fossil and barely worth the breath she is expending to speak. If one day, she *is* able to review these details, it will be at this point in the scene that Keely will notice the old man pausing.

When she sees it—*if* she ever does—Keely will bear down in concentration, running and rerunning the clip. And yes, she will see the old man pause every time. He will not relax his arm or allow it to hang by his side. Instead, his hand will continue to reach toward her. And if, one day long into the future, Keely notices the pause, its length will be less than the time it takes her to draw a breath.

Even hoping things turn out well for Keely, somewhere, way down the line—even if she gains understanding, wisdom, and prosperity— this moment will never be a pleasant scene for her to remember. A wise Keely, far into the future, will most likely cringe, knowing that the young woman she watches in the sequence is about to react to the old man's pause in a most inappropriate manner.

And in fact, as it happens in real time, Keely is quite rude.

A mind is a thing far more powerful than the body it orders about. Like fire and water, a mind's available level of strength is the same whether the force harnessed is to be used for purification or destruction. This, in fact, explains how a mind left untended can create mischief far beyond its own ability to clean up the messes it makes.

Keely's mind was powerful, but it had grown cunning and some-what dangerous through the years. Even Keely had noticed it. *That's just what happens*—she often told herself, with an astonishing degree of accuracy—*when a mind is cultivated in a garden of fear and hurt. And lies. And anger and betrayal. And then when the garden itself was abandoned.* Well, Keely's mind was powerful enough to stop there.

When she was a teenager, everyone said, "That Keely Higgins can put a smile on anything." And she really was able to. She had done so her whole life. She had smiled for her teachers and the neighbors. She had smiled for friends and for guys and for professors and for the old hag at the dry cleaners.

The dry cleaner smile was Keely's private joke. The scowling woman hated everyone in town, and everyone in town pretty much hated her. But she owned the only dry-cleaning service for miles around. So they put up with her clipped replies to questions, paid the bill, and left. Sometime later—perhaps even days later—people would just grit their teeth and say nothing as they dressed for work or church. And they said nothing while wearing clothes that occasion-ally offered up a faint nicotine bouquet when the plastic was removed.

Keely was blinded by an arrogance that refused Jones's offered assistance. The fact that Jones didn't immediately withdraw his hand obviously did not register with Keely. She didn't even notice. Later, in retrospect, she decided that it must have been the pause that had served as a catalyst for her verbal salvo—*No. I am fine. I can see well enough from here.* Only three clipped thoughts loaded into twelve syllables, but fearsome fire so closely launched behind her first words that they functioned as a preemptory strike. What Keely said and how she said it was intended to destroy any capability the old man might still possess of ever speaking to her again.

After all, it was how the fit, dark-haired beauty had managed to survive without a mother since she'd been twelve. When one learned the art of conversation in the suburbs of Chicago, while growing up with two older brothers and a dad whose only connection to anything outside school and work was the Bears, the Bulls, and the Cubs, it was understood that an equal piece of the world's pie would never be won by Keely with gentle tears or quiet patience, oh, no.

In that place and at that time, verbal assault skills made one king—or in this instance queen—of the hill. When it came to competence levels of spoken expression, Keely Higgins, at twenty-seven years of supremely educated age, was regarded in disputatious circles as their own equivalent of a black belt. Without preparation and in under three seconds, she was consistently able to hammer a point into surrender while simultaneously flinging ninja-like sarcasm stars into anything else that moved, before walking away with an arched eyebrow and a knowing smile.

Furthermore, as an exclamation point to any particularly articulate smiting she might have delivered in those days, if an open trash container was nearby into which she could toss her lipstick-stained, half-empty cup of latte from Starbucks, so much the better. For in the rough and tumble world of "conversational crucifixion," style points counted.

It was all bluster, of course. It was Keely's way, the pattern she followed, her coping mechanism. But in jail, there was no latte. Any lipstick Keely might've otherwise been carrying, or even wearing, was long gone, and there wasn't a trash can within reach, in any case.

With more animal instinct than finesse, Keely misinterpreted the old man's slow response. She saw only weakness that demanded bullying and disrespect that deserved punishment. Therefore, with not a single warning shot more than she had already delivered, the angry young woman fired away, words flaming from her mouth with increasing intensity, her locution like a machine gun warming up, its bullets just beginning to shake loose.

"Excuse me," Keely began in a menacing tone, indicating that anyone with a lick of sense would not seriously suspect her of wanting to be excused from anything, "but when one makes a statement like '*I am fine*' or '*I* can see well enough from here,' the concept—being a simple one—should communicate to the recipient of that message—*you* in this case—the reality that the communicator—*me* in this case—is satisfied with the present location of their person. In short, and again, I do not welcome your intrusion, and my vision from this place—where I now sit—is unimpeded."

That's what she said. And the gathered rush in which she said it cannot be overstated.

But *say it* she had. And Jones got the message.

The old man managed a weak smile. Stepping back across the cell, he saw that Keely appeared to be locking herself into place. She held both legs straight. The intact heel on her right shoe dug into the cracks of a floor drain as the torn bottom of the broken left heel claimed whatever purchase it could manage on the rough, nonskid floor.

The young woman's hands gripped the bench seat beside each of her thighs, providing anchor points for her rigid, unbending arms. Keely employed her arms in the same way a builder might use braces or a floor-jack, to jam her shoulders and torso into the wall. Only then, with each body point actively holding down the fort, did Keely allow her head to lean against the chipped paint of the pale blue concrete behind her.

She closed her eyes, effectively "saving" a snapshot of "young woman in a jail cell" that Keely would puzzle over in days to come. It would be one of the many critical misconceptions about herself that she would need to unravel. While to others the way in which Keely had just physically situated her body might be described as tense (or wound tighter than the rubber-band engine on a toy airplane), the young woman honestly regarded her positioning to be an example of "lightening up."

Sitting down again beside her, Jones folded his arms and stretched out his legs, crossing them at the ankles. He snuggled his back into the cement behind him as if it were a well-worn recliner and for an interval, appeared to simply relax. Keely was already asleep or appeared to be.

After several quiet moments passed, Jones began to speak in a way that might remind one more of a front porch on a Sunday afternoon instead of where they actually were. "You know, young lady," he began, "I've always thought that if Moses'd had a little more time on the mountain, he'd have come back with eleven."

"Okay . . . ?" Keely hadn't wanted to respond, but the old man had a way of launching a thought into the atmosphere that demanded attention. She was interested in spite of herself. "And if he had?" she said dully.

"Number eleven would have been *Thou shalt not kid thyself.*" Jones nudged the young woman playfully with his elbow and chuckled. "You're lucky he only had ten. 'Cause if my count is accurate, I'm figuring that at least twice in the past three minutes, you've broken what would have been number eleven."

Again, Keely briefly considered ignoring him, but realizing that hadn't worked so far, she sighed wearily and said, "Twice? Okay. I don't even know what you're talking about."

Jones held up a finger. "Number one. You said, 'I am fine.' Actually, you are in jail. So, no, you are not fine."

Adding the second finger, he continued. "Two. You said, 'I can see well enough from here.'" The old man pursed his lips. "Then you doubled down and told me your 'vision from this place is unimpeded.'"

He said the last part with a formal tone and clenched jaw—doing his imitation of a snob. Keely's face clouded, but he continued to gaze toward the ceiling as if he hadn't noticed and was still contemplating the situation. In seconds, it appeared he had come to a conclusion.

Shaking his head, he said, "Hmm. No. You're kidding yourself there too. In fact, your vision at the moment is as cloudy as your future is becoming."

Keely's eyes darkened and despite her throbbing head, she turned, drawing herself back to get a clear view of the old man sitting next to her. "You know? That is incredibly offensive. I am finished with this conversation."

"Wow," Jones said with a huge grin. "Okay. But I must say that you are *really* good at this."

There was a long pause—an extended moment of tense silence— before Keely, able to hold it in no longer, finally spat the question, "Good at what?" into the air between them.

"Good at what?" she demanded again, practically screaming at the old man before suddenly gaining control, crossing her arms, and leaning back against the concrete block wall. "Not that I even care," she said evenly, now in a normal tone of voice. "Though I will admit a degree of curiosity about what it might be *possible* that I *am* good at. God knows, I'm almost thirty and haven't found anything yet. So? What? What am *I* good at?"

"Kidding yourself," the old man said simply.

Without a glance at the old man and out of steam now—perhaps for the first time in years—Keely said, "'What am I good at?' was a rhetorical question. A rhetorical question is a question that does not require an answer. You answered anyway. Thank you so much. It has been a pleasure meeting you. Good-bye." With that, she closed her eyes.

A few beats later, with her eyes still tightly shut, Keely snorted a small laugh. "Trust me, 'kidding yourself' might be a defense mechanism, but it is not something one can *do*. It's certainly not a marketable skill."

"No, it's not," Jones replied calmly as if the conversation had never paused. "But it'll sure diminish the marketability of the skills you *do* have. Kidding yourself—believing and reinforcing things that are untrue—serves only to banish hope and joy from your present life. Simply put, it makes you feel bad. Worse, it legitimizes the things you've already told yourself about *why* you are like you are and *why* your future is nothing to look forward to."

Without warning, Keely sprang to her feet and ran headlong into the cell door. Stopped cold less than ten feet from where she had begun her charge, Keely thrust her arms through the steel bars, cursing loudly, vile language pouring from the young woman as she turned on the old man once again, but Jones remained unflinching. He never moved.

"First of all," she snarled, "what makes you think *you* have any idea about what I tell myself? Second . . . my future, if there is to be one at all, is decidedly dim. And third, this is none of your business." Increasingly louder, Keely added, "*I* am none of your business. So shut up and leave me the hell alone. Why? Because I am asking you to! For God's sake, please!"

Jones was silent as she jerked herself away and moved to the end of the bench, where she lay facedown and cried bitterly. For a moment, he watched with a frown. Then, slowly, as if he'd thought of something or as if someone had nudged him from his reverie, the old man relaxed. Turning away, he crossed his arms comfortably and leaned back against the wall. Closing his eyes and settling in as if he might take a nap, a gentle smile appeared on his face.

It was not an ordinary smile. At least, it didn't indicate happiness. No, the smile on Jones's face was one of understanding and contentment. It revealed the depth of feeling that wells up in a person when their purpose in a situation becomes clear. Jones contemplated the young woman's last words. She'd told him to stop talking. She ordered him to leave her alone. The reason he should comply with the demands—according to her—was that she had asked him to do so. Not only that, but she had added, "For God's sake."

The old man glanced down the bench when he pondered her exasperated tagline. Keely had settled into an uncomfortable sleep. Satisfied that she was all right, Jones closed his eyes again and chuckled softly. "Keely, Keely," he murmured, after which he recalled her last declaration of frustration and repeated it quietly. "For God's sake." And with that, he sighed deeply and drifted to sleep.

Four

"Identification, please."

The uniformed officer at the desk stifled a yawn as he waited for me to dig the driver's license from my wallet. It was almost 6:30 a.m., full daylight in the eastern edge of the Central Time Zone. According to GPS coordinates, the town of Clanson was 146.7 miles from my home in Orange Beach, about two and a half hours away and well over the state line. Frankly, I had never heard of Clanson, Florida, but here it was. And for a tiny village well off the beaten path, it appeared to have a very nice jail.

The officer was young—early thirties—and noticeably out of any kind of shape one might otherwise choose if not for the convenient option of overeating and neglecting to exercise. Receding on top, his hair in back fell over his collar. The uniform he wore was messy and wrinkled. Not a judgment, just an observation.

The policeman was tired, which was understandable at this hour of the morning, but when he took my license, glanced at the picture, looked back at me, and asked, "Is this you?" I had to bite my tongue. A thousand sarcastic answers were competing for space in my head and beginning to enthusiastically line up behind my vocal cords. I managed to choke them all back, however, and reply with a smile.

"Yep, it's me." Then, taking a stab at being friendly, I said, "Wow. You sure are here early."

He stared at me for a beat, grunted, and handed the license back. Picking up a pen and sliding a clipboard to the middle of the desk, he pursed his lips and asked, "Purpose of your visit?"

I took a breath before answering.

Here was a guy, I knew, for whom "middle ground" did not exist. I'd already assessed the situation, determined its likely outcome, and within seconds of walking through the door, decided upon my role here. Successfully navigating this encounter would require me to way overdo it in the submission department. *A guy like this?* I thought. *Everyone he meets is a favored guest . . . or a threat to his authority.*

The personality trait is not rare or even unique. Privately, I called it the Barney Fife Syndrome (BFS)—a reference to the deputy sheriff that actor Don Knotts portrayed long ago on *The Andy Griffith Show.* During his five seasons as the overly officious lawman in the classic television series, Knotts won five Emmys for his work.

Deputy Fife remains the gold standard for this temperamental psyche, and before me sat a textbook case. Oh, and the fact that this particular example of that psychological manifestation also happened to be wearing a badge. Let's just say that the irony was not lost on me.

"Well, sir," I began, addressing him as "sir," though he was at least twenty years my junior, "I received a call from someone on your staff about a person who is in your custody?"

Now, see how I did that? I referred to the people on duty as *his* staff. The prisoner was in *his* custody. Was I brownnosing? Absolutely.

"Ahh," he said. "You have a friend in jail. Not . . . good."

I have come to understand that the classic cases of BFS appear most often in middle-aged males who, for whatever reason, have never experienced the reins of sovereign command until suddenly, through some miracle of bureaucracy (or absent anyone else willing to walk around at night with a flashlight), they are in charge.

Authority—especially when it is undeserved, unsupervised, and unrestrained—often produces an adrenaline-fueled rush of superiority—power—that can be dangerous to the commonsense wishes of mere mortals like you and me. Therefore, lest trouble ensue, we must always be careful to humble ourselves before this type of person. In other words, no matter how ridiculous the situation, we must remember to display outlandish admiration for their skills and intellect, or we will most assuredly be considered a threat.

"Yes, sir," I said. "Evidently, I do have a friend in jail. He's an old man. White hair . . . ? I'm not really sure what he's supposed to have done."

Despite my experience in dealing with people like this officer, I am sometimes astonished by my own stupidity. True, I recognized my mistake the instant it popped out of my mouth, but it was too late.

The policeman's head tilted upward as his eyes narrowed. Slowly, he gathered himself and stood. Placing his hands on the desk, he leaned forward and spoke menacingly. "What he has *supposed* to have done? You're saying my people arrested somebody that didn't do any-thing? Huh?" He glared at me.

Immediately, I feigned surprise. I might have even cowered a bit. "Oh, no, sir!" I said, my eyes wide. "That's not what I meant at all. Your people wouldn't have done that. I just meant that I don't know what he did. Can I see him, sir?"

I almost laughed out loud when, sure enough, he responded to my little show by visibly relaxing and saying, "Yes, you can see him." Looking at the clipboard on his desk, however, he frowned. "Name of prisoner?"

"Jones," I replied. "Not *Mister* Jones, just Jo—"

"Yeah, I know," he interrupted. "I heard him say it five times." He jerked his head toward several cheap chairs lined along the wall to his right and added, "Have a seat. Visitors are not allowed until 9 a.m."

The officer saw me glance at my watch and grinned when my face fell. It was 6:37. Slowly, I took a deep breath to compose myself, at the same time thinking about *The Incredible Hulk*, still another television program I had watched as a child. "I'm sorry," I stated calmly, knowing it would serve no purpose for me to get mad, turn green, and rip the place apart like Dr. Bruce Banner would have done. "I thought I would be able to see my friend."

"You can," he replied. "At nine."

My eyes narrowed. "Look," I said, not quite so friendly this time, "all I want is—"

"All *I* want is for you to sit down," the officer said loudly as he stood and came around the desk. In place, he paused as if to look me over. Then, with a forward lean much too aggressive for my taste, he peppered me with questions.

"Are you related to the prisoner?"

"No," I replied.

"Are you an attorney?"

"No."

"Do you represent an attorney or represent the office of an attorney otherwise located in the state of Florida?"

"No."

"Are you therefore, in fact, visiting these premises as a civilian observer?"

"I am."

"Then you are classified 14A, a visitor," he said. "And visitors are not allowed until 9 a.m." With those words, he stopped and lifted his chin. Appearing to be satisfied with the flow of words that had just gushed from his mouth, he sniffed loudly, placed his hand on the can of mace holstered in his belt, and turned to walk away. Over his shoulder he tossed his coup de grâce, adding, "I suggest you take a seat."

So I did.

I'd hurried from home, neglecting to bring anything to read. The brochures for bail bonding were interesting, and I studied them a little closer, not certain whether or not I might need one at nine o'clock. Lacking anything else to do, I worked on my smartphone, answering newer e-mails and deleting a lot of older ones. And I watched the clock, glancing often through the glass at the reception desk, keeping an eye on the officer.

Interestingly, the officer's actual duties appeared to be very uninteresting.

I am not exaggerating when I say that I *never* saw him do anything else. He didn't fill out a form. He didn't call anybody. No one called him so he never had to answer the phone. He didn't check on the prisoners. He couldn't have. He never left his desk. Not even to go to the bathroom.

He did nap a couple of times. At least, I think he did. That's assuming the "arms crossed, chin on the chest" thing was not prayer. For his sake, I hoped not. God, I have always believed, frowns on snoring during prayer.

Finally, it was nine o'clock. The officer let me know that he *knew* it was nine because at 8:59, he ceased all motion and pointedly stared at the clock. It was the same clock I'd been watching, but it was amusing to see him suddenly so attentive to it.

I had risen from my seat when he came through the door. He walked straight at me without saying anything and was about five feet away when, before I could decide whether to say anything or reach out my hand to shake his, he did a sharp turn to the left without breaking stride. The move was unexpected, and quite frankly, it startled me.

He hadn't done a full turn. It was more of a forty-five-degree angle, but with the unmistakable flair of military precision. In the waiting area of the Clanson jail, of course, it just seemed goofy. All he'd needed was a sword or a rifle on his shoulder and someone to count cadence, and he could have held his own parade at Fort Bragg.

Anyway, it threw me when he turned, but he never stopped—just continued his steady march to and through the door. He was halfway down the hall before I caught up, and as I matched his steps, I couldn't help thinking, *Hup, hup, hup. Hiyup, hup, hup.* As soon as the thought was in my head, a laugh was out of my mouth. Which was a mistake.

Now understand, it was just a tiny laugh. This was no guffaw. It was not an outburst of hilarity. I was not giggling. Heck, the sound I made would've hardly qualified as a chuckle, but it was loud enough to get the attention of my grim escort.

Suspecting I might be laughing at him (which in a way, I was), he said, "Is something funny?" I didn't answer and thankfully, we quickly arrived at a brightly lit, barred cage that was significantly larger than the others. "This is Holding Cell Number Two," I was informed as we approached. The comment caused me to glance around, but I did not see a Holding Cell Number One. I did, however, see my old friend. He was standing right next to the door.

"Good morning," Jones said cheerfully as we approached.

Five

Good morning? I thought. *He said, "Good morning"?*
Considering the circumstances, I wasn't sure how to respond, but I'd suddenly had the thought that this was somewhat like getting my daddy out of jail. Anyway, he'd said, "Good morning." So, with an impish smile, I replied, "It is for some of us. Is it for you?"

"Of course, it is," he said without the slightest hint of doubt in his voice.

"Oh, brother," the officer said. He smirked and shook his head in a holier-than-thou display of disgust.

"What?" I asked, momentarily taken aback.

"We do not have good mornings here," he explained as if talking to a child. "This is a jail. Here, we deal with the dregs of humanity—felons, miscreants, habitual offenders . . ." He was deadly serious, and I did my best to imitate a person who was seriously listening.

This prevented me from glancing at Jones or allowing my eyes to roll into the back of my head as he droned on. ". . . deviants, the mentally unstable, and those who are generally a menace to society and/or themselves."

Jones was close, within hand-shaking distance of me, but still on the other side of the bars. As the officer ran down his litany of miscreants, I looked at the old man, who raised his eyebrows in an innocent expression that asked, *Do you see what I have been dealing with here?*

I almost laughed out loud but managed an effort at throat clearing that hid my true feelings nicely. This guy was a cartoon. Nevertheless, he did have Jones locked up in the Big House. So I politely asked, "May I have a moment of privacy with my friend?"

For a beat, he appeared to consider whether or not I might have a tommy gun in the pocket of my jeans or a helicopter hovering nearby for a jailbreak, but he squinted, nodded slowly, and indicated a desk in the walkway several cells down. "Sure," he said with a level of suspicion and menace in his voice rarely heard outside Attica's death row or on the chain gangs of Angola. "I'll be right over here," he said and as an afterthought, added, "No funny business, boys."

"What kind of funny business are you thinking about?" Jones grinned. "You want to bust me out?"

Turning to the old man, I shook my head and slightly lifted my arms and hands in what is commonly known as a universal parenting gesture. This move, used most often to deliver a message of mystification to a teenager, says, *Will you be quiet? What in the world are you thinking?* without verbal communication actually taking place.

I suppose that for the first time, I was also feeling somewhat the authority figure in our relationship, so I took a stern posture. "Exactly what is going on here?" I asked.

The old man shrugged it off. "Oh, they nabbed me on a 752."

I sighed. "What's a 752?"

"Loitering in a city park after midnight. 'Course they had me dead to rights on a 751, which is loitering in a city park *before* midnight. They were cagey, though . . . watched me for a couple of hours, then popped me for the more serious offense."

"You're kidding," I said, suddenly outraged. "You are in jail . . . for

loitering in a city park? Isn't that why city parks are built? I mean ..."
I was beginning to sputter. "Doesn't one go to a park specifically *to* loiter?"

Jones laughed and patted my arm through the bars. "No worries," he said. "It was important and anyway, I'll be out soon."

Later, I remembered the phone ringing on the desk down the hallway, the officer answering, and a muffled conversation he had with someone on the other end of the line. At the moment, I simply asked, "*What* was important?"

The old man cut his eyes and casually bobbed his head in the direction of a young woman curled up on a bench in the cell, with her back to me. I looked, but before I could ask any questions, the officer returned, jingling his keys. Still steely eyed, he said, "Looks like you caught a break, old man."

Jones smiled. "That's wonderful. Thank Chief Peebles for me when he gets back from vacation. The mountains are refreshing this time of year."

The officer had unlocked the door, but now he stopped it from swinging open. Staring suspiciously at Jones, he demanded, "How'd you know that was the chief who called?"

"Was it? Ha! Well, who else could it have been?" Jones replied. "The good news is that I am out of *your* hair."

"You know the chief?"

"We've met."

"How did you know he went to the mountains? Nobody around here knew he went to the mountains."

"Where else would he have gone? You live in Florida. People in the mountains come here to vacation. You Florida folks go to the mountains. When it's hot, you go where it's cool. Simple."

I held my breath. I could see the wheels turning in the officer's mind. He wasn't sure whether to believe the old man or not, but he couldn't figure out what difference it would make. Apparently, he'd been ordered to release him. Therefore, with a dark scowl on his face, he did just that.

Jones looked at the young woman on the bench who was still asleep. He nodded at me, smiled at the officer, and strode from the cell.

At the window in the waiting area, the officer said, "Sign this," and Jones did as he was instructed. As we turned to go, the officer had a thought. "Hey . . ."

"Yes?" Jones responded as he turned back.

"I know nobody will tell me why the chief let you go. But I would like to be clued in on how he knew you were in jail. You didn't make a phone call to anybody."

Jones shook his head. "That is a curious thing, ain't it? It's a mystery, Nathan. A real-life mystery."

Startled, the officer said, "Hey . . . how do you know my name?"

Jones laughed softly and reached out to pat the man on the shoulder. "You're wearing a name badge."

Nathan's eyes narrowed, and his mouth opened, but no words came out. I could see his mind whirling in different directions. "Oh yeah," he mumbled, suddenly appearing to be embarrassed. Gathering himself, he shifted to his sterner persona and said, "Okay. I think we're done. Stay out of trouble now, you hear? Don't let me see you back."

We walked to the vehicle, and neither of us said a word as we climbed in, but as soon as my door was shut, I whistled the first line of the theme song from *The Andy Griffith Show*. Jones only shook his head and chuckled.

Driving away, we were around the corner and down the street from the jail before I spoke again. Watching the old man from the corner of my eye, I said, "Nathan was the officer's first name?"

"Yes," Jones replied.

"Hmm. But it was a last name that was on the officer's name badge," I said casually.

The old man poked his lips out as if he were confused. "It was?"

"Yes, sir," I said, with just the bare hint of a smirk. Turning onto the state highway toward home, I let the "yes, sir" hang in the air for a beat before cutting my eyes at the old man. "And you know it was a last name too. The guy's name badge read *Howland*. Howland is a last name."

"Howland?" Jones said. "Huh. Well, where'd I come up with 'Nathan'? That's a curious thing, ain't it? It's a mystery, Andy. A real-life mystery." It was the last thing he said for a while.

Ten minutes passed, then twenty.

Occasionally, I glanced over to confirm the old man was okay. And he was, I supposed. He appeared to be calm. Or perhaps serene might better describe the expression on his face. As far as I could tell, he was enjoying the countryside floating by outside the passenger window.

I didn't get it. Most people, I figured, having been through what he'd experienced would have been exhausted, embarrassed, worried, or in general terms, an emotional wreck. Obviously, the "jail" thing was bothering me more than it was him. I knew the subject needed to be broached, but it would have to be done carefully.

Okay, I thought, *I'm sure he's tired. If he doesn't want to say anything, I don't have to say anything. I can be quiet too.*

Almost immediately, I took my foot off the accelerator. "Jones. Seriously." My mouth was open, but nothing else came to mind. So, brilliantly, I added, "You were in jail?"

To the sound of his laughter, I shook my head and resumed the drive. But I was grinning. No matter how it happened, whatever the circumstance, I was thrilled to be back in the company of this old man.

As I mentioned, I'd not seen him in several years, which was unsettling, but not unusual. If pressed for a description of his modus operandi—at least during the times I had been around him—I'd have to say that Jones just sort of came and went. It was a fact I had come to accept, but never really gotten used to.

Maybe, I'd often thought, that was because I never knew where he was headed when he disappeared or when, if ever, he might come back. Every time he left, I'd wondered if I'd ever see him again. Yet here he was.

The old man was a walking, talking conundrum.

I couldn't count the times I'd tossed a "Where've you been?" into our conversation. I'd underhand him a soft "Will you be here awhile?" and watch it just hang there in the air. Occasionally, I'd try to be tricky and sidearm in a quick shot like, "Do you have a place to stay?" but he swatted everything I threw with the ease of a major leaguer facing a high school kid. On this subject, the old guy never once gave me a straight answer.

Jones crossed his left arm over his right and eased into a more comfortable position. Pursing his lips, he took a deep breath and blew it out noisily. "Did you know that if you buy twelve at a time, you can get bottle openers shaped like dingo dogs for only seventeen cents apiece?"

I did not have a ready response for that unexpected information, but, if accurate, it was indeed one more thing about which I was woefully uneducated, and I told him so.

"Yep," he went on. "It's true. And you can retail 'em all the way up to ten dollars if you want. The dingo dog's face is on one side, and his tail is on the other. The tail's what gives leverage to open a bottle. Makes a nice key chain too."

"What's a dingo dog?" I asked.

"Dingo dogs are indigenous to Australia."

"Oh," I responded and waited, but apparently there was no more.

"Well, it sounds useful," I offered, "but that's a pretty high markup."
Jones bobbed his head as if to acknowledge my shrewd understanding
of this crucial matter.

"Nine, eighty-three," he said.

I was confused. "What?"

"Nine, eighty-three," Jones said again, not even looking my way.
"The profit. Nine, eighty-three is the amount between buying a dingo
dog bottle opener for seventeen cents and selling it for ten bucks."

"Oh," I said, my eyes opening wide. "Yeah, well, that's good. That
kind of margin, heck, you ought to get a couple dozen of them." I was
joking and tried to laugh, but it came out sounding like an odd bark.

Jones turned his head at the noise I'd made and frowned. "I'm
thinking about it," he remarked as if also deciding whether or not his
feelings had been hurt.

Not that it was particularly unusual, but I had absolutely no clue
as to what Jones's point might have been in leading a brief discussion about the market in dingo dog bottle opener futures. I'd been
around the man off and on my entire adult life and being conceptu-
ally puzzled in his presence was not a new experience for me. Many
were the times I'd been concentrating on what he was saying as hard
as I possibly could and *still* been aware that my mind was huffing and
puffing several beats behind.

The traffic flow was somewhere between light and nonexistent.
I'd decided to take the Cracker Kingdom route for the return trip.

His arms remained folded over his chest and at some point, I saw,
he had also crossed his legs at the ankles. His leather flip-flops had not
been kicked off and were still on his feet. They were plain brown and
looked like the same ones he'd been wearing when I first met him. But
I knew they couldn't have been. Briefly, I wondered where one might
even find a pair of flip-flops without a logo.

The blue jeans and white T-shirt were the same as always. And, as always, they looked crisp . . . as if they'd just been washed. The "clean clothes thing" was something that had driven me crazy for years. Again, I looked carefully at the old man's shirt. There wasn't a spot on it.

"How is that?" I'd wondered aloud to my wife more than once. "He wears jeans and a white T-shirt. I've never seen him in anything else. They are worn, but not worn out. And always clean!" Then I'd demand, "Have you ever—even once—seen Jones wearing dirty clothes?"

Polly's response was always the same. "I have not," she'd say. Then she would laugh and shrug her shoulders with one of those "it is what it is" kind of expressions.

Driving along, I smiled at the memories I had of the old man and looked over at him to see his eyes firmly focused on me.

Six

It was a quarter. Had it been a penny or a nickel, she probably wouldn't have bothered. Perhaps a dime might have caught her attention. But a quarter? Absolutely.

The tall, well-dressed woman slyly scanned the Publix parking lot to see if anyone was watching. Concluding no one was, she bent over as if to tie her shoe and snatched the quarter from the curb. Standing with her prize, the woman looked around again. Had anyone seen her? Apparently not, and she cackled as the quarter went into her purse.

If ever there was a woman seeking the attention of others, it was Blair Houston Monroe. Thus, there was a bit of irony involved when, at that particular moment, she did not want to be seen. Of course, it revealed a lot about the woman that she thought anyone might be watching her in the first place. Similarly, it revealed a lot about the people of Orange Beach that from the instant she appeared—wherever or whenever that might happen—no one ever seemed able to look away.

Blair Houston Monroe, according to most of the local townsfolk, should have been registered as a tourist attraction in some official capacity. At six feet two inches tall, her stature was overshadowed only by her thin figure.

Her eyes were dull green and seemed to fit her narrow face. Despite the woman's perfectly applied makeup, a description of those eyes in relation to her face had made the rounds several months earlier. "Like two pale emeralds set into the blade edge of a hatchet," someone had remarked. No one knew who'd said it first, but those hearing (and passing on) the vivid characterization declared it not only an accurate portrayal of Monroe's features but her personality as well.

It was a recognized fact that most people—certainly upon the instance of a first sighting—simply stared at the sixty-eight-year-old woman in disbelief. Monroe was, after all, certainly easy to spot. Besides her already significant height, everyone agreed that it was her hats that made the woman appear taller than seven feet. And she owned dozens of them, all magnificently beaded and feathered in such a way as to capture the attention of everyone within eyesight.

Women's hats, at least the big ones with long feather plumes, have not been in style since the middle of the last century. There are, however, two places in our modern world these conspicuous headpieces can still be seen: once a year at Churchill Downs on the Saturday of the Kentucky Derby and almost every day somewhere in Orange Beach, Alabama.

Then there is what the locals call "Blair Houston Theater." When the woman is spotted in Publix or shopping at The Wharf, it is not unusual for an Orange Beach resident (or several) to discreetly follow her. The object of their exercise is to see a tourist's face the moment they encounter Blair Houston for the first time—bonus points awarded for capturing their reaction on video.

Many have reported visitors abandoning their shopping carts, frantically running to find a friend or family member who absolutely must come *right now* to see the giant woman and her hat! The tourists' reactions are discussed, compared, and laughed about again and again. Blair Houston Theater is often called the longest, continually running live production between Nashville and Miami.

Without full historical knowledge of Orange Beach and its relationship with Monroe, one might be tempted to believe this poor, never married, seemingly friendless woman to be undeserving of the laughter occurring behind her back. Therefore, several facts are crucial to gaining proper insight.

First, not one person polled would deem Blair Houston Monroe to be undeserving of their laughter.

Second, while, yes, the laughter does indeed occur behind her back, it is only because virtually everyone in Orange Beach is terrified of her front. *Callous, venomous, vindictive, loathsome, spiteful, malevolent,* and *malicious* are a few of the words used to describe her. As my next-door neighbor, Brian Bakken, recently remarked, "And those are her *good* qualities!"

Additionally, this is not a "poor" woman. Not in the monetary sense in any case. Quite the contrary is true. Locally, some say, "Her ancestors were from Texas," as if that might explain her financial situation. More on that in a moment.

Her "Texas thing" is a source of consternation for many. Despite Blair Houston having lived in Alabama for most of her adult life, she flies the Texas state flag beside her home in Orange Beach and displays a huge metal and concrete Star of Texas in the middle of her massive front yard.

The general feeling—certainly in this state—is that here, you can yell "Roll Tide" or "War Eagle," but those are your only choices. If you intend to wear an odd shade of orange or hold up your fist with index and pinkie fingers extended, you need to take Highway 59 to

Interstate 10 and drive west until you hit Beaumont on the Texas state line. There you can yell "Hook 'em, Horns" until the cows come home.

She was the only child of a man who had wanted a son. He named her after his state and himself. Blair Houston Monroe's father was the heir to a mining fortune. His name was Blair *Dallas* Monroe. The choice of names seemed strange to some at the time, but not to the Monroe family. It was a tradition. After all, his father had done the same thing.

Her granddaddy, Blair *Austin* Monroe, had lived in a shack outside Van Horn, a settlement began in the mid-1800s as a support for the San Antonio–El Paso Overland Mail Route. As the story went, the only luck he ever had turned out to be the only luck he ever needed. It was 1903, and on a freezing midwinter evening in the mail office, Blair Austin Monroe won three poker games, back to back to back.

The loser, unable to pay in cash, offered instead a deed to one hundred acres located several miles north of town. Monroe accepted the deed as payment and rode out the next day on a borrowed mule to inspect his newly acquired land—a remote pile of pale green rock called Tumbledown Mountain.

When he arrived, he thought he'd been cheated, but as it turned out, the green rock was talc, a pure mineral worth considerably more than anyone imagined. In 1914, mining began on Tumbledown Mountain, and many decades later the Monroe Holdings are producing more than ever before.

Today, talc is an ingredient in tire rubber, paint, and cosmetics, and as a brightener for white paper. It is used in ceramic tiles, roofing materials, and as a lubricant in applications where high temperatures are involved. As it turns out, the most well-known use for talc—as a powder—accounts for only a small fraction of its worldwide demand.

Still, it is that specific use most people associate with the wealth of Blair Houston Monroe. Or, as she is often snidely called, the Talcum

Powder Heiress. "That figures," someone said recently. "Talcum powder is the perfect symbol for that old woman. She's always on everybody's butt."

It was true. Blair Houston Monroe was rich . . . and she was mean. But she was an equal-opportunity kind of mean. She hated everybody.

With the quarter securely tucked away, Blair Houston pushed the Publix shopping cart beside her car, moving from back to front, and stopped it just behind the rear door on the driver's side. The big luxury vehicle was not only unlocked, it had been left running for the entire fifty minutes she had been in the supermarket.

This was not unusual. Once, someone asked Blair Houston why she left her car running while she was in a movie theater or at church or while shopping. She turned on them and asked a question of her own. "When you leave your house, do you turn off the air conditioner?"

Somewhat confused, the person shook his head. No, he did not. "Well," Blair Houston snarled, "I don't turn the air-conditioning off when I leave my car."

The tall woman stepped around the cart. Her intention was to open the rear door in order to transfer the cart's contents to the vehicle's back seat, but as she reached for the door handle, something caught her eye. It was down and to her left. Casually, Blair Houston backed away from the car to look again.

Yes. There, under the driver's door—almost under the car—was another quarter. Taking a quick glance to make sure no one was looking, Blair Houston bent to perform the old shoe-tying trick a second time but froze halfway down.

Her white, wide-brimmed hat—the one with seven long feathers from a pheasant's tail—was being dirtied by the side of the car. Blair Houston paid it no heed, however, and remained in place for several seconds before reversing course and slowly standing erect, once again casing the parking lot for overly nosy people.

Her mind was scrambling through possible solutions to solving the only problem with what she had just seen. There was more than one quarter. There were several quarters. There were also dimes and maybe a nickel or two, but these coins were farther under the car than the lone quarter under the driver's door.

Like a pirate finding buried treasure but planning to keep it all to himself, Blair Houston made a decision. She knew what she would do, but first, everything she'd bought in the store had to be emptied into the back seat. Quickly, she did so and shoved the empty cart onto the grass. Not because she was in a hurry—no, this was Blair Houston's custom. "Let the people who work here return the cart," was her attitude. "They have a job. I'm allowing them to do it."

Practically diving into the driver's seat of the running car, Blair Houston began to execute her plan. There was a vehicle nose-to-nose with hers and would, she had calculated, provide excellent cover. She would back up just far enough to get the car out from over the coins and just pick them up.

Blair Houston figured there was almost three dollars under her car. "Oh, my Lord in the sky," she said aloud as the big vehicle slipped into reverse. "Whosoever has money shall never have enough. From the fifth chapter of Ecclesiastes, the tenth verse."

It was one of about fifteen or so passages from the Bible that Blair Houston had memorized, and she quoted them frequently. To her, Bible verses were like weapons and could be used to justify anything she said and did. They were also handy for condemning the thoughts and deeds of almost everyone else.

This time, it had been Ecclesiastes 5:10. Despite knowing very well that she had omitted more than half the verse, Blair Houston Monroe did not care. It was what she always did when quoting from the Good Book—she used the part she liked. Any part of the Bible she did *not* like, she would change or leave it out entirely.

When the car had been sufficiently backed out of the space, Blair Houston put it in Park and got out as quickly as she could. With one step to get around the open door, it took only three of the woman's long strides to reach the coins. They were uncovered and out in the open. *I have to get this done now*, she thought.

Turning her head one way, then the other, Blair Houston judged her "grab and go" safe to begin. Just before sinking to her knees, a car she thought was about to pass by stopped behind her vehicle. "Good afternoon, Ms. Monroe," came a voice as the vehicle's window rolled down. "Do you need help?"

It was the local Methodist minister, her own pastor, Burke Ruark.

Blair Houston took a couple of steps to her right, ready to block the way if she had to. *And I might have to*, she thought. *Just don't get out of your car.* "Good afternoon, Brother Burke," she said as sweetly as she could manage. "Thank you so much, but no, I am fine."

"I couldn't help but notice your car halfway out of the space. Is something wrong with your engine? Can I check under the hood for you?"

"If you lifted the hood, would you even know what you were looking at?" Blair Houston blurted. Pastor Ruark rocked back a couple of inches. That and the shocked expression on his face were impossible to miss. *That didn't come out like I wanted it to*, Blair Houston thought as she gritted her teeth and tried to make it look like a smile.

She honestly didn't care whether she hurt his feelings or not. Blair Houston just wanted him to go. Acting as if she were getting back inside her vehicle, the woman waved. "No, I don't need you,

Pastor. You can go." That hadn't been the perfect thing to say either. She could tell by the pastor's wide eyes as he nodded and drove away.

"Who cares?" Blair Houston muttered as the minister drove out of the parking lot. She waved at the vehicle in case he was watching in his rearview mirror and thought, *There's not a preacher alive who could look at that much money on the ground and not covet it. It looks too much like what's in the collection plate.*

She turned, and as she came to the front of her vehicle, Blair Houston Monroe was still admonishing her pastor. "Thou shalt not covet!" she said under her breath. "That'd be Exodus 20:17."

The coins were scattered over an area of about eighteen inches. As she bent down, the possibility that the money had been lost by someone else never occurred to Blair Houston. She simply did not care. Reaching for the nearest quarter with her thumb and forefinger, she somehow missed it and tried again. Her finger slid over the smooth twenty-five-cent piece again, but this time, she saw that it had not moved.

Blair Houston eased her thumbnail under the serrated edge of the quarter and pushed. The coin did not budge. It was stuck. The woman's eyes narrowed as she tried a different quarter with the same result. She pushed at a dime with her left hand. Nothing.

She stared at the money for a moment and blinked, but when she swept her palm across all the coins at once and not a single one moved, she was enraged. Blair Houston Monroe gave a two-handed scratch at the money and didn't dislodge anything but three of her ten artificial nails. Another shot at it and two more popped off. The rest were ruined.

Blair Houston got to her feet, stomped her size 12 platform shoes, and yelled something unintelligible. The woman was livid, and her hat seemed ready to fly away by itself, but for some reason, it never occurred to her that she might stop the craziness at least long enough to examine the coins and see *why* they were stuck.

Or perhaps she already *knew* why and that was the reason for her tantrum. Whatever the case, Blair Houston Monroe kicked it up a notch. Literally. She went after the coins with her big, hard shoes.

Combine the aggressive footwork of a demented clogger with the body type of an old NBA player, throw in a continuous stream of bad language, and put a big hat on it all, and one can conjure up a fairly accurate representation of what was happening in the Publix parking lot.

And it all might have ended there if Blair Houston had not heard him laughing. Not that one could blame the kid—she was a sight! But when Blair Houston turned suddenly to her left and spotted the young teenager leaning across a car hood, taking video with a smartphone twenty feet away, she saw red—nothing but red.

Everything *but* red faded into the background as the sixty-eight-year-old woman bellowed in anger and propelled herself toward the boy. Headfirst in the air, Blair Houston Monroe tried to make the whole twenty feet in one leap but only made it halfway across the hood of the vehicle parked next to her.

"Nice dive, Mrs. Goliath," the kid taunted as he continued to record the action. "Five more tries and you'll almost be here!"

If she hadn't lost it before, Blair Houston Monroe most surely did then. She screamed and stomped her feet up and down several times right there in the same place. Then the skyscraper of a woman pulled the hat off her head and threw it at the boy.

His eyes widened as the hat flew toward him, for in addition to the hat, there had been some kind of wig hair sewn into the edges. When it had been seated on her head and combed in, the wiglet matched Blair Houston's hair perfectly. Now, however, as the teen deftly caught the hat and hair she had flung his way—and did so with one hand—it was just a trophy of war.

The kid shut down his phone camera with a flick of his thumb and, just as quickly, reached into his shirt pocket and tossed something small and light to Blair Houston. She did not catch it but managed to bat it down. Picking it up immediately to examine, she saw that it was an empty bottle of Super Glue.

She threw it back toward him and bellowed again, but the boy had danced away another twenty feet or so. When he was at what he obviously considered a safe distance, he turned the video back on, but this time he pointed it at himself. With his other hand, he positioned Blair Houston's hat so he had it gripped by the crown.

Puffing his chest and facing the mean, old woman, the kid held his trophy high.

The brim of the hat sagged, and the hair sewn into its edges hung straight down. Situated like he wanted at last, the kid spoke in a loud voice, saying, "And after the boy had defeated the giant, he drew the Philistine's sword and took the giant's head as a prize."

As Blair Houston came after the kid again, he stayed out of her reach until he could finish what he wanted to say. And, amazingly, he stopped laughing long enough to shout, "That's First Samuel 17:51. Woo hoo!" he added and ran away as fast as he could.

Blair Houston could only stand there as her nemesis escaped again. Too many times now, she had seen red during moments like these, and she had grown to dislike the color immensely. "Just wait," she muttered to herself.

Yep, she was determined. And if it was the last thing she did on this earth, Blair Houston Monroe was going to catch that red-headed kid.

Seven

I was a bit startled. "What are you looking at?" I said.

"You," Jones snickered.

I waited for an explanation, but that was all he said, and soon we were riding along in silence again.

Another quick look, and I saw that he was smiling. And . . . humming? Yes, he was humming. One wouldn't have imagined he had a care in the world. His clear blue eyes flashed as his head swiveled from one natural delight to the next.

As I mentioned earlier, this return route home was not the one I had traveled earlier that morning. While we would be on blacktop all the way, even a main drag through the center of a small town—at least this far from I-10—was considered a back road.

It had been less than an hour since we left the jail's parking lot. Therefore, according to the straight-line standard of a flying crow, we had not yet reached the midpoint between Clanson and Orange Beach. We were still far from the white sand and salt air of Alabama's Gulf Coast.

This was an area in which the topography is quite opposite from the image of the sunshine state most people carry in their heads. This . . . was Cracker Kingdom.

Great expanses of palmetto palms fill the landscape for miles. Rarely more than eight feet high, their long, slender, olive-green fronds reach skyward like a million sturdy fingers. For thousands of years, these virtually indestructible plants have met winds of ill intent and come out of every assault no worse for the wear.

These laureled prairie lands are often dotted by slash or small stands of loblolly pine, but the dense vegetation is broken only by natural pastures, many of which hold cattle and provide feeding opportunities for wildlife.

Occasionally, one will also spot signs of human habitation— structures set well off the road—usually freshly painted and almost always in white, the same color they have been for more than a hundred years. These are old, well-kept masterpieces of simple architecture. And locally, they are not referred to as houses or homes. Rather, they are "homeplaces," and the family histories rooted there are well known and greatly respected.

And of course, there are giants that dwell in this place.

Slowing the truck as we neared the first of the behemoths we had spotted, I watched as Jones's eyebrows lifted high enough to erase the wrinkles from his face. There, directly to our front, were some particularly large specimens.

Simply standing there, they waited patiently as our vehicle approached. It was as if they'd already figured time to be on their side, like they knew that any weary traveler wishing to pass this way must first make it directly through the middle of their gathering. Staring, I counted at least a dozen of the titans crowding each side of the road and noted that they looked for all the world as though they could stand there forever if they had to.

Not a one of them was an inch under one hundred feet tall, and as we drew closer, it became apparent that several of the giants had already locked arms across the road. Their barrier, however, would be too high to stop us and I knew it. When the time came, we would simply drive under their reach. I had done it before and because I'd never had one fall on me, I was confident about making it to the other side.

As usual, though, I was in awe of the giants and wanted to see them up close. And so, before immediately running the gauntlet, I made sure there wasn't a vehicle behind me, slowed, and steered the Ford from the blacktop onto the roadside.

The steady throbbing of the truck's engine provided background for the deep resonance of the oversized tires as they popped gravel on the road's shoulder with loud, offset rhythms that quickly transitioned into peaceful whispers as the big vehicle left the highway's pavement, its undercarriage swept by the seed tips of tall, untended grass.

The acoustics were familiar. It was the racket of a drum set, pedal bass pounding like a metronome until joined by the snare—all of it a jarring mashup—until suddenly tamed by the steady massage of swishing brushes on cymbal steel.

Easing to a complete stop, I shifted into Park and grinned at Jones, who was peering through the top of the windshield, slowly shaking his head.

Still without talking, the old man and I opened our doors, unconsciously inviting the civilized, well-conditioned air of the truck's interior to mingle freely with the wilder version of itself that was panting like a wolf, waiting just outside for the collision about to come. Wild air is not pure or pristine. It is common, humid stuff filled with pollen and bugs and electricity, and it holds the power to overcome one's senses.

My eyes widened a bit with that first invisible impact in an unconscious recognition that my brain had begun to reassess the physical surroundings and was now computing data.

Having unbuckled and leaning left from the driver's seat, I swung my legs to the side. It was in that ordinary instant I remembered a specific thought the old man had once planted in me. It was a musing of the type he had termed a "ponderation."

He'd told me that "hearing" was confirmation of a "right now" kind of thing and that if reexamined *later*, all the details remembered could be viewed and turned over in a person's mind. He'd said that one could quite often use the littered pieces of that moment to construct a compass that would provide direction, even in situations that had yet to unfold.

And it was with that particular observation—at least in *my* mind—that we stepped from the truck and moved from one world of sound into another. It was like escaping from a blistered bubble of percussion-fueled jazz in a New Orleans barroom and free-falling into the soft, almost telepathic resonance of Carnegie Hall.

The sun had not yet reached its midday zenith, but any dew that might've lingered in the grass was long gone. In the still air, heat was rising and with it came the fragrance of pine and crumbled red clay intermingled with the fecund smell of a decaying sweetgum tree that had outgrown its roots and tumbled into stagnant water some weeks before.

It was the first week in May. Those of us privileged to live in this temperate zone knew that an early summer had arrived. While not yet as hot as it would be in June—or certainly July and August—most of us, at one time or another, had silently vowed never, ever to move farther south than this.

"Go through here," I said to Jones and motioned for him to take the lead down a dirt pathway that seemed to meander toward the giants. He cut his eyes up and locked onto mine for the barest second and smiled as he passed and moved onto the narrow trail.

After walking a hundred or so steps and closing about half the distance to the giants, Jones stopped and put his hands on his hips. Watching from behind, I paused too. Wisps of his longish, snow-white hair flared as a soft breeze rose from nowhere and disappeared just as quickly. His head leaned lazily to the left, and I saw him nod in a few short but very definite motions.

"Oh, yeah," the old man said. "I know these guys."

Before I could ask a question, Jones resumed his walk, but this time at a much faster pace. I was right behind him, but when he had begun to move, the distance he put between us left me scrambling to catch up.

No more than a minute later, the old man stopped as suddenly as he had taken off. Within seconds, I was beside him, and there they were, larger and certainly more imposing than they had seemed from the road. The sunlight was directly in our eyes and so bright that the dense shadows cast by the giants were cavelike in comparison.

"Jones . . ." I began. But the old man held up his hand. He was asking for silence, and I complied. As I waited for him to say something or continue forward, I became aware of the heat. There was only the barest wisp of a breeze, and the sun felt heavy on my skin and clothes.

After a short time Jones gestured for me to follow and stepped forward again, this time more carefully. As we moved into the shade, I looked up and almost gasped. Shafts of light poured through the dark green leaves and, sifted by long tendrils of Spanish moss, danced in the air around us. Seeing sunbeams filtered by nature's own stained glass was as if we had entered a heavenly cathedral.

Quercus virginiana, a magnificent tree more commonly known as the live oak, is an icon of the deep south. Dark green leaves fill its branches year-round, and the trees regularly reach heights of more than one hundred feet. Single specimens are almost a rarity. Most often, live oaks are found loosely grouped around others of similar size. Because of their incredible age, the largest specimens are usually members of the smallest groups.

I counted seven here, not a one less than twenty-five feet in circumference. Live oaks are bigger by far than anything Gulliver ever witnessed; and these giants were absolutely stunning.

We were only a few feet into the shadows, and the temperature had dropped by at least fifteen, perhaps even twenty, degrees. Jones smiled at me, and I could only shake my head in wonder. I had experienced the anomaly before, but it never got old. Live oaks have been effectively working to cool hot air long before the invention of an air conditioner—a modern machine built to approximate what the tree has been doing for thousands of years.

On a still, hot day, the air directly under the canopy of a live oak can register as much as twenty degrees cooler than the immediate area in full sunlight. Live oaks manage this miraculous feat by a process known as transpiration. In it, moisture is moved from the roots of the tree, through the trunk, and to tiny pores on the underside of the live oak's dark green leaves. There, the water changes to vapor and is released into the atmosphere.

Jones walked over to the largest of the trees and gave it a pat on the trunk before pointing to the underside of the giant oak's biggest limb. "Amazing, isn't it?" he commented as he followed the limb with his finger until he was pointing at its other end. I stepped a few feet away to get a better view and could only shake my head.

Where the branch extended from the trunk, its circumference was bigger around than a washing machine. The limb had grown at a right angle from the trunk and, for decades, managed to parallel the bare earth fifteen feet below until at last, its weight succumbed to the law of gravity and curved downward in a gentle parabola until finally touching down.

It had taken more than a hundred years, but the live oak's massive limb had finally been grounded. If an airplane's landing could be filmed in slow motion and technology allowed the slow motion to be viewed at the pace of a growing tree, the analogy would be perfect. For just like the maneuver all student pilots must practice—actually landing for several seconds before immediately taking off again—the branch performed its own version of a "touch and go."

Earthbound for the first time in a century, the limb never slowed but maintained its speed, riding the runway for a dozen feet or more until, after thirty years of running flat on the ground, it leapt into the air once again.

I knelt beside the part of the limb that was on the ground and must've appeared to be in shock. Jones laughed. "Care to guess how long it is?" he asked.

"I wouldn't have a clue," I answered, shaking my head.

"Go out to the tip," he instructed. "I'll wait for you here. You have a three-foot stride?"

"Pretty close," I said.

"Use it," the old man instructed. "If you get it right, I'm thinking fifty-four steps will take you right to the tree."

A bit more than a minute later, I had reached the wide base of the live oak with astonishment. I had counted my steps out loud and the closer I got to my old friend, the wider his grin became. Stopping my short walk right in front of him, I paused, looking directly into his eyes. "Fifty-four steps," I said. "Do I need to frisk you? Are you carrying a range finder?"

Apparently, that was funny to him too. "Fifty-four steps," I continued, "at three feet per step. That limb is 162 feet long, which is obviously incredible, but right now, I'm more interested in how you called the length so exactly."

Jones looked up at me. He grinned and waggled his eyebrows. "I told you before," he said, gesturing to the trees. "I know these guys!"

My eyes narrowed, but the old man continued. "This biggest one here is thirty-two feet around at the base, and while the others are not quite as large, they're all about the same age."

"How old might that be?" I asked.

"Eight hundred years or so," Jones said.

I didn't ask how he knew. Instead, I just readied myself to listen and for my own sanity attempted to keep from my mind the curious thought I'd had about Jones for so many years: he is a bit beyond incredibly wise, willing to think through and answer any question from anyone who asks, yet he remains absolutely close-mouthed about himself.

With the intention of prompting the old man to talk, I lobbed an easy question over the net. "Eight hundred?" I served.

"Or so," he returned, grinning as if he had read my thoughts, which, I reminded myself, was not out of the realm of possibility.

Jones actually laughed out loud and moved away, motioning for me to follow. "Why don't we sit by the waterfall for a few minutes before getting back to the truck?"

"Sure," I said, heading downhill after him. "By the creek, you mean? I don't think there's a waterfall here."

But there was.

"Beautiful, isn't it?" Jones said. "Pull up a rock and have a seat."

Glancing around, I realized there was no need to pull one up. The rocks were everywhere, and most of them too big to move anyway. Staring at the waterfall, I sat down slowly.

It wasn't large as waterfalls go, perhaps a few inches higher than three feet. Therefore, the water didn't gush across the rocks at the top or roar into the pool at its bottom. Instead, it fell with a unique resonance that seemed strangely familiar. At first, I couldn't place the sound, but when I did, I realized my heart had recognized what I was hearing before my mind made the connection.

It was a sigh, but one without the expression of sadness or disappointment usually associated with the word. Instead, this communicated a calmer, more hopeful emotion . . . like satisfaction. Yes, that was it. The little waterfall's never-ending voice sounded exactly like a sigh of contentment.

Despite the mood of the place, something was bothering me. "Jones," I said, "I'm pretty sure there's not supposed to be a waterfall here."

The old man raised his eyebrows. It was a look I'd seen before, one of amusement mixed with a keen interest in what I might be confused about this time.

"What I mean is . . . I didn't think waterfalls existed in places like this."

"Places like what?" he asked.

"Well . . . you know . . . this." Looking around, I tried to explain. "It's sort of swampy here. There're no mountains, and waterfalls are usually in the mountains, aren't they?" Gesturing at the giants, I said, "'Places like this have trees like these. Mountains *don't* have trees like these."

I paused for an answer, but it looked like he was waiting for me to say more. So I did. "Seriously, Jones. Have you ever seen a crystal-clear stream with a waterfall running through a grove of live oaks?"

"Actually, I have," he answered. But before I could ask where, he continued. "The first time I saw this kind of a setup was a long time ago on an extraordinary piece of property. Friends of mine owned the place for a while. They were a young couple. Sweet people, both of them. But bad thinking led to bad decision-making and . . ." He lifted his hands a bit, letting them fall in a helpless gesture.

"What happened to them?" I asked.

"Oh," he said, "they lost their home. Lost everything, actually. They ended up having to move out . . . move away. And they did. They started over in another place . . . not nearly so nice, though . . ."

Jones's voice had trailed off. He was facing the waterfall, but it looked like he was staring into the past. Watching him closely, I tried to remember if I'd ever seen the old man sad before and couldn't recall a single time. He sure seemed sad now, though. Fortunately, that mood lasted only a moment.

The old man took a deep breath, glanced over at me, and delivered a soft smile. "Anyway," he said, "the day after they moved out, I had the opportunity to walk the entire property by myself. As I said, it was extraordinary.

"I remember walking through the live oaks and listening to the waterfalls under them—there were several—and when I finally left that afternoon, it was with the thought that waterfalls and meandering streams were beautiful decorations, but live oaks were a symbol of permanence."

"What do you mean?" I asked.

The old man smiled and waited a couple of beats before answering. "An acorn is the tree's first form. It has value as a food source or to propagate the species." He looked up into the branches above them. "As a mature tree, it increases its value by providing shade, oxygen, ever more acorns, and a peaceful place to contemplate the universe."

The old man picked up a stick and studied it for a moment, turning it over in his hands. Looking up at me, he continued. "Even after its death, there is value that can be provided by a live oak. The wood can be transformed into homes or furniture. In this way, the tree can live and serve for centuries longer than it did in its original form."

I didn't reply, and for a few minutes Jones was silent too. Finally, he ended our conversation with this: "Live oaks can seem randomly placed, but like people, there is a reason for their deployment in a particular location. Just as live oaks bear the brunt of wind and storms only to produce the strongest of wood, great people can take the worst life has to offer and produce value and hope for their fellow man."

Jones stood and brushed off his jeans. "Yep," he said, "the live oak has been my favorite right from the beginning."

Eight

For some unexplained reason, people who for many years have vacationed at the beach have come to expect more than just a beach. Enter The Wharf, presently number three in our local "big deal" category. Filling out the top two spots, as they have since before voting for such a thing was ever considered, are the sand and the water.

Despite being relegated to "big deal number three" with virtually no prospect of moving up in the rankings, The Wharf is the only other candidate on the list able to honestly claim "destination" status. While there are many attractions scattered up and down this part of the Gulf Coast, there remain only three targets on our map that can, by themselves, lure a traveler: The sand. The water. And The Wharf.

At The Wharf, there is not only a hotel but a condominium where visitors can rent rooms for as long or short a time as they'd like to stay. There is a beautiful marina to walk, a ten-thousand-seat outdoor amphitheater that hosts major musical artists, a big and very high zip line, a movie house with fifteen theaters, mini-golf, and if it's not the world's largest Ferris wheel, it's at least the biggest one I've ever seen.

There's a nightly laser light show on Main Street, live entertainment in several establishments, and places to eat. There are places to have coffee and places to eat breakfast, or places to do both. There are places for lunch, places for dinner, and places for dessert. All these places, of course, are scattered among all the places to shop.

If variety is key to whether or not you enjoy a shopping experience, you will love The Wharf. In a general sense, the store owners are an eclectic mix of happy locals who have created a welcoming atmosphere in which one can purchase everything from ladies' shoes to wooden carvings of fish. The possibilities span from T-shirts all the way to fine art and everything in between.

If a three-hundred-pound grill is on one's shopping list, Sand Dollar Lifestyles offers the Kamado Joe in every size. There's a store that sells nothing but hot sauce and a totally different one that offers only jerky.

There's a shop for plastic drinking glasses (and they are awesome!), several that deal in home furnishings, and others that offer nice clothing for men and women. In fact, the only thing The Wharf did *not* have was an old-fashioned Five & Dime general store.

Until, apparently . . . now.

I was driving north on The Wharf's Main Street at the posted speed—a cautious five miles per hour—and my eyes stopped on an object just coming into focus. Up and to the left, hanging above the sidewalk on the second floor, was a sign. Fashioned from whitewashed wood and lettered in simple strokes of navy-blue paint, it read "Jones's Five & Dime."

I braked to a stop and stared. *There is no way*, I thought. *He just arrived two days ago.*

As soon as we had gotten to town, Jones asked that I drop him off at the state pier. He was meeting someone there, he'd told me, and insisted he would be fine. "I'm in town for a while," the old man said.

"Let's catch up in a day or two." Typically, "tomorrow" was as close as he came to a suggestion for a time and place.

There was a polite, double-tapped beep from the horn of a small car behind me, and I realized I'd been holding up traffic. Waving an apology, I pulled into an empty parking space and wasted no more time, walking directly to the middle of Main Street before stopping.

Despite the traffic on both sides whizzing by at five miles per hour, this wide median is a safe area, grassy, and lined by towering palm trees. From here, I knew I'd be better able to get a look at Jones's store before I found the escalator. Turning, I shaded my eyes with my left hand, but the angle was not good. The afternoon sun was right in my face and just too bright.

Backing up—only a couple or three feet at the most—I was able to stand in the distinct shadow cast by one of the palm's enormous trunks. I peeked around its edge and could see that the glare obscuring the sign was still there. Nevertheless, I was happy with the momentary relief I'd found from the sun.

Remaining in the shade, I ventured farther from the tree and looked north, up Main Street to the traffic roundabout that circled what is perhaps the most beautiful—and unusual—works of art on the Gulf Coast. The Wharf's centerpiece is not one but two colossal statues of tail-walking marlin, both sculpted from brilliantly polished stainless steel. They were life-size too. And—if you can imagine twin, thousand-pound fish leaping from the asphalt at the same time—very realistic!

Concentrating, my eyes ran back and forth from the second-floor balcony entrance of the new Five & Dime to the palm trees lining the median of Main Street. From my vantage point, and taking only a few seconds, I decided which one of the trees was closest to the front door and counted from it back to the marlin.

Then I did the same thing in reverse, counting palm trees from the steel marlin to my imaginary point straight out from the store. There were eight. Which meant that starting from the marlin and moving north to south, one need only count eight palm trees along the way before coming to a complete stop. With a simple quarter turn to the west, one would be facing the second-floor entrance to Jones's place.

Eight palms south of the marlin at The Wharf. West side of Main Street. Second floor. These were the simple directions for a person wishing to visit Jones's Five & Dime. *As I wish to do*, I thought. *Right now.*

There were two couples on the escalator. *Nope*, I thought. *I'm not waiting behind those people.* That decision made, I gobbled the stairs three at a time. At the top, slightly out of breath, I went to the railing and looked out, fixing my current position and surveying where I had been standing moments before. With a glance up the sidewalk, I spotted the sign and moved quickly that way.

I checked the sign above the entrance, making sure I was in the correct place before entering. As I pulled the door open, a cowbell that had been tied to the inside handle swung on its string and clanked against the glass. It was a sound I remember from my childhood, back when almost every place of business had a cowbell tied to the door. To the uninitiated, I suppose, the sound of a six-inch, rectangular, thin copper bell banging against a moving door might seem a harsh and archaic way of announcing that a customer has arrived.

On the other hand, there are many people—and I can be counted among them—who are contemptuous of the light beams crisscrossing the entrances to most modern establishments. Honestly—if it meant never again being assaulted by the electronic noises triggered when we walk through those light beams—most of us would bring back cowbells in a heartbeat.

As the glass door closed behind me, I could hear the distinct sound of an oscillating fan, the volume of its humming motor rising and falling as the face slowly rotated from left to right and back again. As I moved into the store, I knew The Wharf's central air-conditioning was responsible for the comfortable temperature, but, still, there was something about the whirring of the fan.

Suddenly I realized what it was. The cowbell, the fan, and, among other things, the black skillets hanging on the far wall . . . these were familiar connections for me. I felt as if I had stepped directly into this place from a time machine. I didn't see Jones—or anyone else—so I just moved past the counter and looked around.

I marveled at the store's interior. It was practically a duplicate of the Five & Dime I remember walking to with my grandfather as a kid. In a way, I half expected to turn around and see him.

There were aisles and aisles of stuff. What kind of stuff, you ask? *Every* kind of stuff.

Linens were stacked beside garden tools across from an aisle of food and cleaning supplies one might expect to see in a supermarket.

I walked past wire, rope, nails, ice chests, fishing tackle, and bait. I laughed when I saw a box of dingo dog bottle openers. The picnic necessities had been piled near the swimsuits and flip-flops. A nice selection of picture frames was available. School supplies, plastic spoons . . . it was more than one might imagine and all of it heaped into this not-so-huge space. As I said before, every kind of stuff, including what seemed like a million different kinds of candy and toys.

I headed back to the cash register, having seen a small service bell on the counter. Another antique, the bell was one of the old silver models that rings with a hand slap on its top. Perhaps that would summon my friend. I didn't know what else to do, but I was becoming more confused by the minute.

When I left home this morning, I had driven to the pier and walked around on the beach, hoping to find Jones. I stopped at Sea N

Suds and talked to Willie, Linda, *and* Elaine, but not one of them had seen him. Willie suggested I drive through the state park, which I did, took old Highway 59 to Canal Road, and headed east. I glanced at Willow Calloway's dock as I went by and drove all the way to Melanie Martin's Interiors before finally picking up the old man's trail.

Melanie had seen him headed east along Canal Road about an hour before. "I just came from that way," I said.

"Well," she reasoned, "he was actually closer to the water than he was the road," she said. "I might not have spotted him at all, but he was with the Sutherland boy."

"Really?" I said, becoming more confused by the moment. "How does he know Ollie?"

"I have no idea," Melanie said. "You know," she added, "that is one red-headed kid. At first, I thought, *Oh look, there's Jones walking around with a ball of fire*, but then I realized it was just Oliver." I thanked her and headed back to my truck grateful for a friend like Melanie, who never failed to make me laugh.

The Wharf was the only place they could have gone, I figured, which was how I had ended up here. Jones's Five & Dime, however, was a surprise. When had he opened this place? I had just gotten him out of jail the day before. How long had *this* been here? Orange Beach is not a city; it's a town, and not much slips by folks who live in a town. Especially something like a new store. And double-especially when the store is at The Wharf.

As I'd wandered the aisles, not only had I become curious about when and how Jones had gotten this much stuff in here, I was increasingly baffled about how it was possible for the old man to sell merchandise at the prices I had seen listed. As far as I could tell, about half the items were overpriced. *Dramatically* overpriced. But everything else in Jones's Five & Dime could be purchased for five cents ... or ten cents. No kidding.

I was about to ring the bell when I heard the squeaking of a door opening somewhere toward the back. "Hey, Andy," Jones said. He was leaning out of a small closet on the left side of the store and waved me to him with something in his hand. Almost immediately, I saw what that "something" was—cash.

The old man had a handful of bills. "Seems like you've had a good morning," I remarked, gesturing to the money.

"It *has* been a good morning"—Jones chuckled—"and this is our first day. We just opened." He handed a stack of the money to me. "Count that, will you please?"

"Sure," I said and began to do so. The bills I counted were all fives, so it didn't take long. I pushed them back and said, "Two hundred eighty-five dollars."

"Thank you. Two, eight, five," Jones said and ducked back into the closet. There, he wrote the figure down on a notepad, drew a line under several numbers, and did some quick addition. Announcing the sum by reading it to me, he said, "Nine hundred, thirty-four dollars and seventy-two cents."

"And you just opened this morning? Wow." Changing the subject, I asked, "Hey . . . you just said it was 'our' first day. Who is 'our'?"

He shrugged a bit and wiggled a hand in the air. "Ahh, you know. . Our . . . me . . . Our *is* me. At least for today." He shoved the money in a bank bag and tossed it under a small refrigerator that sat on a table in the closet. I couldn't help but notice the huge, silver coffeepot on top of the fridge.

"It's 11:38 now," the old man said. "You want to go somewhere for lunch? I have just enough time before I have to be somewhere else."

Jones had been looking straight at me when he announced the time. Always fascinated by however he managed this trick or whatever it was, I didn't even comment. Instead, I touched my cell phone to light up the screen. 11:38 exactly.

Jones never wore a watch. Instinctively, I did what I always did when he called the time like this and turned to look for a clock positioned somewhere that he might have seen it. Of course, there wasn't one. It felt like I'd seen him pull this off a thousand times, and there was *never* a clock—not one that I could find anyway.

It was something the old man had been able to do as long as I'd known him. Every now and then, he might look at the sun before he announced the time, but I'd come to believe that was more for effect than anything else. After all, he didn't need the sun. Indoors, at night, on cloudy days . . . it made no difference. I'd never seen him a single minute off the mark.

"I will go to lunch," I answered, "but what are you going to do about the store? Just close up?"

"Nah," he said with a wave of his hand. "I'll just leave a note at the register. Want some coffee to go?"

"Wait . . . you'll just leave the door unlocked?"

"Sure," Jones said, seeming surprised that I was surprised. "With a note at the register. My new people start tomorrow. Want some coffee to go?"

"You've already hired someone?" I asked.

"Yep," he said. "I have a teenaged boy starting after school tomorrow, and I'm about to hire a very sweet young lady I met recently. She and I are becoming reacquainted this afternoon. I'm really looking forward to working with her." As I opened my mouth to ask another question, the old man said, "Hey . . ." and paused.

I closed my mouth and raised my eyebrows. "Hmm?"

"Are we going to lunch?" he asked.

"Yeah, sure," I answered, not certain why he had posed the question.

"Good," he said. "Want some coffee to go?"

"That'd be great, thanks."

Shaking his head as if he were exasperated (though I wasn't sure why), Jones said, "Excellent. I'll get it."

Leaning into the tiny closet, he retrieved two mugs from the several that were stacked and set them on the front of the table. An old box-style, hand coffee grinder was at the back of the table. Jones removed the grinder's small drawer and tilted it toward me. "I just ground the beans right before you came in," he said. "Smells good, doesn't it?" I agreed that it did.

The old man opened the spout in the silver kettle and filled the two mugs with what I must admit was the most aromatically perfect coffee I have ever encountered.

"You drink yours little-kid style, right?" he asked.

"I do," I answered and laughed as Jones faked a shiver. A couple of minutes later, I took the first sip from the cup he'd handed me. "Oh my gosh!" I exclaimed. "What kind of coffee is this?"

"Little-kid coffee," the old man said with a grin. He threw the jab and sipped from his own cup without even looking at me. He apparently thought it was funny though. Jones drank his coffee black and had always teased me about the sugar and milk I wanted in mine. "I got some soft drinks in the little fridge," he added. "You want me to add some Coca-Cola into your cup? We could cool it down even more . . . make it a little sweeter."

"That's very funny," I said.

"Thank you," Jones replied. "I thought so too." We both laughed.

"I meant, what *brand* of coffee is this? It's the best I've ever had in my life."

"You know," he said, "I don't mean to brag, but I don't doubt it. The taste is a merging of my own private blend of coffee beans, how I have them roasted, and my old silver kettle. I don't pick the beans myself, of course, but I do choose the combination that goes into my coffee. Bring your cup, and call Polly to meet us for lunch. I'm hungry."

Jones stopped at the cash register and, after placing his cup on the counter, took a pen and note card from a shelf underneath. As he scribbled something on the card, I threw this one in from the blue: "Jones . . . how did you get this stuff in here so fast? And a sign hanging out front? You know I'm going to be disappointed if you were in town loading merchandise into this store and didn't tell me. The boys and I could have helped."

Jones smiled and continued to write. "Nope," he said. "First day I was back in town was day before yesterday. You were driving, remember?" He finished with the note card, looked up, and saw the question remaining on my face. "This was no problem," he said. "I just had the stuff shipped in. I asked Jim Bibby to find some guys to move it all inside." He started toward the door. "Sea N Suds?"

"Perfect," I answered and pulled my phone from a pocket. I held it so that he couldn't see it, but before I could ask, the old man laughed.

"11:46," he said. "Let's go." He laughed again because he knew he'd been right on the mark. Without stopping to gloat, he headed for the door.

I moved as if to follow, but when the old man's back was turned, I ducked back to look at what he had written. The note was anchored at its top with a single piece of tape and read:

I'll be out the rest of the day. Prices are listed on the merchandise.

The cash register is to your right, so feel free to make change.

Bags are under the counter. I apologize for asking that you serve yourself.

I will return tomorrow. Or perhaps the next day.

Jones

I shook my head in wonder and hurried to catch up.

Nine

"Please rise. The Court of the Second Judicial Circuit is now in session. The Honorable Judge Carolina Gritney presiding."

Seated at a table near the front of the room, the defeated young woman stood before ever looking to see what was happening around her. Glumly, she thought, *At least what I'm wearing is clean.* As positive affirmations go, it was the best Keely Higgins could do at the moment, and while the realization provided only a vague sense of relief—as opposed to being filled with joy and gladness—it was a fact for which she could be grateful.

Yes, Keely's clothing was clean. And that was something. After all, she did not think orange was her best color, could feel that size medium was too big, and had long been aware that one-piece, beltless jumpsuits were not her style. In addition, Keely hated the Crocs on her feet. But the city of Clanson had issued the attire, insisted she wear it, and here she was.

About thirty others, responding to the bailiff's call, got to their feet at the same time a tall, middle-aged woman swept into the room wearing a robe that, while not completely black, was at least a couple shades darker than her skin. While the bailiff continued to stand beside the door through which she had entered, the judge took her seat in a large swivel chair behind a desk on an elevated platform.

Before the judge even picked up her gavel, Keely had three thoughts in rapid succession.

1. *She isn't wearing any makeup.*
2. *I'm not wearing makeup either.*
3. *But I look like hell, and this woman is going to hate my guts.*

The gavel came down with a bang. "Be seated please," the judge said and smiled wearily. "Those of you who came of your own volition, thank you for being here. Those of you who have been required to attend will be sorry."

Judge Gritney did not speak these words with particular animosity. Instead, she said them with perfect peace—like someone else might say, "The weather's been good lately"—as she quickly allowed her eyes to scan the room before organizing a few papers on the high desk known as the bench. There were a few nods to accompany the knowing expressions shared between those gathered in the courtroom. It was as if they had heard Judge Gritney deliver the lines before.

And they had. In fact, the judge had become well known in and around the area for these words and was quoted quite often. Even at Clanson High School, the vice principal repeated her two most famous lines almost every afternoon.

"Those of you who came of your own volition, thank you for being here," he would tell the students assembled in Room 222 at 3 p.m. Those who were there to be tutored or for an after-hours study hall usually seemed to appreciate the sentiment. But because the daily gathering was also used for detention, Mr. Steinhaus would always add, "Those of you who have been required to attend will be sorry."

Nevertheless, no matter where the words were delivered, by whom, or to what group of people, there was usually an equal number of smiles and frowns in response. Certainly, in this instance, Keely was already sorry she had been required to attend. Sorry . . . and alone.

Seeing the judge preoccupied, Keely glanced around and saw two people immediately across the aisle to her right. Both were seated behind a table identical to the one at which Keely's left ankle was chained. Closest to her was a middle-aged man. He was of medium build, wore his gray hair neatly trimmed, and was dressed in a dark suit and red tie. *A cheap dark suit and an ugly tie,* Keely thought.

On his far side was a woman Keely quickly decided was at least ten years older than her but not quite as old as the man. He was obviously her boss or partner and they were prosecuting attorneys, she figured. It was an assumption based on little more than the crime dramas Keely watched on television.

The woman's hair was muted blonde, shoulder length, and pulled back into a ponytail. She wore a tan skirt and matching jacket over a simple white blouse. No necklace, no bracelets, no rings. Her shoes were chestnut brown, with tapered two-inch heels.

Keely looked away from the pair, but not until her mind sneered as brutal an assessment of the woman as she had made about the man seconds before. Her exact thought was, *A plain nothing doing a nothing job in a nothing place.* At that moment, it did not occur to Keely that the woman might have considered her to be a "nothing" as well. Certainly, neither the man nor the woman had bothered to glance her way.

A quick scan of the courtroom behind her, however, and Keely immediately understood what held the attention of everyone else. Without exception, it seemed, the forty or so men and women she saw present for the hearing were looking at her. And not in a kind or sympathetic manner. No, to a person, they openly displayed varying degrees of disgust and hostility.

Keely saw a close blur of movement to her left. Turning, she reflexively jumped as a young man about Keely's age rushed into the empty chair beside her. Simultaneously, he swung a somewhat scuffed, burgundy briefcase onto the table and pressed the buttons on either side of the locks. The gold-plated fasteners swung open with thunking sounds, and before a conscious reason had time to register, Keely's eyes were flooded with tears.

Quickly, she turned down and away from the man beside her. Other than a nod when he sat down, the young man had paid her no more attention than the prosecutors. Keely stabbed at her eyes with the heel of her hand as if something had gotten in them and coughed to further camouflage her emotional reaction—one that surprised Keely almost as much as it would have anyone else had they seen her tears.

What was that? she thought before instantly knowing what must have happened. The morning after Keely had been thrown in jail, she had asked for, and received permission to make, one phone call. There was no boyfriend. She did not consider calling her boss or anyone at work. Her father had been dead for years, and unfortunately, she didn't know the fathers of any close friends.

Standing in the jailhouse hallway that morning with an officer watching her every move, Keely mentally ran down her list of possibilities and came to the empty realization that she didn't actually have any close friends. She also decided against contacting her oldest brother, Jackson.

She had not talked to him in several years, and, not so coincidentally, that occasion was also the last time he had talked to her. His final communique had been delivered immediately after a somewhat heated discussion and immediately *before* he turned on his heel to stalk angrily away. In his defense, Jackson only used a single five-letter word in his good-bye.

On the other hand, he did say it and repeat it. Then, not so much as an afterthought but more in the vein of a carefully considered action, he said it again. And the way Keely remembered it, he had expressed each repetition of the sentiment with escalating emphasis and a dramatic increase in volume. The word started with a *b*.

That is why on the morning of her one phone call to the outside world for help, Keely discarded the notion of asking Jackson for anything and went right to the easier mark. Timothy, her younger brother, would help. She knew he would. So she dialed his number and used her one phone call on him.

Her bail had been set at five thousand dollars—a number she thought ridiculous, but then, she couldn't remember exactly what she'd done either. In any case, Keely didn't have five thousand dollars. Sure, she could have paid a bail bondsman 10 percent of that figure and gotten out of jail if either of her brothers had been willing to sign as a guarantor. But she didn't have five hundred bucks, and her brothers weren't willing to help. Tim had said no for himself before making it clear that in this matter, he spoke for Jackson too.

Then he had hung up on her. It had made her spitting mad, which was her default emotional state whenever anything was too sad to contemplate. And this was. Abandoned by the only family she had left. Of course, as much as she hated them in the moment, she would always remember her brothers as kids. And that was what had made her cry.

When the burgundy briefcase buttons had been pushed and the locking mechanisms thunked open, Keely clearly saw herself at six years of age in the family den. She was a fair maiden being protected by her knights, the courageous Sir Jackson and handsome Sir Timmy. For hours, the boys fought dragons for her using the only weapons at their disposal—the miniature catapults mounted on their father's briefcase. Over and over, until they'd all laughed themselves silly, the little girl's heroes launched spitball boulders into fiery attackers, recocked the catapults, and shot them again.

It had been the sudden mental image of them as children that had summoned Keely's tears. But the concept of family as a protective reality was more fantasy now than it had been when they were kids. She was alone and knew it. Time to toughen up.

"Mr. Haywood?" From the bench, the judge's voice interrupted Keely's thoughts. "Mr. Haywood," Judge Gritney continued without waiting for a response, "this is the second time you have been late for my court. I am aware that you are a new resident of this state and so may not be aware of our customs. The first time you were late . . . last week . . . I attempted to take into account your being newly graduated. However, being on time is common courtesy, not a class you might have failed in law school at the University of Alabama."

"Your Honor, I'm very—"

"I am still speaking to you, Mr. Haywood!" the judge boomed. "Do not interrupt me in this courtroom!" She stared hard at the cringing attorney and took her pause to a length that had everyone in the courtroom holding their breath.

Finally, Judge Gritney continued. Her volume was reduced, but the intensity with which she delivered her message remained the same. "Now, Mr. Haywood. In only a few moments, I will demonstrate to you and this court that I have a willingness to begin this day again. I will be cordial. But Mr. Haywood, as nice as I may appear, sir, do not make the mistake of assuming that I do not keep track of my bygones. Because I do. In fact, I catalog each and every one. Even at this very moment, Mr. Haywood, you are free to walk out of here and find another county in which you can practice tardy law. Perhaps you will find another judge who blithely allows bygones to be bygones.

"But if you stay here, Mr. Haywood, you would do well to remember that while other courtrooms may suffer fools lightly, I do not suffer them at all. You have been assigned the role of public defender in my court twice now. And as I pointed out a moment ago, you have been late on both occasions. That's two strikes, Mr. Haywood. If I ever see a third one, sir, I will take you out of this ballgame so fast your head will spin. Because if you cannot hit the slow, underhand pitches this county is tossing your way, I will allow you the opportunity to find another county's team to join.

"I will not ask if I have made myself clear or if you understand. We have wasted enough of this team's morning. It is time to play ball.

"Good afternoon, counselors," she said with a smile to the opposite table. "How is the district attorney these days?"

"He is well, Judge, and asked us to send you his regards," the attorney in the dark suit said.

"Excellent," Gritney responded. "Please thank him and express the court's appreciation for all his hard work." Turning her attention back to Keely's table, the judge spoke again to the young man.

"Mr. Haywood," she said brightly. "Good afternoon."

"Good afternoon, Judge."

Keely heard the wariness in Haywood's voice.

"Mr. Haywood, when I arrived this morning, I missed seeing an expected item on my desk. Do you know what I missed?"

"No, Your Honor."

"I missed seeing a written plea of 'not guilty' from this defendant."

At that, Keely—like everyone else in the courtroom—turned to look at the man seated beside her. She didn't know enough about the law to understand why this would have been important, but she could see that the attorney understood. And she wondered if the bench was far enough away that the judge might also miss seeing the blood drain from his face.

Without offering him an opportunity to comment, Judge Gritney said, "As I am sure they taught you in Tuscaloosa, Mr. Haywood, a written plea on my desk this morning would have allowed us to avoid this formal hearing." The judge took a deep breath as if resigned to her fate. "But we *are* here, Mr. Haywood, and without any further delay, I am about to read the formal charges. Is your client ready to plead?"

Ten

A llow me to state for the record that of all the ages I would *not* want to do over again, thirteen is at the top of the list. A thirteen-year-old human—at least the male of our species—is much like a lion of the same age equivalent and gender. Even his voice is uncontrollable. And sometimes at night, when he is alone in the dark, what he imagined as a roar squeaks from his throat, more a cry for his mother than a declaration about becoming king of any jungle.

At thirteen, there is an unforeseen low tide of self-esteem that arrives with a rising level of uncertainty about the world in general. These demons of doubt produce irrational fear—a gradually occurring, false narrative of terror that might have come to town unannounced but is now steadily making its presence known.

Viewed dispassionately, as one might watch a germ under a microscope, irrational fear can be understood as an invention of the mind—a self-seeking missile with load-bearing capacity that adjusts on the fly and will use however much weapons-grade material the mind has provided to completely destroy its target.

Irrational fear is a creative misuse of one's own imagination, and while most often destructive, this type of fear is actually armed with a shut-down switch that can be flipped, held fast, and locked. It's a mental gear that can be triggered only by intentional thought and contains the power to banish trepidation forever.

Unidentified and left alone, irrational fear often finds a grip and begins to squeeze the guts of a boy and lead him to another deception—this one about the opposite sex. The lie convinces him that the beast in *his* belly is a greater foe—and far more difficult to vanquish—than the harmless monarchs and swallowtails fluttering at the same time in delicate tummies of girls.

Yes, life until now has been experienced from inside the safety of a carefully managed playground, but at thirteen, the boy hears and feels the gates to that sanctuary being unhinged. Seat belts fastened or not, all indications are that the ride from this point on will be faster and rougher and portioned out with a significant reduction in mercy.

As the consciousness of a thirteen-year-old pegs deep into the red zone, the world he once thought to be wide and welcoming now feels cramped and unsteady—like an outhouse being nosed by machine onto a conveyor belt and shoved down society's fast-tapering throat. He finds himself struggling for space, and the adults, who not too long before had circled him with protective arms, aren't as friendly as they used to be. Neither are they as funny.

But then, right about the time he has gathered the courage to speak up—perhaps to talk with someone about what he is noticing—a huge funnel suddenly appears directly ahead, and the boy knows without question that he had darn well better fit into the neck of it. Just like the other kids seem to be managing. And, of course, he does.

With a forced smile on his face and in nicer clothes than he'd have ever chosen to wear, the boy is ground down the chute with little say in the matter. For at this point, it's the fate of almost every thirteen-year-old to get dumped into one big doughy mess with the other kids roughly his same age, all wearing somewhat similar clothes and having mastered a predictably limited vocabulary.

Once in, not long after the mixing blades begin their relentless work, he resigns himself to the inevitable and decides to ignore the pain, no longer attempting to surface and ride the top of the wave or swim to the edges of the bowl. The recipe was decided upon long ago; blending is now underway.

With the always interesting addition of assorted nuts and flakes tossed into the mixture along the way, the goal, of course, is to be properly rolled, cut into shape, and baked through the industrial conveyor ovens of middle and high school in order to be inspected at the other end and labeled a "perfect cookie."

At that magnificent moment, society's hope, of course, is that he—along with all the others—might now take the opportunity to do it all over again, but *this* time for real money, at a state-sanctioned university to which he can remain in financial debt for the rest of his life.

And during the "rest of his life," if that man ever becomes confused by his lack of employment due to the level of difficulty he has encountered meeting people or contributing to conversations deeper than those about television programs or ball games—

If he is ever discouraged by the inability to communicate an idea effectively or understand the basic economic realities controlling his very existence—

Then, at least, he can be content knowing that if a government agency ever again requires him to read a novel by John Steinbeck or to explain why he failed to perform a simple bookkeeping task, he will at least be able to identify a theme, like "weariness" or "the American dream," and claim that once upon a time he was indeed able to pass Algebra II.

Oliver Sutherland was thirteen years old.

I'd seen Oliver around Orange Beach for a couple of years. A lot of people come and go in a resort town, and after a time, there is a sameness to all of them. Oliver, however, was in an obvious category of one.

It wasn't because Oliver was tall—even though he was. Or because he was beanpole thin or sported freckles that evenly covered his arms and face.

No, the detail that stood one to attention upon a first glimpse of Oliver was his hair.

To simply say Oliver Sutherland was a redhead and let it go at that would do an injustice to your imagination. So how do I put this? Describing Oliver's hair as red would be like saying Goliath was kind of a big guy. Or that Rembrandt was a pretty good painter. Only if flame produced pigment instead of heat could one possibly characterize the color of this young man's head.

And to quell any suspicion that my portrayal is exaggerated, I'd ask you to remember Melanie Martin's reference to Ollie's head resembling a ball of fire. In addition, consider the fact that even while engaged in casual conversation, the townsfolk of Orange Beach do not compare the color of Oliver's most recognizable feature to anything else. Instead, all things are compared to it.

For instance, instead of wasting precious minutes browsing through the variations of red offered by the nail salon on Canal Road, a lady need only pop in and declare, "I need a bottle of polish the shade of the Sutherland child's hair," and the bottle would be fetched.

On a Friday night last October, I was standing on the sidelines at an Orange Beach High School football game. To the delight of about fifteen hundred fans, our hometown Mako offense was driving for a score. During a timeout, I looked toward the fence and happened to see a woman I didn't recognize talking to one of the middle-school cheerleaders whose squad was cheering with the older girls for this game.

It was a short conversation, and the young cheerleader jogged close to where I was standing. "Hi, Mr. Andrews," she said, and I responded. The girl turned toward the bleachers and put a hand above her eyes to shield them from the stadium lights.

I wasn't sure if there was a problem, but in Orange Beach, the adults still watch out for each other's children. "I saw the lady wave you over," I said, before adding, "Is everything all right?"

"Oh, yes, sir," she said. "That was Mrs. Sutherland—Oliver's mom—they live down the street from us. She said she has to go home and wanted me to tell Ollie to ride with us." Her hand was still above her eyes.

"And now you're trying to find him in the crowd, right?"

"Yes, sir."

"Well," I said, "just look for the hair."

The cheerleader giggled. "I am," she said, and about five seconds later, pointed into the bleachers. "There he is," she said, and I looked toward the location she was indicating.

Oliver Sutherland was twenty or so rows up and about thirty yards down from where we stood. He was in the middle of fifteen hundred people, but it did not matter. The kid's head was a beacon.

Not only was Oliver easily spotted, he was very recognizable. Everyone who didn't know him, knew *of* him, mostly because of his reputation. Usually, when a person is said to have a reputation, the assumption is that it's a bad one. That is not the case with this young man. His reputation was a good one—especially among the adults.

Oliver was extremely smart, though his grades at school did not bear evidence to the fact. Only into his teens, Oliver was a brilliant conversationalist, and when the opportunity presented itself, his quick wit was apparent. He smiled often and laughed easily.

The only issue anyone seemed to have with Oliver was that there didn't seem to be any kind of an issue. Ever. Dr. Charlie Cooper spoke for most of Orange Beach when he said, "Great kid. *Great* kid. But you can just look at Ollie and tell he's up to something." So Oliver had a reputation for mischief even though he'd never been caught at anything.

Never been caught. Those three words explain why people around town were convinced that Oliver certainly got away with a lot. Curiously, however, since no one could produce a single example of anything he'd actually gotten away with, neither was anyone able to define "a lot."

Word had gotten around about a conversation held one morning at Café Beignet. Apparently, Pastor Ruark had made a remark about Blair Houston Monroe not liking Oliver. To which Mike Martin responded, "That don't mean nothing. Blair Houston don't like nobody. I'd hardly hold that against the child."

The child? Well, there you have it—a perfect example of our earlier topic. You see, referring to Ollie as a child is a big part of the problem with that age. Because at thirteen, he *wasn't* a child anymore. But neither was he an adult.

Not all kid; not quite grown-up. It's a juxtaposition that goes a long way in explaining the reasoning (in that young, teenaged way of not reasoning at all) that made it possible for Oliver to have decided he was in no danger, even while his arm—up to the shoulder—was pushed through the intake vent of a currently functioning commercial air-conditioning unit.

I suppose many of us are fortunate to have survived some of the things that seemed perfectly logical to us as teenagers. The "Old Enough to Know Better" speech that is often given by a parent—or sometimes another authority—is an after-action declaration derived from sound adolescent sociology. Unfortunately, its power is most often used too late to prevent trouble but is always just in time for a hearty I-told-you-so.

Similar confusion can be found in comparisons of "old enough" and "young enough." Opposite meanings, to be sure, but certainly another way of explaining the decision-making process Oliver engaged just prior to his present activity.

Oliver was "old enough" to have quietly navigated several hundred yards of pine thicket, alone in the dark, and accurately arrive in a specifically predetermined location behind the middle school. At the same time, he was "young enough" to confidently stick his hand deep inside a working machine running 100,000 BTUs per hour and not think about electrocution as a possibility.

There were four monstrous air-conditioning units lined up at the back of the school. Oliver had plans for three of the four. The gym and locker rooms, the school office complex, and the music wing, which included the glee club and the band room. Most of the actual classrooms would be spared. *You got to have some folks to laugh*, he thought. *Can't have everybody throwing up and crying.*

With his arm deep inside, Oliver did something that seemed to require force with his hand. He rocked forward a couple of times, heard a hiss, and backed his arm out. Moving to his right, he repeated the procedure twice more and was finished with what he had intended.

Even though the vast majority of his product was vented into the school, Oliver was surprised to feel a smidge nauseous from the tiny whiffs he had received. Any hunter could have told the thirteen-year-old that most of the game animal, mating-scent, urine-based products could melt someone's head from their shoulders. There was nothing that compared to the stench. Nothing.

The deer lure "Doe in Heat" is rough. However, it is child's play compared to "Sow in Heat," a can of which Oliver had in his hand at the moment. An aerosol can of "Sow in Heat" purchased at Campbells Hardware and Sporting Goods costs less than ten bucks per can, and three were all he needed.

When Oliver depressed the caps and the three cans emptied their contents into the vent system that powered the air-conditioning for three-fourths of Orange Beach Middle School, he retreated, easing through the pines on a direct route home. Ollie was tired but happy. The "Sow in Heat" alone would have been enough. As it turned out, the foul hormonal mixture was the cherry on top of his original idea.

When Oliver had seen in the newspaper that the state park was live-trapping feral hogs, he searched until he found the traps. The "catch pens," the article had said, were surveyed only once a day—in the mornings. Therefore, Ollie checked them every afternoon until he found six small pigs in three different traps at the same time.

That night, Ollie removed all six pigs and divided them into two burlap sacks. Each, he estimated, weighed more than forty pounds, and it took him two trips through the woods to get both the wriggling, squealing bags to his staging area.

From inside the school earlier that day, Ollie had unlocked three windows in three widely spaced locations. From the art department, he had also pocketed a wide-tipped, black permanent marker.

When Ollie slipped the pigs numbered "1" and "2" through the first window, he made a mental note to be early for school the next morning. In the second location, as the pigs marked "3" and "4" touched the floor and sped off, he smiled. The pigs were lightning fast, and the vegetable oil he was pouring on each of them before they were released would make tomorrow's show a lot longer.

Easing around to the third unlocked window, Ollie greased the last two pigs. Placing them inside, he watched carefully as they raced away, turning into a lighted hallway before disappearing from view. Ollie saw the large numbers printed on their sides very clearly. The oil had not faded the ink at all.

Pig number "6" and pig number "7" were good to go.

Eleven

The judge was opening a folder as she asked the question she had posed to attorneys hundreds of times before: "Is your client ready to plead?"

Reading glasses in place, she had no expectation that she would hear anything other than a perfunctory "Yes, Your Honor." For a brief moment, however, the judge heard nothing. Then the sound of a throat being cleared. Without moving her head, Judge Gritney lifted her eyes and peered over the rims of her glasses.

"Your Honor, if I may?" Haywood asked.

Removing the glasses from her face, the judge pursed her lips and shook her head. She leaned all the way back in her big chair, made a show of checking her watch and with a magnanimous gesture—arm high in the air with an open palm—simply said, "Yes?"

"Your Honor," Haywood began nervously, "I was informed about this case—and the fact that it was being assigned to me—only thirty minutes ago ... ahh ... which is why I was late ..." He paused, but there was no reaction from the bench, so he continued. "That is also why there was no plea from my client on your desk this morning. And so, no, Your Honor, my client is not ready to plead. We haven't even met."

Keely had no trouble following the attorney's words—and every one of them was the truth—but the expression now evolving on Judge Gritney's face was not encouraging. From the start, weary aggravation had been apparent in the judge's demeanor. It was this new information, Keely saw, that had begun to redline the woman's level of frustration.

It was plain to see that the judge was unhappy with what she'd just been told. She looked at the bailiff before attempting, without success, to make eye contact with the two prosecutors, but their heads were down. They wanted no part of this.

Any attorney who has ever felt the wrath of unchecked judicial power could have predicted what was about to happen. Added to everything else, they all thought, Judge Gritney now had a dump-truck load of incredulity in gear and was about to drive it over the attorney for the defense.

The justice system is not known for its patience and understanding. Grace and mercy are also in short supply, and that is especially true when, for whatever reason, a judge has it in for an attorney. That certainly described the situation everyone believed was unfolding at present. But Judge Gritney surprised them all.

She picked up the folder, paused as if deep in thought, and put it back down without having opened it. For a moment, she stared at the defense attorney and for the first time, seemed to notice Keely. The courtroom was silent as Judge Gritney took a glass of water and drank several swallows.

"Mr. Haywood?" she said at last.

"Yes, Your Honor?" he answered.

"Mr. Haywood . . . did you know my daughter?"

"No, Your Honor," he answered without hesitation, "but I do know she was in law school at Alabama."

Gritney narrowed her eyes. "Are you trying to make me angry again, Mr. Haywood?"

The attorney did not look away. His eyes were soft as he shook his head. "No, Your Honor. Not at all."

The judge took another drink of water from the glass. "She was a year ahead of you in law school. I am not sure how you came to work as a public defender, Mr. Haywood, nor do I know what your future intentions might be, but my daughter was eager to practice law as you do. She had no judicial aspirations. It occurred to me a moment ago, that had my daughter lived, she'd probably have ended up dealing with the same issues that plague you today.

"As a young counselor, she would have been an afterthought in the public defender's office, assigned at the last minute by an overworked government bureaucrat to come to the immediate aid of a client without even having met the client. And without a doubt, she would have been expected to perform this miracle in front of a grouchy old judge who had forgotten what it was like to be young and need a bit of help."

The judge picked up her water glass and held it for the courtroom to see. It was empty. Placing it carefully in front of her, she looked at her watch and said, "Mr. Haywood, I am out of water. Despite the early hour and the fact that we have not accomplished much, I intend to recess this court in order that I may refill this glass. Mr. Haywood, do you believe an hour to be enough time for me to do that?"

"Yes, Your Honor," the attorney said. "An hour would be perfect."

"Court is in recess for one hour," Judge Gritney said, striking the gavel. Without further comment, she retreated through the door behind the bench and disappeared into her chambers.

"I'm Carl Haywood," he said without shaking her hand. He removed a few pieces of paper from the burgundy briefcase and scanned them quickly. "You are twenty-seven-year-old Keillor Higgins, currently residing in Atlanta, Georgia, formerly employed as a loan officer with Pace Bank and Trust. I don't have much beyond that, but we're on the clock, so you need to fill me in quickly."

"Call me Keely. Yes, Atlanta. And it's not 'formerly employed by.' I still work for Pace."

Haywood continued to read the papers but shook his head absently. "Nope," he said. "Not anymore. Pace Bank and Trust is a financial institution registered with the FDIC. You were a loan officer. Therefore, they were notified within twenty-four hours of your being arrested and charged with a felony. They already have this." The young attorney flipped through a couple of pages, pulled one, and placed it on the table in front of his client.

It was Keely's mug shot, taken soon after she had been arrested. The image was horrendous, worse than she could've imagined. Keely turned her head and pushed the photograph back to the attorney. She neither commented nor doubted his assessment concerning her job status back in Atlanta. As Haywood tucked the mug shot into his brief-case, Keely thought, *Yeah . . . if the bank has that, I'm unemployed for sure.*

"Is there anything you want to tell me about the other night?" Haywood asked.

"I was drunk?" the young woman responded with a flippant expression.

Haywood frowned. "I gotta say, I think everybody has already figured that out." He looked at his watch. "You take all the time you want though. Smart aleck seems your style. I can't wait to see how that works for you when I tell the judge that your lack of cooperation wasted her hour."

"Okay, okay," Keely said. "I'm sorry. First, I didn't know getting drunk was a felony."

"It's not."

"But you said I was charged with a felony."

"You are." Haywood paused, but Keely did not respond. He looked at her more closely before asking, "So . . . you're telling me you don't remember what you did?"

Keely shook her head.

"Okay . . . well, you were drunk and disorderly, which in the state of Florida, is *not* a felony. Then you hit a police officer, which, everywhere in the world, *is*."

Keely stared blankly. "I totally don't remember doing that."

Haywood checked the time again. "Well, the judge will be back in here soon, and she will want a 'guilty' or a 'not guilty.' As your court-appointed attorney, I can only recommend you avoid any statement to *this* judge that begins with 'I totally don't remember.'"

"Is the officer hurt?" Keely asked.

"No," Haywood replied, "but everyone in this small town is mad as hell about it. Understand . . . you have no friends or relatives here. You were just passing through and stopped for whatever reason. Evidently, however, within two hours of arriving in this charming community, you were intoxicated and assaulted one of their police officers. So now you're facing this judge, in this town, with this crime." The attorney shook his head in a combination of disgust and defeat. "You'd be better off right now if you'd just gone to some big city and robbed a bank."

Twenty minutes after the judge returned, the charges were read, and Keely shocked everyone but her attorney by pleading guilty. For a moment, there was silence in the courtroom. Judge Gritney removed her reading glasses. "Mr. Haywood?" she said, not unkindly. "Have you counseled your client about the consequences of a guilty plea in this case?"

"Yes, Your Honor," the young attorney answered.

Directing her gaze to Keely, the judge said, "Ms. Higgins, are you fully aware that today's proceedings are not a trial but a hearing, and that a guilty plea will immediately place you at the mercy of this court?"

Keely nodded.

"Speak, Ms. Higgins," Judge Gritney instructed. "My stenographer does not record movements of the head. Do you understand that by issuing a guilty plea, you can be formally sentenced today?"

"Yes."

The judge looked hard at Keely for several seconds before shifting her stare to the attorney and using a few more seconds on him. "Mr. Haywood," she began again, slowly this time, "did you inform Ms. Higgins that this court . . . that I . . . if allowed to pronounce sentence in this case, my judgment is likely to be harsh?"

Haywood held Judge Gritney's gaze and stated, "Yes, Your Honor. I did."

With a slight softening of her voice, the judge asked, "Did you tell her *why*, Mr. Haywood?"

The young attorney's eyes fell. "No, Your Honor," he said. "I did not."

With that, Keely felt an unusual hush settle over the courtroom. Glancing to her right, the assistant district attorneys were staring at their hands, folded in front of them on the table. Beyond them, not a single person within Keely's view was looking toward the bench. Some heads were down. Others turned their eyes to the ceiling fans. A few more seemed focused on the window.

The defense attorney appeared to be studying Keely's folder, but his eyes were unmoving. At first, Keely assumed everyone was avoiding eye contact with her. In the next instant, however, she understood that was not the case. With a sinking feeling, though she couldn't imagine why, it was Judge Gritney, Keely decided, whose face no one could bear watching at the moment.

Twelve

It felt like a long time, but in reality, might've been only fifteen or twenty seconds before the judge moved. Holding a single sheet of paper in front of her, she said, "Ms. Higgins, because of your guilty pleas to both charges against you, this court has latitude with regard to the state's sentencing guidelines. On the Disorderly Intoxication charge, I can only fine you as much as five hundred dollars and keep you in a county jail for as long as sixty days."

Keely's heart was hammering. She was hearing the judge as if from a long tunnel and it occurred to her that she might faint.

"Battery of a Police Officer," Judge Gritney read from the paper before placing it down and looking again at Keely. "This charge is not only a felony; it is a disgrace. My limit here is a fine of five thousand dollars and up to thirty years in the state penitentiary."

Tears began to track down Keely's face.

"The fact that the felony charge is alcohol related," the judge continued, "makes your actions especially egregious to me, Ms. Keely, and I will be honest, when you pled guilty, I was not only pleased but saw my way clear to have you on your way to Ocala tomorrow."

Leaning forward, she added, "Ocala is a bit south of Gainesville. It's where the state of Florida houses our female inmates."

Keely's head was down, and tears fell into her lap. She had never felt so alone in her entire life. *Alone*, she thought. *No help and no hope.*

"I stayed in my chambers during our recess, Ms. Higgins. And for some reason, I did a little research of my own on you."

Keely lifted her head and looked at the judge.

"I found that you grew up without a mother, your father is dead, and your brothers want nothing to do with you. Not only do you lack the personal finances, apparently, you do not even have a single friend willing to attract the interest of a bail bondsman. You have twenty-seven thousand dollars in credit-card debt—this despite all six cards listed in your name having been canceled."

Judge Gritney selected a sheet of paper from her right and examined it briefly. "Certainly, by now," she said, "you must be aware of your pending unemployment."

Keely could only nod. Judge Gritney looked to Haywood, who spoke on Keely's behalf. "She is, Your Honor. We discussed that probability during the recess."

"Thank you, Mr. Haywood. Your client can consider the termination already in place. The only good news I see among this considerable mess is that you were *not* behind the wheel of a car when you were arrested.

"Nevertheless, while you can still technically operate a motor vehicle, a representative from your former employer retrieved the company car with which you were entrusted. Conveniently, they had a key of their own, and their paperwork was in order. I signed the release first thing this morning."

Judge Gritney, now directing her comments back to Keely said,

"So . . . I look at your life, and I see this: extreme arrogance, disregard for others, and lack of respect for authority. These, of course, describe effects of abusing alcohol. I see a person with no family, no friends, no money, and no job.

"To me, it would seem a kindness to send you to prison." Judge Gritney paused before continuing. "However, I am also aware that you've had no prior arrests."

At this, the judge paused again. The three attorneys in the room appeared now to have become curious. The spectators seemed suspicious. Keely, whose tears continued to flow, remained hopeless about the situation.

"Ms. Higgins . . ." Everyone in the courtroom listened with rapt attention as the judge looked toward the ceiling and seemed to gather herself. Finally, she continued. "Ms. Higgins, I am going to tell you something I only wish I had the opportunity to tell my daughter. It is this: second chances exist.

"That having been said, it is a common misconception that everybody deserves one. On the contrary, they do not. In fact, considering the human condition and our many sins, *most* of us do not deserve a second chance.

"A second chance is an expression of grace. It is unmerited favor. When bestowed from one person to another, a second chance involves the undeserved generosity of the giver. While I do not believe one is owed a second chance, I do believe that a person receiving a second chance has the responsibility to make the most of that opportunity.

"Mr. Haywood? Would you and your client rise? I believe this court is ready to sentence Ms. Higgins."

Even with the assistance of her attorney, it was all Keely could do to stand up. And once she did, she wasn't sure she could stay up. While her sobs were under control, the tears continued to course down her cheeks. Facing the judge, she desperately wanted someone to pat her arm, to tell her everything would be all right. Keely realized, with almost unbearable sadness, that even at this critical moment in her life, no one in the world was even willing to hold her hand.

"Ms. Higgins," Judge Gritney began, "we have already discussed the latitude this court has in your case. With that in mind, there are two possibilities that exist for you today. Prison...or a second chance."

Almost immediately, Keely opened her mouth to speak. "Not so fast," the judge said, holding up her hand. "Remember . . . a second chance involves the generosity of someone else. And if there is a 'someone else' for you, that person must be in this courtroom right now. Why, you ask? Because only those who are here at the moment care enough about this case to have concerned themselves one way or another." Again, there was confusion on the faces of almost everyone in the courtroom.

The judge explained, "No one was physically harmed by your actions, Ms. Higgins, and knowing there was no property damage either, I am willing to grant you probation if..." Judge Gritney placed emphasis on the "if." "If . . . there is someone in this courtroom who is willing to offer you a job at their own place of business. You must keep that job and successfully satisfy its requirements for at least six months."

As they waited, Keely and her attorney had similar thoughts. *This lady is going to prison*, Haywood concluded. *The people in here do not like her at all.*

Cruel was the first word that came to Keely's mind. *Giving me hope only to snatch it away? No one in this courtroom will give me a job, and this judge knows it. She's just . . . cruel.*

Judge Gritney looked at the spectators and felt immediately that she'd made a mistake. Her attention had not been on the gallery. It never was. It had never needed to be. She watched attorneys and juries, witnesses, victims, and those accused of a crime. That was what a judge did.

Her intention had been to give this young woman some much-needed direction to go along with the second chance. In her mind, she was arranging a sentence of mandatory mentoring. Now, she feared, her own compassion had gotten the best of her. Worse, if this did not work—and all of a sudden, she didn't believe it was going to—her "grand plan" would leave Higgins headed to prison while she gained a reputation as a judge who was bitter and vindictive.

After a quick silent prayer, Judge Gritney announced, "The court is offering this unique solution as a second chance for this young lady, that is true . . ." With a nod of her head, the judge indicated Keely. "However, it is an opportunity for someone present today to lead this community."

She waited. No one moved.

"Surely, there is a person in this courtroom with a job to offer Ms. Higgins."

As the silence grew deafening and its meaning became apparent, Keely began to sob again. Haywood looked as if he wanted to bolt. Judge Gritney scanned the courtroom one last time—including a glance at the bailiff and stenographer—and saw nothing in their faces but anger or apathy.

Slowly, the judge drew in a deep breath and prepared to address the woman she had honestly hoped to help . . . the one she was now duty bound to sentence to prison.

Keely swayed unsteadily. Fearing his client was about to collapse, Haywood reached out, placing his right hand under Keely's left elbow.

In her elevated position from the bench, Judge Gritney had no choice but to watch the scene unfold, but when she witnessed the unexpected sympathy—the expression of kindness—the young attorney displayed for his stricken client, she was touched in a way she'd never experienced in her professional life. Without warning, the gnawing dread in the pit of her stomach became a lump in her throat. Her eyes watering, she opened them wide to avoid the judicial disaster of tears rolling down her face as she pronounced sentence.

"Ms. Higgins . . ." the judge began and paused. She was attempting to control the slight quaver in her voice and momentarily glanced away from the young woman. Tears blurred her vision as she blinked, fighting to contain them. Despite not seeing clearly, movement caught her attention.

The judge faked a cough. It was enough to get a handkerchief and wipe her eyes. Looking more carefully, she saw the movement again and leaned a bit to her left. Toward the back of the courtroom, positioned in a seat that placed Higgins directly between Judge Gritney and himself, was a white-haired gentleman with his hand up.

He was leaning to his right and had waved a couple of times. Realizing the judge had seen him, the old man raised his eyebrows and gave another motion with his hand.

Judge Gritney's brow furrowed slightly. *Where did he come from?* she thought. The judge knew she had not seen him only a few moments before, though she had carefully scanned the gallery. Quickly deciding she missed him because Keely had been in her line of sight, the judge addressed the old man. "Sir? Can I help you?"

"I have a small store," the old man said as he stood. "She could be helpful there."

There was a rustling sound in the courtroom as everyone turned to see who had interrupted the court's proceedings. The expressions around the room didn't change much. Only Keely reacted, but her air of stunned disbelief was hidden from the judge, and no one else was looking her way to notice.

"What is your name, sir?" Judge Gritney asked. "I don't believe I am familiar with your store. Is it located here?"

"I am Jones, Your Honor. Not Mr. Jones. Just Jones," he said pleasantly. "And no, ma'am. My Five & Dime is in Orange Beach, Alabama."

Keely didn't know what to say or whether to say anything at all. Certainly, she recognized the old man. Should she go anywhere with someone who had been in jail? Then Keely realized she was also "someone who had been in jail" and decided she would keep quiet. Anything was better than prison, she figured, and if this Jones character was the only way she could avoid it, fine.

"Your Honor?" It was the woman from the district attorney's office. "We object to this particular arrangement on the grounds that this man's place of business is out of state."

Judge Gritney withered the prosecutor with a look. "Your objection is noted and ignored. This court does, however, appreciate being reminded that Alabama is out of state." Redirecting her attention to Jones, she attempted to smile and began her most pressing question. "So, Mr. ahh . . ."

"Jones," he said.

"Yes. Mr. Jones, to be—"

"Jones, Your Honor," the old man broke in. "No mister to it. Just Jones."

Judge Gritney looked startled. She was not used to being interrupted but seemed more than willing to grasp at this straw that had seemingly appeared from nowhere. Taking a calming breath, she started over. "All right. Jones . . . ," she said, and seeing the white-haired gentleman nod his approval, continued. "To be clear, you are giving Ms. Higgins a job?"

"Oh, no, ma'am," he replied. "I do own and run a place of business, but I don't have a job to give anyone."

A flash of irritation crossed the judge's face. She glanced at the bailiff, who dutifully rolled his eyes.

Keely, of course, was still facing the old man and heard his words as clearly as the judge. Curiously, however, a wave of nausea and panic hit her full force, only to subside within seconds. At the very instant the bailiff had rolled his, Keely had been looking directly into the blue eyes of the old man. And the left one blinked.

More precisely, it winked.

Did I see that? Keely asked herself. Very quickly, she noticed the sly but innocent manner with which he was looking at her now and decided that yes, she had seen exactly that. *Yes,* she thought, *he winked at me.*

"Sir," Judge Gritney said, which in itself was a statement. Her irritation was coming into bloom. "If you are toying with this court, and I find you in contempt, you will be seated in *her* chair tomorrow morning." The judge had pointed to Keely, who had turned back toward the bench. She said, "Sir, is there even the slightest reason I should continue here?"

Once again, Judge Gritney was not expecting an answer to her question. Jones, however, jumped in with a reply before she could say any more. "Yes, Your Honor," he said. "And I think it's more than the slightest reason. In fact, it is the reason you gave earlier."

She frowned, not remembering what she might have said that this man might reference. "I don't recall saying anything of the kind, sir."

"Well, ma'am," Jones said. "I believe you expressed the desire not to be a grouchy old judge who has forgotten what it was like to be young and in need of a bit of help. That's what you said, isn't it?"

At that moment, there were quite a few people in the courtroom who seemed to be immediately seeking shelter from the hurricane they felt sure was about to blow from the bench. Just as surely, there were some who were disappointed by her self-control.

Judge Gritney's jaw dropped only a bit before she had it firmly back in place. *Either this guy is putting me on,* the judge thought, *or he's as sharp as a tack. Let's find out which it is.*

"I do not understand," she said. "I thought—I believe we all thought—that you were offering to help Ms. Higgins."

As he responded, Jones smiled as if nothing troubled him in the least. "Oh, Your Honor, I apologize for the confusion," he began. "I *am* offering to help the young lady. And the first way I will help is by making certain that Ms. Higgins understands the truth as it applies to basic economics, which is basically this: As the owner of a business, I do not have a job to give. I have results I require."

For several beats, Judge Gritney stared stoically at the old man, but then a spark appeared on her face and a grin slowly began to take shape. When it was ear to ear, she nodded at Jones before looking once more at Keely. The judge's face now reflected less of a grin. Her countenance was more one of hope and challenge. *Do not blow this,* she seemed to be communicating.

The judge spoke as if to everyone at once. "The court clerk is available now to gather details the county requires. Signatures will be necessary along with information the county will need to follow up on all aspects of this case. Bailiff, please release Ms. Higgins." Looking to Jones, she said, "Sir, thank you for your help."

At last, the judge looked at Keely again. Seeing the young woman mouth the words *Thank you,* the judge nodded, took her gavel, and slammed it down. "This court," she said, "is adjourned."

As Keely's ankle was being unlocked, she shook Haywood's hand and thanked him.

"I have no idea what just happened," he said with a chuckle, "but

I'm glad it did." More seriously, he added, "Will you be okay? I mean ... do you know this old guy?"

"Oh yeah," Keely said quietly. "He's good. We were in jail together."

Haywood's face blanched, and he held up a hand. "Just don't tell me any more. Really ... I don't want to know. Anyway, good luck."

He closed the burgundy briefcase and was about to leave when Keely remembered a question. Stopping him with a gentle hand on his arm, she said, "You know, there is something I'd like to know."

"Okay," he replied.

"Now that things are turning out well," she said, "I'm curious. During the recess, you told me that I'd have been better off if I had robbed a bank because I was facing this judge, in this town, with this crime. What did you mean?"

Haywood put the briefcase back on the table and looked at her thoughtfully. "This morning," he said finally, "do you remember when Judge Gritney asked if I had known her daughter at law school?"

Yes, Keely nodded. She remembered.

"Well," he continued, "as I said, I never met her. That isn't to say I don't remember her. I do. I'm sure the people in this town remember her too. She grew up here. The judge's daughter was kind, she was intelligent ... she was even beautiful."

"Was ... ?" Keely lowered her voice. "What happened?"

Pausing, Haywood's face showed a level of sympathy for Keely he had not really felt until now. He knew that what he was about to reveal would be painful. Yet, as sad as the information was, he hoped it was painful. Perhaps, he thought, it would be the fuel this second chance needed.

Keely looked stricken ... dreading what she suspected she was about to be told.

Haywood shook his head and took a deep breath. "Three years ago," he began softly, "Caitlyn Gritney was killed in an automobile accident just outside of town. She was home for the weekend. Some kid who'd been at the beach ran a stoplight on the bypass. Caitlyn died instantly. The teenager walked away from it."

Keely didn't move. She was horrified, but somehow she knew it was about to get worse.

Haywood looked at her carefully, making her wait. "Yeah," he said finally. "You think you know the rest of it, and you're right." Pausing one last time, he added, "The kid who killed her was drunk off his ass."

Thirteen

The following morning, I was sure I'd arrived at the store before the old man. Standing outside at a quarter 'til nine, I peered through the big front windows and assumed the place was empty. I did have a clear view of the small closet on the left but paid it no attention because the door was closed. At 9:00 sharp, however, it opened. Jones appeared from within and headed in my direction with two steaming mugs.

He stopped at the register and placed the coffee on the counter, waving me inside.

"G'morning," I said as I entered and, having found the door unlocked, commented, "I didn't know you were already open."

Jones pushed a cup toward me. "I always am," he said.

"But—" I started.

"I don't lock the door," he said, as if that were explanation enough. "I'd rather people be able to shop when they want to."

I didn't even know what to say to that but wondered if he was sleeping in the store. In the past, I'd invited him to stay with my family at our house when he was in town, but he never did. Neither did I *ever* know where the old man stayed instead. For a moment, I wondered if the coffee closet was as small as I had assumed, realizing I'd not seen more than the open door revealed.

I determined that I'd look inside the next time I had the opportunity. At the moment, I was interested in meeting whomever he had hired. Glancing around, I asked, "Hey, is your new person here?"

"Not quite yet." He smiled. "She'll be a bit late this morning. Your coffee okay?"

I took a sip. "Oh yeah, thanks. Again, it's *really* good." Eyeing Jones over the lip of my cup, I took another swallow. We were both leaning against the counter. Trying my best to seem nonchalant, I said, "Wow. Late on her first day?"

He just nodded. Glancing around, he said, "We need a table in here. It's not real homey sitting around a cash register."

"Sure," I said. "A table'd be nice." I was curious about the old man's reaction to his new hire's breach of etiquette. I'd never heard Jones's thoughts on punctuality. I'm an on-time kind of person and guessed that was probably why, but I didn't doubt he had an opinion on the topic. Knowing I would most likely be leaving before the mystery woman arrived, I decided to fish for a preview of the coming attraction. "What do you think?" I prompted. "I mean, about being late and all?"

"She'll be here," was all he said.

I nodded, somewhat disappointed that he didn't roll his eyes or something, but he never did that kind of thing. The possibility did occur to me that he was being easy on her. After all, he had called her a "very sweet young lady."

"Tell me about your coffee," I requested. This, I was also curious about. "What did you mean when you said you choose the combination of beans that go into your coffee?"

"Well," Jones began, "there are more than seventy countries in the world that commercially produce coffee. Even though there are only four major types of coffee beans used, everything from the type of the plant, soil composition, temperature, the amount of humidity, rainfall, and sunshine—even the altitude at which the coffee beans are grown—affects what the coffee tastes like when it is brewed. The combination of characteristics is so intricate that one plantation's beans can vary in taste from one row of trees to another."

He raised his eyebrows. "That enough?"

I grinned and said, "That's amazing. Is there more than one country's beans in your blend?" He nodded slowly. I had decided long ago that I would keep asking the old man questions until he shut me down, and I could tell that he was thinking about it, so I forged ahead quickly. "Where do you buy it?"

"It is shipped to wherever I happen to be," Jones answered. "I have several bags I roasted myself in the coffee room. Would you like to take a couple of pounds to Polly?"

"That would be great," I said. "Really, thanks. And what do you call it? What kind of coffee can I tell her it is?"

"It's just java. No name to it."

"Jones!" I said. "Come on! It's got to have a name. It's incredible coffee. So name it."

He laughed and thought a minute before answering. "How about . . ." the old man said, making me wait, "Just Jones Java?"

"Yes!" I laughed. "That'll work!"

Before we could spend any more time discussing coffee, the cowbell rang at the door. And to me, it sounded like the door had been hit pretty hard. I followed Jones toward the front. When we rounded the end of an aisle, the old man kept his pace, but seeing the young woman I assumed was the old man's new employee, I slowed considerably. One did not have to look twice to know that the new arrival was not what one would describe as "happy."

"Hello, Keely," Jones said. "Welcome to Orange Beach."

He had stopped several feet in front of her, and I'd noticed that his tone, while not overly so, was warm and friendly.

"Yeah," she said. "Hi."

I was aware that my eyes had opened wide, but I was able to stop my jaw before it dropped to the floor. *"Yeah, hi?" What?* I looked closer. Keely, did Jones say her name was? Well, Keely looked rough. Her hair had definitely not been washed, maybe for several days. And I was not close enough to make a call on whether or not her clothes were clean, but I w*ill* say that the slacks and blouse she wore looked like she'd spent the night in them. While camping. In a box.

"When did you arrive, Keely?"

"About sixty seconds ago," she said.

My jaw clenched a bit harder. I'd sensed a smart-alecky tone and didn't like it, but Jones just chuckled like it was cute.

"No, Keely," the old man said. "I meant, when did you arrive in town?" Jones spoke to her with a level of patience that was—at least in my opinion—stunning considering her sullen attitude.

"Oh," she said flatly. "Last night."

"Where'd you spend the night?" Jones asked. "Have you eaten?"

The young woman had not taken her eyes from Jones since she'd walked in. I saw her hesitate with her answer and Jones lift his chin as if to say, did you hear me?

"Yes, I have eaten," she said. "I had enough cash for that. I slept in the car you arranged for me."

That explains the wrinkled clothes, I thought.

For the first time, she broke eye contact with Jones and glanced around. "What do I do? Do you want me to start now?"

Ignoring her questions, Jones said, "We will chat about your responsibilities this afternoon." Removing an envelope from the right back pocket of his jeans, he held it out. "Take this," he said, and she

ANDY ANDREWS

did. "It's three hundred dollars; however, it's not a gift or a loan. It is an advance on your earnings here."

The young woman gripped the envelope in her right hand. Seeming to stare at the floor, she spoke. "How do you think I am supposed–"

"Ms. Higgins?" Jones interrupted in a gentle, clear voice that prompted her to look into the old man's eyes again. "Keely," he continued with a smile as if nothing had happened, "I have complete certainty that you will figure it out. You will figure out where to take a shower and where to wash your clothes. You will decide the most practical place to stay . . . remembering that you must make three hundred dollars last a week.

"The vehicle you are driving–as I am certain you've already noticed–has no air conditioner and is not in the best of shape. It is, however, owned by a friend of mine and is yours to use free of charge while you are in town." Jones waited a moment. Receiving no response, he added, "You're welcome."

I watched with fascination as the young woman jerked her head up, eyes flashing. She pointed the envelope at Jones, and her mouth was almost in gear when, suddenly, she stopped. Swallowing whatever she was about to say, the hand holding the envelope fell to her side.

"Man . . ." Keely said, shaking her head. "Yeah, thank you. I'm sorry for not saying it. What do you want me to do now?"

"I want you to take off until after lunch," he said. "Drive around. Familiarize yourself with Orange Beach. It's not a big place, so it shouldn't take long. Be back at one o'clock, and we'll make some decisions then. Good?"

"I guess," Keely said and turned toward the door, but hesitated.

"Are you okay?" Jones asked.

"I guess," she said again. Then "Thanks for . . . um . . . what you did."

113

"Of course." Jones stepped forward and patted the young woman on the arm. Smiling softly, he said, "I very much look forward to seeing you after lunch . . . *promptly* at one."

She nodded and again moved to go.

"Oh, Keely. One more thing," Jones said. The young woman already had both hands on the door and turned. Indicating me with his hand, he said, "I'd like you to meet a longtime friend of mine. He and his family live here in Orange Beach. This is Andy Andrews."

I was still about thirty feet away from her, and she appeared ready to bolt, so I didn't walk over to shake her hand. I just smiled and nodded. "Nice to meet you, Keely," I said, and she burst into tears.

"No, it's not," she said. "And I'm sorry." She pushed hard out the door and to the accompaniment of the cowbell, she said it again. "I'm really sorry."

Jones watched her hurry down the sidewalk and out of sight before turning to me. He said nothing, but I noted his slight smile and the sparkle in his clear blue eyes. "She will do well," he said and walked to me, closing the gap between us.

"Okay," I responded tentatively. "Good."

I didn't know what else to say, but I wasn't sure who this Keely person was. I didn't know where he had found her and, from what I had just witnessed, I certainly did not know how Jones had come to the conclusion that "she would do well." I wasn't going to say so, but I seriously thought this woman was carrying the air of disaster.

"Did you watch her closely?" Jones asked.

"Oh yeah," I said a bit smugly and looked at my watch.

"So you caught the parallel," he said. Then, obviously having noticed me checking the time, he added, "It's 9:48. If you have a ten o'clock interview with John O'Leary, you'd better go. It's about to come a gully washer, and that might slow you down. How about the parallel?"

My eyes narrowed. "How do you know I have a ten o'clock with John O'Leary?"

"I talked to John at eight," the old man said simply. "Did you catch the parallel?"

"The parallel . . . ?" I said, frowning as I moved to the door and looked up. Not a cloud in sight. "I guess not. And it doesn't look like rain."

Jones eased me out the door, taking back the coffee cup that had remained in my hand. "Come on now," he said. "Quick. Who does she remind you of? And yeah, it *will* rain. Hard. It'll be a frog strangler."

"Hmm." I glanced at the blue sky again and considered the question for a few more seconds. "I don't know," I admitted. "Nobody really. Why? Who does she remind *you* of?"

Jones laughed as he reached up to grab my shoulder. "Keely's not as outwardly angry, I don't suppose. But . . ." Releasing my shoulder, he shrugged before crossing his arms.

"But . . . what?" I said. "Who? Who does she remind you of?"

Jones laughed again. "You!" he said. "Keely reminds me of you! Why, she even needs a pier to sleep under!"

I gave him a disapproving frown as I turned and began to jog down the sidewalk. I wanted to get the last word for once, so over my shoulder I called, "Not me. She's not like me at all!" Hearing him laugh, I added, "And it's not going to rain either!"

But it did.

Keely clanged through the front entrance at 12:59. Stopping just inside, she looked carefully at her watch and breathed a sigh of relief. She was not late. She was, however, soaked to the bone. "Hello?" she called out weakly. "Jones?"

"Hang on, Keely . . . I'm grabbing you a beach towel or three," she heard Jones say from somewhere in the back of the store.

"Thanks," she said and furrowed her brow. She hadn't seen him. Had he seen her come in? She *was* dripping all over the floor, but how did he know?

Seconds later, the old man came hustling down the aisle to her left and was talking before he even reached her. "You either like being wet or the car wouldn't start and you walked. Which was it?" he asked, handing over the first towel.

"Thanks," Keely said and wiped her face and arms before draping it over her head. "The second. And I ran."

"I'm sorry," he said as he handed the second towel to her. "That's a long way to run in the rain. Listen, you can't stay in those clothes. The restroom is in the back on the right. Take the far right aisle to get there. Halfway back you'll see ladies' slacks, blouses, sundresses, sandals, and ahh . . . underthings." Jones shook his head as if he were embarrassed. Keely lifted her eyebrows and smiled.

"Anyway," he continued, "get whatever you need. There's a hair dryer and brush on the cabinet in the restroom. Neither have been used. I put 'em there this morning. Toothbrush and toothpaste are yours too. Makeup is aisle six. Just get what you want. Go on, before you get cold." He shooed her toward the aisle and said, "I have coffee ready when you want. You take a lot of cream, yes?"

Keely slammed on the brakes just before turning into the aisle and paused for a beat before peering over her shoulder at Jones. "Yes . . . a lot of cream," she said warily. "And how would you know how far I ran in the rain?"

Jones crossed his arms slowly and brought his right hand to his face. Tapping his chin thoughtfully with his forefinger, the old man said, "Well . . . let's see now. Judging from your degree of wetness, I'd imagine you were in the rain for at least twenty-five minutes. Your hair has been blown from right to left and a north wind arrived with the rain, so that means you were undoubtedly moving from east to west."

Keely's eyebrows began to lift as Jones continued. "You appear to be conscious of your health. That tells me you probably didn't skip lunch. You'll be working to make your money last–and you don't look too tired–those two facts say you ate a salad."

The old man noted the young woman's dropped jaw but didn't mention it. His eyes narrowed as if he were deep in thought. "Keely, while you were out, did you happen to notice the driving range and par three golf course about a mile and a half up Canal Road?"

"I did," she said cautiously.

Jones brightened. "My conclusion is that your car is probably parked right next to the driving range at Duck's Diner. Their salads really are excellent. Good choice."

Keely was stunned. "That is astonishing," she said. "Oh my gosh!"

Jones issued a humble little chuckle. "Well, that's just the power of observation, my dear." He shooed her toward the back with his hands. "Go. Change into something dry. We have work to do. I'll make a call about the car."

Keely turned, but Jones stopped her with what she thought was an out-of-the-blue piece of advice. "It's always good to keep receipts," he said.

Not knowing how to answer, the young woman simply nodded and said, "Yeah, I guess," and began again to turn away.

"No guessing about it," the old man said. "You don't want to lose a receipt only to need it come tax time. So don't lose one."

Keely's brow furrowed. "I won't," she said, and when it appeared the odd exchange was over, she turned away for good and, in fact, had rolled her eyes rounding the corner of aisle six. She was completely out of sight when she heard the old man's voice again.

"It'd be a shame to lose the receipt that's sticking out of your back pocket."

Jones heard her footsteps stop, and for several beats, there was no sound at all. He leaned over the counter and watched the corner of aisle six with his chin in his hands and a grin on his face.

Sure enough, within seconds, Keely slowly rounded the corner, stopped, and held a small piece of paper up in front of her. She was nodding, and her left eyebrow was arched. With a tight smile, Keely spoke. "*Just* the power of observation, huh? Yeah. Observation my–."

"Hey, hey, whoa," Jones interrupted and collapsed in laughter.

Keely turned away so the old man would not see her laughing. *Maybe this won't be so bad after all*, she thought after she'd finally made it to the restroom with the things she had selected from the shelves. She'd been choosing makeup when Jones brought her a cup of coffee. Both had attempted to keep straight faces, but both burst out into laughter at the same time.

It is good to laugh with someone, she thought as she tied the laces on a new pair of running shoes. *It's been a long time*. Standing, she looked herself over in the mirror. "Ready to start," she said softly, but before opening the door, Keely carefully folded the damp receipt for $6.95 she'd almost lost and put it in the side pocket of her canvas purse.

Exiting the restroom, Keely thought, *If things work out here, I might display it one day*. The more she considered it, the broader her smile became. *Four, ninety-five for the salad, another two bucks for the tip. It would be funny all framed up*, she mused. *Especially with that Duck's Diner logo at the top of the receipt*.

Fourteen

It's just a suggestion," the old man said, chuckling at the reaction it had drawn. "Just one more option in life's ever-evolving bag of tricks."

Jones had just mentioned to Keely that she might consider joining a health club or gym. It was another instance in what was already becoming a long list of moments when the old guy gave direction or suggested a course of action that was so off-the-wall that it sent a "disconnect command" to her brain. At least, that had been true at first.

Now, however, Keely recognized the fact that every time the old man explained his *thinking*—what he called "the foundation that exists beneath the words we speak"—what might have seemed patently ridiculous moments before was often transformed into the utterly obvious.

"To find the best," Jones had convinced her, "one has to search for the truth." She'd quickly found out that just because she thought a certain way or believed a particular thing—that didn't necessarily make it the truth.

On her second day at the store, the old man had made an off-hand comment that almost immediately gave Keely a greater desire for finding and understanding the truth in every category of existence she might explore.

He had said, "If a person has any inclination toward the best that life has to offer, a constant and never-ending search for truth is a must. For while one can know the truth and never achieve the best, it is not possible to achieve the best without knowing the truth."

"That makes sense," she had replied. "How did you figure that out?"

"It's what I do," Jones said with a smile. "I am a noticer. While others may be able to sing well or run fast, I notice things that other people overlook. And, you know, most of them are in plain sight."

The old man cocked his head. "I notice things about situations and people that produce perspective. That's what most folks lack—perspective—a broader view. So I give 'em that broader view, and it allows them to regroup, take a breath, and begin their lives again."

When Jones had mentioned the possibility of joining a health club, Keely's first thoughts were flooded with the same dismissiveness that had clouded her mind for years. But Jones had begun teaching her to crush the negative energy that threatened to make her discouraged and pessimistic.

There was a reset button for her brain, she was learning, and it could be pressed by mentally acknowledging the fact that another "opportunity" to consider was at hand, and it was time to pay attention. It was a thought process he had convinced her to try, and she was cautiously optimistic about becoming . . . well, optimistic, because it sure seemed to be working.

Keely shook her head as if to clear it, looked into the old man's eyes, and concentrated. Her dark hair, still not completely dry from her shower, shone in the morning sun. When she'd arrived twenty minutes early, Jones had greeted her outside with a cup of his coffee. After greetings were exchanged, for a time, they stood at the front railing without talking, just looking down onto Main Street and enjoying the coolest part of the day.

A bit later, after the conversation had started and she prepared herself to listen, Keely was pleasantly surprised to acknowledge being excited to hear how the old man would explain his health club suggestion.

At first, every journey to whatever conclusion Jones was determined to make clear had been a "forced march" for her—the equivalent of a teenager being ordered to sit on the couch and listen to a parent. Quickly, however, Keely had been so intrigued by the accuracy of reasoning the old man came to that she began to follow—then attempt to understand—his thinking.

The idea of joining a health club was a perfect example. In her financial situation, it was the last thing she would have considered. And that's how she started her side of the conversation. "Shouldn't I save the exercising and wait to buy cute gym clothes until I knock down some debt?" she asked. "I'm already walking a lot."

"Well, let's think this through," he said. "Knocking down your debt is a big part of what needs to be done as quickly as possible. Where are you sleeping?"

Keely frowned. "In the car, but what's that—?"

"Showering?"

"At the park. Either at the pavilion or at the State Pier."

"Eating?"

"Wherever. Burgers mostly. I'm not—"

"Laundry?"

"Um . . ." Keely shrugged. "Just kinda piling it in the car for now, but there's a laundromat about a mile past Duck's . . ."

Jones pursed his lips, considering what he was about to say. "There are sometimes good reasons for certain moves that are beyond the obvious," he said. "Many people just don't have the smarts or the guts to make those moves. That's true of chess, and it's true in life. Here's the thing . . . health clubs are everywhere—three of 'em right now at The Wharf—but you don't have to exercise or participate in a clothing competition to join one."

Jones paused. When Keely didn't respond, he continued. "To become a member of a health club, you don't need a letter of reference. Nobody does a background check. You just need the money to join. And because the fitness business is super competitive, their prices can sometimes be very, very low."

Keely stared hard at the old man but was still without a clue as to why she might consider joining a health club.

"Keely," he said, "you are thousands of dollars in debt. That's the bad news. The good news is that you have no car payment, no mortgage or rent to pay since your roommate immediately replaced you, and all your credit cards have been canceled."

Her eyebrows went up. "My cards being canceled is good news?" she asked wryly.

"Yes," he said emphatically, "because the bleeding has stopped. "Now, you have the opportunity to pay back what you owe and live a new life. One without all the financial foolishness that contributed to your most recent trouble."

"Ahh . . . wait a minute," Keely said, cocking her head. Despite her recent vows to herself that she would listen to this old man, what he had just said had irritated her. "There was no financial foolishness involved in my recent trouble. None of what happened had anything to do with money."

Jones smiled gently and as if curious, asked, "Did I offend you by intimating that it did?"

"Yes," Keely said, as if suddenly clear on the matter. "Yes, you did."

"I am sorry that you were offended, of course," Jones said, "but there is a truth in that too. You'll soon find that wise people are rarely offended by the truth, even if it is a previously unknown truth to which they have yet to become adjusted. A wise person seeks to make peace with the truth, especially when it's personal and even when it hurts."

Before she could speak, the old man continued. "As you and I have discussed, the truth is foundational. In the instance of your most recent trouble, from the moment you left Atlanta for the beach, enjoyed your short vacation, headed back, stopped in Clanson, and ended up in that bar, every drop of gasoline you used, everything you ate and drank, everything you did, and every place you spent the night—at least until you arrived in Clanson—was 'paid for' by credit card."

"So?" Keely said.

"So . . ." Jones said, "you did not actually have the money to make the trip. The entire jaunt was based upon the financial smoke and mirrors of a misused credit card. If you had disciplined yourself to pay cash for the trip, your trouble would have been over before it started. Because you did not have any money. You only had credit. Credit is not money.

"Financial discipline can keep a person out of trouble that doesn't even seem to have anything to do with money. On the other hand, financial foolishness will create trouble in places a person would never imagine."

Keely didn't say anything, but she understood. She felt awful, but she understood. With her lips tightened, a single tear ran down her cheek. She swiped at it with her sleeve and nodded. "You're right," was all she said, but it was all the old man needed to hear.

Jones patted her forearm a couple of times and moved the conversation back to their previous topic. While his last few sentences had cleared fog from Keely's past, his next few shared a promising thought pattern for her immediate future. Almost as soon as they were out of the old man's mouth, she became excited and, considering her present circumstances, thought Jones's idea was brilliant and life-changing.

He said, "It's just a different way of looking at the same old stuff." Then, the old man explained, "Health clubs have showers and provide soap, shampoo, and conditioner. They have towels and hair dryers and big, bright mirrors. Most of them have washing machines for their towels, and some hire part-time help to do the laundry."

Keely listened carefully and was becoming even more excited.

"Some health clubs provide fruit," he continued. "Apples, bananas, oranges, even yogurt . . . Healthy energy for their members, you know."

Already thinking ahead, Keely asked, "You don't mind if I get another job? Part-time, I mean?"

"Of course not." Jones grinned, then added, "And soon, you'll need to figure out a business of your own as well. You know what your duties are here. Pay attention to those first and I'll help along the way in some other areas."

The very next day, Keely joined a fitness center only to have her membership fee refunded when she agreed to be the combination cleaning staff and unofficial security guard.

"Security guard?" Jones had asked. "What's that about?"

Keely laughed. "I don't get a uniform or a gun or anything, but it sounds cool, doesn't it? The thing is this: the cleaning job doesn't start until 10 p.m. That takes about three hours, including the laundry, and"—she grinned—"I have permission to wash my clothes there too. Anyway, the owner said that I should be extra careful when I leave because it'll be so late—then she mentioned that they couldn't afford a security company yet.

"When she said that, I said, 'Hey, if you'll put a fold-up cot in the back room, I will *be* your security company.' She loved the idea, and now I'm getting paid for that time too!"

Keely's first major task at the store had been to familiarize herself with the inventory. She did, and tried her best not to say, "Seriously?" every time she looked at a price. She quickly learned the system of accounting Jones wanted and offered to take on the chore of ordering and receiving new stock, but the old man told her that that was his only area of expertise.

It was fine with Keely, of course. Her watchword was "whatever" because, in reality, she didn't mind. After all, she figured to be gone in six months. Meanwhile, things seemed to be working out well. Keely also really liked Oliver, the kid who came in after school—even though she had wanted to strangle him the first day they met.

She was surprised to see the teenager cleaning her windshield when she left the store at the end of that day. She was touched by his apparent kindness and told him how much she appreciated his effort. Oliver accepted her thanks with a humility Keely thought rare in a teenager. The young man even hurried to the other side of her car, opened the driver's door, and helped her in.

Only a moment later, Keely backed out of her parking space to what sounded like the car's engine exploding and falling apart. When she stopped the car, however, the horrible noises stopped too. Catching her breath and calming her heart rate, Keely saw that Oliver was not only doubled over laughing, he was holding his smartphone and was capturing her near nervous breakdown on video.

At first the young woman was furious, but when she stomped to the other side of the vehicle and realized what he had done, she began to laugh too. On both passenger side tires, Oliver had duct-taped small balloons and several dozen walnuts onto all available space. With one revolution of the two tires, it had sounded like the car was about to fall out from under her.

Oliver had approached Keely when she began to laugh. "Welcome to Orange Beach?" he asked and stuck out his hand.

Keely shook it and said, "Yes. And thank you." With a big smile, she waggled her eyebrows and added, "Just remember what they say about payback."

After the exploding car prank, Keely and Oliver became fast friends. He worked after school and all day Saturdays, so the two were together often. Both were amazed at the number of customers who came and went. In addition, they were shocked by the variety of items the customers asked for and actually found.

To the best of her recollection, Keely could not remember a single time that a customer wanted an item the store didn't have. Weirdly, there were several instances when she'd just issued an apology for some particular something she knew they had not stocked, when Jones would pipe up and say, "You know, I ordered one of those three days ago. Let me see if it's in the shipment that came in this morning."

The old man would hurry to the back of the store only to return within minutes carrying a wood carving set or a violin case or a set of metric wrenches. Once, she was sipping her early cup of Just Jones Java and working on the books at the register, when an elderly man entered the store. Jones quietly joined them as the man began to talk.

He was pleasant and polite, but there was a deep sadness about him that Keely had spotted immediately. He told them that he didn't want to be a bother and that, really, he was not even expecting to find what he'd been looking for, but that several people had suggested he check here before giving up.

"What are you looking for, sir?" Keely asked.

The elderly gentleman sighed and hesitated as if he were almost embarrassed to say, but at last, he spoke. "An ostrich egg." When Keely's eyebrows raised involuntarily, he chuckled sadly. "Crazy, I know," he said. "Still, I never thought they'd be this hard to find."

"Just any old ostrich egg?" Keely said and the man chuckled again.

"Like I say, I know it's crazy, but I had to try. I've seen several online that I can't afford. Not sure there's time now anyway."

"How so?" Keely asked while Jones remained silent beside her.

"My wife is sick. Not much time left," he said. "We got married fifty-nine years ago and went to Africa for the honeymoon. Spent all our money getting there and getting back. Only souvenir we bought on the whole trip was an ostrich egg. The yolk stuff was blown out, it was dry, and the lady who sold it to us had painted a beautiful sunset on it. Cost three whole dollars."

"You don't have it anymore?" Keely asked.

"Nah," he said with a shrug, "somehow or 'nother it fell off the shelf. Busted into a jillion pieces. Like to've broke her heart. Anyhow, that was twenty years ago, but she still talks about it. How pretty it was . . . how she loved holding it . . . feeling the cool smoothness. I thought, *Man, if I could get ahold of another ostrich egg.* I guess I'm done lookin' though."

He blinked hard and seemed to come out of his reverie. "I didn't mean to hold you folks up," he said and began to back away. "Nice store you got here. I'll come back sometime."

"Hang on a second, if you don't mind," Jones said, and Keely slowly turned toward him. His finger was tapping his chin, and he appeared deep in thought. The elderly gentleman had stopped and was watching Jones curiously. "Like a dark gray, almost black, ostrich egg? Yellow, orange, and red in the sunset?" The man nodded dumbly.

"Keely," Jones said as if he couldn't quite remember, "there's supposed to be some African art pieces in that big crate that came in last night. I have no idea what kind of art pieces. Have you unpacked it yet?"

Keely slowly shook her head, no. Glancing at the gentleman, she could see his eyes had narrowed. Was he hopeful or suspicious? She couldn't tell.

"Why don't we all go back and unpack that crate together?" Jones said and headed that way. "You never know," he added, waving for them to follow.

The crate was heavy wood, and Keely wondered who had pulled

it inside. It took a hammer and a crowbar—both in stock—to remove the lid. After the top layer of packing material was removed, items began to appear. Carefully, they lifted out a package of bamboo flutes. Next came a ceremonial headdress of woven grass and decorated with dried flowers. There were carvings, large and small, a few painted shells, and a medium-sized canvas book about zebras that appeared to have been done by a child.

Keely had been bent over the side of the crate, handing out one item after another to the two old men. She was almost at the bottom when they heard her gasp. She stood up quickly. "What's wrong?" Jones asked and looked at the other man who also had a concerned expression on his face. "Keely?"

"Nothing," she said, but appeared spooked.

"Nothing?" Jones asked.

"Umm . . . nothing wrong," she said, looking back and forth between the two men. At last her gaze settled on their visitor, and she pointed into the crate. "It's for you. In there, I mean. I think what's in there is for you."

The man looked to Jones, who nodded. "Go ahead," he urged.

As he slowly bent at the waist, the man maintained eye contact with Keely, then Jones until he was almost touching the packing material in the crate's bottom. As he adjusted his gaze, he saw something peeking through the shredded paper and touched it. The object was hard and its surface smooth, and when he brushed the paper away, an African sunset bloomed underneath his hand.

Without breathing, the elderly gentleman eased both hands into the crate and carefully removed a darkly colored ostrich egg that had been painted on one side with the most glorious sunset the man had ever seen—yellows and oranges and reds.

For a few moments, not a word was spoken. Finally, the old gentleman broke the silence. "I don't know what to say. I hope I can afford it."

Keely's eyes were wide. Jones chuckled softly. "Well," he said, "these items come in already priced. I really don't have anything to do with it." Gesturing toward the egg, he said, "Check it. There should be a price sticker already on it."

The man turned the ostrich egg in his hands, carefully rotating it to see the other side. When the movement stopped, the old gentleman did not move either. Though his head was down, Keely was watching closely and saw a tear fall from his face and onto the egg.

He brushed it away with his sleeve, but Keely was concerned. "Is it okay?" she asked. He nodded. "I mean, you can afford it?" His head still down, he nodded again.

Relieved, Keely looked to Jones and whispered, "How much is it?"

Jones shrugged and shook his head with an "I have no idea" expression on his face. He motioned to the man and quietly said, "You'll have to ask him."

"Sir?" Keely said, and the man looked up with tears streaming down his face. "Sir," she continued, "I'll be happy to ring it up and gift wrap it nicely."

"Thank you, miss," he replied. "That would be very kind."

"And what is the price on the egg, sir?"

The elderly gentleman turned his unusual gift to where Keely could read the sticker, and as she leaned forward to see, he spoke the price aloud. "Three dollars," he said. "It's impossible, isn't it? But that's what it says . . . three dollars."

Fifteen

It was a Saturday morning. Oliver was due to arrive any moment, and Jones had stepped out the back door of the Five & Dime to empty the trash. Pausing as he did so, Jones caught movement from the corner of his eye. The trash emptied, he turned to stretch, giving himself a moment to survey the situation.

Thirty feet to his right, there was a man slumped behind the steering wheel of a modest blue car in the first double row of the parking deck. Jones saw that he was middle-aged with thinning hair and his car was still running.

Pastor Burke Ruark sat alone in the car as he had for the last forty-five minutes. The well-worn Gaither Vocal Band CD was in the player and their song "Chain Breaker" poured through the vehicle's heat-cracked stereo speakers. He could leave now, he told himself. He had done what he came to do.

He had seen the old man everyone called Jones. He'd heard countless stories about how the old man had helped people turn their lives around. It was said that he would often do so in a single conversation. One part of him desperately wanted to follow the old man inside. Lately, however, it was the other part of him that had begun to call the shots.

For as long as he could remember, Burke Ruark had fought down the portion of himself that wanted to quit everything he had started, to run away from every situation he faced. Nowadays, however, as sad as it was, he was beginning to accept the judgment of the voice in his head—the one that told him he was a follower, not a leader. Burke had tried to swim against the current, but he was obviously a "watcher," not a "doer"; a "sometimes," not an "always." He was an "I'll try," not an "I will."

Burke knew he had lost confidence, but his sense of adventure had deserted him too. He woke up with no energy. Where was the nerve he'd had as a younger man? Several years ago, a local news reporter had written that Pastor Burke Ruark had "audacity." When his family had read that, the description made him proud. Burke didn't feel audacious anymore. Had he lost his courage? Or was it all just a bluff to begin with?

He was an "if I am able," not a "without a doubt." He was a "perhaps in the future," and had not been a "today's the day!" in a very long time. Burke Ruark had turned into a cautious person in charge who often said, "We need to stop and pray about it." Somehow, he had backed away from the leader he used to be, the man who would step up and say, "Let's get started *now*. We will pray while we work."

What happened to me? he wondered. *I accepted a calling.* A tear escaped his eye. Rolling down his cheek, along his nose, and into the corner of his mouth, the tear tasted salty—almost bitter—but he was not surprised. He was an ordained minister of the gospel, and in a profession that cried out for anointed lions, Burke Ruark had become a designated sheep.

He wasn't certain how long his eyes had been closed when the pastor was startled by a rap on the window beside his head. He jerked hard to his right and, for a heartbeat, did not know what had happened or where he was. Had he been asleep? He didn't think so, but as he looked to see what had startled him, Burke also noted the song blaring from his speakers. It was "Chain Breaker." Again. Or still. And it was loud.

In a sleepy daze the pastor couldn't quite shake, he reached to turn off the radio and wondered why the volume was so high in the first place. He glanced to his left and saw the old man's face framed in the rain-flecked window. Jones smiled at Burke and gave a little wave.

The pastor took a deep breath and made a "hang on a second" motion with his hand. Turning off the ignition stopped the music and the sound of the car's engine. The last thing he'd heard before silence enveloped the car was the end of the chorus. "If you got chains, he's a chain breaker."

Burke opened the door, and the old man stepped back, allowing him to exit the vehicle.

"I'm sorry," Jones said. "I didn't mean to alarm you."

"Oh, no . . . ahh . . . no problem. I wasn't asleep." Burke turned to the car. He was still in a fog and wasn't certain what he was doing. Thoughts whirred through his head like a tornado of litter. *Why did I get out of the car . . . and why did I tell him I wasn't asleep? Did he ask?* the pastor said to himself as he faced toward the old man again. *Was I asleep?*

"You're Burke Ruark. The pastor." The old man wasn't asking. He just stated the fact and stuck out his hand. "I'm Jones. Nice to meet ya."

"Um . . . nice to meet you too," the pastor said. "I've sure heard a lot about you."

Jones smiled. "I hope most of it was good."

"Oh . . . yeah," Ruark said. "I didn't mean to imply—"

Jones interrupted him with a laugh and punched the much younger man lightly on the shoulder. "No worries," he said. "I didn't take it that way. Hey . . . can I help you with something?"

The pastor paused. He wanted to get back in the car and drive away, but he felt as if his shoes had been glued to the concrete upon which he was standing. Pastor Ruark strongly sensed a turning point in his life and thought, *I either say something now, or I never will.*

Burke paused and looked at the patient face in front of him. He'd heard so much about this old man, now here he was and despite his exhaustion and fear, Burke was mesmerized. The old man's clear blue eyes spoke to him without words and the wrinkles on his face seemed a road map into his soul. Jones, he decided, had a ministry of presence.

"Ahh . . ." He stammered a bit as he began. Then, with a deep breath, Burke Ruark uttered words he had never imagined coming from his mouth. "I think I need help." There was a desperate look in his eyes as he added, "Can I sometime . . . um . . . talk to you?"

Cool and as comfortably casual as anyone could be, Jones smiled and said, "Of course! I'd be honored to talk with you." Suddenly, the old man got a crafty look in his eye. "Do you like coffee?" he asked.

"Sure," the pastor replied.

"Good," Jones replied. "I'll have it ready Monday morning. Say seven thirty, here?"

"Ahh . . . yeah, great," Ruark said. "I really appreciate it."

"It's set then," Jones said and clapped the pastor on the back, turning him back to his car. "See ya Monday morning," he said, and the pastor nodded as he got into the vehicle and turned the ignition key. The engine sputtered a bit at first, but when it caught and came to life, the stereo roared. Embarrassed that he could not turn off the music or even down, Ruark simply put the transmission in Drive, waved, and hurried away. Jones waved back and watched Ruark make the turn and head down the ramp of the parking deck.

The old man laughed when the blue car passed by him one level down. He turned and walked toward the back door of his store. He knew how hard it had been for Burke Ruark to do what he'd just done. Some adults, Jones knew, could make a request for help upon becoming aware they needed it. Others struggled along, hoping they could handle their crisis alone, until finally understanding they needed to talk through the situation with someone else.

On the other hand, Jones knew that this man was in a different league. A member of what sociologists call a micro-minority, he was one of the one-tenth of 1 percent of all the people in the world most likely to *never* ask for help of any kind. For he was a pastor.

No matter the denomination, members of the clergy are available to their community, willingly offering help and hope to others during times of trouble. They are, however, aware of the personal and professional danger should certain members of the community become aware that the leader is dealing with troubles of his own. What happens, many have quietly wondered, when the helper needs help?

"Good morning, Hot Shot," Jones said to Oliver as he entered from the rear. The young man was in the middle of aisle two, mopping the stained concrete floor. "Thanks for doing that."

"Well," Oliver said as he paused with an impish smile. Eyes on Jones, he pointed toward the register though it could not be seen from where they were. Then, perhaps a bit louder than he needed to speak, he said, "You're welcome and good morning to you, too, but she put this in my hand the second I walked in the door. Mopping was the old lady's idea."

"I heard that!" floated across the Five & Dime. The old man and the teenager snickered, but almost immediately Keely came around the corner of the aisle. "While I may be an old lady to you," she said, attempting to hide a smile, "twenty-seven years old is quite the young woman to at least 70 percent of the population."

They stared at each other for a beat or two before dissolving into laughter. "Finish what the 'old lady' told you to do," Jones said to Oliver, "and join us up front."

Still chuckling, Jones and Keely headed for the register. Before anything else could be said, Keely pointed back over the old man's shoulder. Her eyebrows were arched. "So . . . we have a table now?" she asked.

Jones smiled. "Yes, let's christen it. Meet me there. I'll get the coffee."

As the old man turned to head for the coffee closet, Keely touched his arm. "Wait," she said quietly. Jones stopped and watched Keely peer around him. She wanted to make sure Oliver was out of earshot. He was, and when Keely returned her gaze to the old man, it was with a mixture of suspicion and awe.

She was still touching him, but as she spoke, instead of removing her hand, Keely leaned in close and gripped the old man's arm as if she thought he might get away. It was not an aggressive posture, rather, Keely had taken his arm without a conscious decision to do so. In reality, the young woman's bearing was that of a mother determined to get the truth from her child.

"When I left last night," Keely began, "there was no table. This morning, right in the middle of this store, there *is* a table. But it is not a normal table, one like after clearing a little space for it, a person or two might carry the table into that space by themselves. No, this is a table that the top alone probably weighs a thousand pounds! And what are its legs made of? About five hundred hardback books, that's what!" She glanced back to where Oliver was diligently mopping, then just as quickly back to Jones.

"Another thing," she said. "While the books used for its legs could obviously be carried into the store a box at a time, I am fairly certain that tabletop will not fit through any of these glass doors." Keely paused, staring at the old man as if waiting for him to crumble and explain everything, but his expression was one of peace and innocence with a twinkle of amusement in his eyes.

"How did this happen?" Keely pleaded. "How did you get it in here and set up? It's impossible!"

Jones smiled . . . even chuckling a bit as he casually peeled Keely's fingers from his arm. The more she'd talked, the harder she had squeezed. "First of all–" Jones began, but he was interrupted by a happy yelp from the center of the store.

"Oh my gosh!" It was the voice of Oliver. "Hey, Jones! When did you get this? Holy moly! Man, this is huge! Keely!" Oliver said loudly. "Come see this table!"

Keely looked at the old man as if some vital state secret had just been uncovered by a rogue nation. For his part, however, Jones continued to smile. Crooking an index finger at Keely in the familiar gesture indicating "follow me," he headed toward Oliver's continuing chatter.

"Keely, look at the table legs," Oliver said as soon as she and the old man appeared. "There must be a thousand books under there." The young woman gave Jones a look that said, *See? I told you this was weird.*

In truth, the table was massive, but without the traditional two long sides and two ends, it was roughly seven feet long by five feet wide. Oddly, the table's outside margins were without predictable definition. Easily more than twenty feet in circumference, the table's perimeter curved and swooped.

A white linen cloth covered the table's top, hanging exactly twelve inches below the table's edge at every point. With an appreciation for fabric, Keely was fascinated by the intricate needlework that had gone into the tablecloth.

Sewn with the tiniest of stitches, the cloth's seam perfectly followed each bend of the table's edge. Why the table was created with an outside boundary that undulated–giving it a shape that required a master tailor to fashion its linen cover—Keely had no idea, but the tablecloth fit snugly and was itself a work of art.

Because of the cloth, the actual tabletop could not be seen; therefore, neither Keely nor Oliver knew the basis of its construction. Was it steel, wood, fiberglass, plastic, or something else? It was covered, and by just looking, there was no way to know. As for the table's legs, however, *their* material source and method of assembly were obvious.

There were only two very wide legs that stretched from one side to the other at each end of the table. The design was simple. The legs were fabricated entirely by stacking one hardback book upon another until together, they created a level and stable platform for the tabletop.

So transfixed were they by the new table, neither Oliver nor Keely had noticed the old man's absence until he returned carrying three cups of steaming hot Just Jones Java. He motioned them to chairs, and Keely said, "I feel like we should cover this tablecloth some way. It looks like an antique." To Oliver, she said, "We can *not* spill coffee on this material."

Jones rubbed his hand across it. "I think it's made out of something stainproof," he said, but Keely didn't believe it. She took a first sip of her coffee and did not take her eyes off the old man.

With another small swallow, Keely tapped a fingernail on the tabletop and asked, "What's the scoop on this, Jones?" He smiled and set his mug directly on the tablecloth. Following suit, Oliver put down his cup as well.

Keely cringed, mentally rolling her eyes as she acknowledged to herself the fact that Jones and Oliver were both male. That seemed the only explanation as to why both would be oblivious to the dark brown stains on the pristine landscape of white linen tablecloth that were visible each time they lifted their cups. She had been served without a saucer or napkin, and there was no coaster in sight. Therefore, with a feeling of feminine superiority, Keely rested her cup on the thigh of her jeans as Jones began to talk.

"First of all," the old man said, "the tabletop is not a thousand pounds. It only weighs four hundred and fifty."

Oliver snickered and leaned toward Keely. "*Only* four-fifty," he said and she smiled.

"And..." Jones said, waiting for their attention. "And there are not five hundred books being used for legs. There are only two hundred and thirty-one."

"Only, again," Oliver said to Keely. She nodded before "shushing" him with her hand.

Her eyes narrowing, Keely said, "Okay then, how did—"

Jones interrupted. "One more thing. Isn't it somewhat ridiculous to say the tabletop will not fit through any of our doors when it is obviously sitting in the middle of the store?"

"Who moved it in here for you?" Keely asked.

"Yeah, who?" Oliver parroted.

"If you must know," the old man said with eyebrows lifted, "I asked Jim Bibby if he would round up some guys last night to move it in." Oliver and Keely each took a quick breath as if they were about to speak, but Jones beat them to it. "And before you ask," he said, "I've owned this table for a long time but only recently decided to put it here."

Finishing the last of his coffee in several swallows, the old man ended their conversation as well. "This will be the table around which we will solve the world's problems," he said, using an old cliché, then added, "Along the way, however, we're going to solve some of our own.

"For a while at least, every day but Sunday, we will do morning coffee around this table." Looking at Keely, he said, "I'd like you to be a part of this. At first, it'll most likely be you, me, and a guy I just met out back, but I'd imagine there will soon be others."

Jones turned to Oliver. "Ollie, until school's out, you and I will find our time to talk. After that, though, you are welcome too!"

The old man held out his hands and said, "I'm calling it 'seven thirty in the mornings' for now. Starting Monday. But for now, let's get to work."

Sixteen

To painfully thin, forty-eight-year-old Richard Mac, life itself was devoid of excitement. At least, that was how he saw it. While he blamed a job for the boring existence that was his, most people in town saw things differently.

They had a hard time believing that the position of assistant guidance counselor at Orange Beach Middle School lacked variety and felt the responsibility for any tedium lay more at Richard's feet than with the career choice he had made.

Few disagreed with the observation made by Dr. Charlie Cooper years ago. It was just "guy talk" in a duck blind—nothing serious intended—but the comment got around quickly. "Richard Mac is a good guy," Dr. Cooper said, before famously adding, "but he is duller'n dirt." Of course, because of his profession, Charlie found his smart remark elevated to the level of "medical opinion," and it had not been forgotten.

She looks familiar, Richard thought, watching a woman who appeared to be in her midthirties as she was buzzed through the school's main doors. She wore dark green leggings and a matching pullover. She was beautiful . . . but in an uncomfortable kind of way. This was not someone a man introduced to his mother.

He stared at the woman until she passed through the doors of the inner office; her close proximity forced him to look away. Richard racked his brain to figure out where he had seen her.

The clothes she wore were not loose fitting. In fact, Richard thought that the leggings and the pullover were too tight. After he watched her a moment more, however, he decided the ensemble was *not* too tight. It was a fine fit after all. In addition, the dark green contrasted nicely with her auburn hair.

She stopped several desks down and was talking to Marlene, the receptionist. It gave Richard another chance to study the woman. He didn't want to compare her to Marlene but the two *were* right next to each other. Marlene was rather plain, and this new arrival . . . well, she was not.

Richard had dated Marlene several years earlier, and the romance had lasted for almost a month. Granted, that was longer than any other relationship he'd ever had, but after three Saturday evenings and one disastrous Tuesday afternoon, Marlene dumped him. Adding insult to injury, she proceeded to remind anyone who would listen that, in Richard's case, "boring" was not a point of view; it was a diagnosis.

As he watched the two women together, Richard remembered how his feelings had been hurt and couldn't help but focus on Marlene for a moment. *At least I don't wear my hair in a bun*, Richard thought.

The beautiful woman's hair, however, looked wonderful. It had some kind of lighter colored streaks in it and when she moved, the streaks looked like flames dancing through her tresses. As for the cut, some of her hair was longer, some of it shorter. It was all tangled and wild and two different colors. He didn't know how one would describe this kind of hair, but he knew there was a word for this kind of woman: *untamed*, Richard thought. Immediately, the old game show came to mind, and he imagined himself the off-stage announcer giving the answer in a low, whispered voice to the television audience at home. *The password is "untamed."*

Richard continued to struggle with how he knew her but was concentrating so hard that he had neglected to notice when she walked toward him until she spoke. "Hey," she said, stretching out the word.

He flushed deeply. There was something about the way she greeted him that would have horrified his mother. But, he told himself, his mother was not there. And he could smell her perfume. "May I help you?" he asked.

"Yes, please. The lady over there told me that you were the checkout person, and I need to check out Oliver Sutherland. Are you the principal? My goodness, what an important position!"

Richard swallowed hard. Halfway into what she had been saying, the woman had leaned over the desk. After asking if he was the checkout person, Richard hadn't heard another word. "Who?" he said.

"I need to check out Oliver Sutherland."

"Oh, yeah," he said. "Red hair. You're his mother?"

She was, the woman said, and Richard stood to shake her hand. Sitting back down, he thought, *She's tall too.* The correct form and a pen in hand, Richard asked, "Is this a doctor's appointment, Mrs. Sutherland? Just a checkout for the rest of the afternoon?"

"No," she said, her voice suddenly breaking. She removed a tissue from her purse and while dabbing at her eyes, explained. "I know it's only Monday, and I know it's barely nine o'clock, but as soon as I dropped him off this morning, I received a call that Ollie's grandmother is about to pass."

The woman leaned toward Richard again. "That's Ollie's grandmother on his father's side who, as you probably know, is already gone." She blew her nose.

"I'm afraid my poor little Ollie will need to be out for the rest of the week." With that, she turned, sat down on Richard's desk, and proceeded to have a breakdown. With her face buried in her hands, the woman struggled for control while right behind her, still seated, Richard struggled for control as well.

He reached to pick up the phone on his desk and was thrilled to see that his hand passed a mere six inches—maybe less—from the green of the leggings that appeared to have been painted on the crying woman.

At the reception desk, Marlene quickly rapped her knuckles on her desktop three times and said, "Air is on. Here we go again."

So captivated was Richard, however, by the goddess sitting on his desk, his brain barely registered the warning. Neither did he notice his coworker calmly tying a red bandana over her nose and mouth. Richard pushed three numbered buttons on the phone. After several seconds, he spoke into the receiver. "Mrs. Engle?" he said. "Please send Oliver Sutherland to the office. His mother is here to check him out."

Placing the phone back into its cradle, Richard stood and came around to the front of the desk. "Mrs. Sutherland," he said. "Oliver is on his way. I'd like to offer the thoughts and prayers of Orange Beach Middle School to your entire family, ma'am."

"Thank you," she said and sniffed. Frowning, she sniffed again. Looking suspiciously at her tissue, she sniffed it. Only then did she address Richard. "What is that smell?" Before he could answer, she put her tissue over her nose and in a loud voice, said, "Gross! What *is* that? Oh my!"

She had the tissue clamped solidly over her nose and mouth now and was frantically looking up, down, and around. She saw Marlene watching her. Marlene also had some kind of cloth over her nose and mouth. Richard had nothing handy and had begun to feel as though his skin might soon match the green of this woman's clothes.

Practically screaming at Richard, she cried, "What is happening? What are you people up to?"

"It's pig urine, we think," he said, and she stopped.

"What?"

"Pig urine," Richard said. "We never found pig number five, and it's as bad as ever. The thermostats are set to seventy-two, but when the air conditioners come on—as they just did—the odor is overwhelming."

The woman gagged and ran for the door just as Oliver came in from the hallway on the other side. He saw her running out and yelled, "Mom!" Speeding by Richard, he threw a "What did you do to my mom?" at him and was gone.

Richard pulled several tissues from a box on another desk and held them over his nose and mouth as he walked over to Marlene. The bandana she held to her face was smeared with Vicks VapoRub. "Wow," he said. "That was crazy."

"Yeah," Marlene agreed. Their voices were muted as they did the best they could avoiding the stench that blew from every vent in the office. "How long is this going to last?"

Richard eyed the vent closest to his desk. "The city people say they'll have to take care of it during the summer."

"Ugh," Marlene said. "There's two more weeks before school's out." They thought about that for a minute before Marlene had another thought. "Hey, I didn't know *she* was Oliver Sutherland's mom."

Richard frowned. "What do you mean?"

"She dances at Club Zoo."

"What's that?"

"Have you never been there?" Marlene asked, and Richard shook his head. "Well," she said, "it's kinda hard to picture, but they have cages hanging from the ceiling in several locations around the club. Instead of animals, they have go-go dancers in the cages. Anyway, she's one of the dancers." Marlene paused, then said it again. "Wow. Oliver Sutherland's mom is a dancer."

"Yeah," Richard said. But that's all he said because he had just remembered where he had seen Oliver's mother. Several months before, he had gone to a friend's bachelor party. It had been Ollie's mom who danced out of the cake. It was the track suit that had thrown him off. She hadn't been wearing it at the party. That . . . or anything else.

Outside in the parking lot, Oliver ran to catch up. When he did, the woman was wide-eyed. "Ollie," she said. "I thought I was going to throw up."

"I'm sorry," Oliver said with an expression on his face that made him look like he really was. "When that air comes on in the office . . . whew!" He fanned his nose with his hand and smiled.

"I cried," she said. "Not because of the smell. I just need the extra money."

He looked over his shoulder at the school. "Good, Dana. That's really great." Stopping at the woman's car, Oliver looked around. "Again, this is all between you and me, right?"

The woman smiled wearily and nodded. "Of course."

"Okay," Oliver said, pulling a wad of bills from his pocket. "Here's the eighty bucks we agreed on for the basic acting job . . . and . . . another forty for the crying!"

The woman took the money and put it in her jacket pocket. "Call me anytime, Oliver."

"Thanks, 'Mom,'" he said, and winked.

As he turned to go, the woman spoke again. "Ollie," she said. "Are you *really* only thirteen?"

Seventeen

"That tree limb," Jones said. "The one above the bush with yellow flowers."

Oliver didn't look long before declaring, "Nah, there's no way."

Jones turned toward the young man very slowly. His mouth and cheeks were set in a concrete countenance of offense and challenge, but it didn't bother Oliver at all. He saw the sparkle of good humor in the old man's eyes.

"Oh reeeally . . . ?" Jones said. "If I don't make it, I'll give you ten seconds to grab all the candy you can at the Five & Dime. But if I do make it, you have to pick some of those yellow flowers and take 'em to your mother."

Oliver's face lit up with the first possibility, but when the second was rolled into play, his eyes narrowed. "Why's that?" he asked.

Jones continued to study the limb, moving his head a bit, gauging the height of the branch as well as its distance. When he answered, the old man's tone was nonchalant, but his words formed a picture designed to touch a place deep inside the boy. "'Cause I'm an old guy and don't need nothin'. But your mom—excepting for you—is alone.

"So you see—" Jones selected a big pine cone from the many lying about and placed it carefully on top of the sandy trail. The old man looked down at the pine cone, then up at the tree limb that had grown across the trail. It was about eight feet off the ground.

Taking three big steps backward, Jones continued to speak to the red-headed boy who was watching him closely. "The way I figure it is"—he looked at the pine cone again, then the tree limb—"I'm doing you a big favor."

The old man made two giant steps sideways, leaned a bit forward, and looked again from the pine cone to the branch and back to the pine cone. His arms hung loose as he slightly rocked back and forth.

Standing several feet away in order to have a clear view of the action, Oliver said, "What's the big favor?"

Still focusing, the old man said, "Well, when I kick this field goal and win our little contest, I will have made things happier for you at home. Because when the man of the house—that's you—brings the woman of the house—in this case, your mom—flowers, she appreciates the man to a greater degree. He feels appreciated and is thus . . . happy."

Holding up a hand, he said, "Now if you'll just give me a second . . ." Jones took two quick steps in his flip-flops and kicked the pine cone hard, catching it full on its lower third with the bare half of his right foot. The cone sailed high and true, crossing over the limb with room to spare.

Jones held both hands straight up in the air like an official. "And the kick is good!" he yelled, dancing in place just a tiny bit.

"Yeow!" the teenager said. "That had to hurt your foot."

"Nope," the old man said. "It didn't. But nice try at changing the subject." Grinning at Oliver, he pointed toward the flowers and added, "Pay up, Ollie. Start picking."

Oliver had been faithful to his responsibilities at the Five & Dime. On the two Saturdays he had worked so far, the redhead had arrived early, worked energetically, and stayed until Jones insisted he head home. Ollie was at the store every weekday afternoon as well. It was obvious that he loved being there. One might even say that Oliver Sutherland was drawn to the place.

After being in Orange Beach for a couple of weeks, Keely shared an observation with the old man. "School is out at three," she said.

"Yes?" Jones responded.

"But you watch," the young woman went on. "Ollie will be here before 3:15."

Jones waited for her to continue. When she did not, he prompted, "And your point is?"

"It's just funny to me," Keely remarked before interjecting, "Funny 'strange,' I mean. Not funny 'haha.'"

The old man nodded.

"It's just funny that Ollie doesn't get out until three; school is more than a mile from here, he has no ride, no bike, but the kid gets here before three fifteen every day. What does he do . . . run flat-out the whole way here?"

Jones chuckled.

"I'm just saying that he needs this place," Keely concluded. "Or you . . ."

Jones paused before tossing that one back. "Or you," he said and allowed the thought to hang in the air for a moment. "Either way"– the old man grinned–"Ollie *is* always on time."

On this particular day, however, the teenager had been early. Really early. Arriving shortly after eleven o'clock, when asked why, Ollie had explained that some kids were granted an entire week off to prepare for exams. As soon as the words had come from his mouth, Keely was opening her own with the intention of challenging what he'd said.

Before she spoke, however, the old man laid his hand on her arm to hold her back. "Good for you, Ollie," he said. "Since you have a bit of extra time and I need to get some fresh air, why don't you join me on a walk down by the canal?"

Though her eyes narrowed, Keely agreed to hold down the fort while they were gone, and, in any case, that is how the old man had begun to maneuver the boy into picking flowers in the first place.

Within a couple of minutes, the teenager held a large bouquet of long, stiff stems, many of which held two—some even three or four—bright yellow blossoms. The flowers were the size of a baby's palm and shaped like bells. Pointing the handful of lemon-colored blooms toward the sun, Oliver studied the translucent quality of the petals. Beautiful though they were, the young man did not smile. His only words were, "Can we go now?"

Jones nodded in response and began to walk. The old man's blue eyes cast about, taking in the trees, the sky, and the slow-moving water of the Intercoastal Canal. His mind, however, was fixed firmly on the teenager beside him. Reaching a bit of shade, Jones leaned against a big pine and said, "Whew. Hang on a sec. I need to take a break."

Oliver turned to face him. "We just started back."

Ignoring that, Jones said, "Seems a pretty good deal to get a week out of school just before exams, right before summer. And you said only some kids got the week off? How'd the principal choose which kids?"

Oliver glanced to his right, before looking directly at the old man. "He said it was a combination of grades and club participation." Transferring the flowers from his right hand to his left, Ollie rubbed the bridge of his nose, adding, "I'm in chess club, rugby club, and a club that discusses current events . . . so I qualified."

The flowers went back to his right hand and with the fingers of his left, he scratched the side of his nose. "A/B average," he said. "Three clubs. I qualified."

Jones stared at the teenager without moving or smiling. "Does your nose itch?" he asked, finally.

Oliver frowned slightly and rubbed his nose again. "I guess..." he said and tried to laugh. "I guess it does."

Jones nodded. "Of course it does," was all he said, but he continued to stare at the young man.

Oliver shook his head, still attempting to smile. "What does that mean?"

Jones cocked his head, but his eyes never left the teenager's face. "As a noticer," he said, "here is a curious thing I have noticed throughout the years. While in the process of answering a direct question, people tend to glance left if they are trying to remember certain things that happened. Looking to the right, however, is what most people do if they are attempting to construct a story."

Oliver did his best in that moment to appear interested, but Jones spoke again. "A story constructed on the fly holds another marker too. Oddly enough, quickly fabricated answers to uncomfortable questions often cause nasal capillaries to expand. A rapid increase in blood flow to the skin's surface almost always causes it to itch."

The teenager had figured the old man was flying blind, but now, Oliver knew exactly where he was looking to land. Sure enough, Jones hit the runway hard. "All that 'good grades and multiple clubs' stuff?" he said. "You delivered it all with consistent glances to your right. And you scratched your nose the entire time. You were lying, Ollie."

Briefly, there was rage in the teenager's eyes, but just as quickly as it had appeared, the fury was gone. Or, at least, it was masked. Oliver casually tossed the flowers onto the ground and stepped on them. "I'll get my mother something different," he said and turned, hiding his face from the old man.

As the boy moved to walk away, Jones asked quietly, "Why's that, Oliver?"

Oliver stopped, and, briefly, his whole body appeared to sway.

"Ollie . . . ?" Jones's voice was clear but filled with a compassion that seemed determined to take another's pain as his own. "Why would you want to get something different for your mom?"

The tall, lanky redhead turned back to face his friend and took a deep breath, attempting to control his emotions. "Because I hate . . ." he began but could not finish what he'd intended to say. As sobs overwhelmed him, the teenager rushed into the arms of the old man and yielded to a confusion and despair he had never imagined.

"What, Ollie?" Jones asked again. "What is it that you hate?"

With an anguished wail followed by whispered words, the boy answered in a way that, at that moment in time, no one but the old man could have ever understood.

"Yellow flowers," Oliver said. "I hate yellow flowers."

Eighteen

It was a conversation with a couple of friends that clued me in to the fact that there was a new piece of furniture in the Five & Dime. Bigger news, however, was dominating the discussion as I arrived.

I had just come from the airport after having been out of town for almost two weeks. Polly had asked me to stop by Publix before I got to the house, and as I walked in, Pastor Burke Ruark was standing with Bennie, the store manager, outside his office. They waved me over.

Both seemed amused and as we shook hands, Bennie asked, "Have you formed an opinion?"

"Of course," I said in a very confident voice.

Both men leaned in. "Tell us," the pastor said.

I looked both ways and leaned toward them. "Banana pudding."

Like twins from a bad sitcom, both guys frowned and straightened at exactly the same time. Then, in a unison so perfect it was as if they'd rehearsed, they said, "What?"

"Banana pudding." I nodded. "In my opinion, the greatest dessert ever invented."

"What are you talking about?" Bennie said.

"What are *you* talking about?" I countered. As they looked at each other and back to me, I spread my hands apart. "Fellas . . . you asked if I'd formed an opinion, and the answer is yes. Obviously, at this point in my life, I have formed many. However, you didn't ask for my opinion on any specific topic. Therefore, I chose one of my favorites."

Bennie turned to Burke as if I were not there and said, "Tourists know he lives in Orange Beach. Sometimes they come in here and ask about him. I'm always nice. I never tell anyone how strange he is."

"Thank you," I said with a smirk.

"We are asking about the star," Burke informed me, shaking his head wearily.

"I just came from the airport," I replied. "I have no idea what you guys are talking about."

"Oh!" They laughed and began talking at once, stopped, and started in again before Bennie held out a hand to silence Burke and took up the narrative. "Someone stole the Star of Texas from Blair Houston Monroe's front lawn last night!"

"Whaaat?" I croaked. That shut me up for a minute.

"Yeah, everybody's talking about it," the pastor said. "There's nothing left but a big hole in the ground and a pile of sandy dirt."

"That star was huge," I said. "At least three and a half feet high . . . maybe four with that concrete base. And it was right in the middle of that massive lawn."

Bennie laughed. "It was the only thing on that massive lawn!"

"Blair Houston is sooo mad," Burke said. "I drove by her place this morning when I heard about it, and she was screaming at the police officers."

Bennie laughed again. "Man, don't you know they wanted to spray her down with that pepper stuff?"

I was flabbergasted. "Wait . . . that was a solid iron star mounted on a concrete slab, secured by anchored steel cables in the ground. How would somebody have gotten it on a trailer?"

Both men grinned. "They didn't," Burke said, and I frowned.

"He's right," Bennie agreed. "Nobody used a trailer or a truck."

"How do you know?" I asked.

Bennie narrowed his eyes and pointed at me. "No tire tracks," he stated, pausing to let that sink in. "All that pretty grass. That wide expanse of lawn. As heavy as that star was ... there's not a single track in that yard."

"Yeah, anything stout enough to haul that thing would've left tracks," I noted. "But how would anyone get it out of there without leaving tracks?"

They paused only a beat before, again, answering in unison. "Helicopter."

Closing one eye, I made a "mmm" sound. I was doubtful. "It would have taken a Chinook," I said, referencing the huge tandem rotor aircraft familiar to those of us who live near military bases. "And if a helicopter had lifted it out of the ground, don't you think the noise and commotion would've attracted some attention?"

Both men appeared to be disappointed. "Yeah," they agreed, and Bennie added, "Dangit."

The subject changed briefly when I glanced at my watch. I still had my shopping to do before I could head home. "Coffee at the Peace Table in the morning?" the pastor said to us.

"Seven thirty." Bennie nodded. "I'll be there."

When they looked my way, I opened my eyes wide and with a leading tone in my voice, said, "Banana pudding ... ?"

They stared.

"Guys! Once again, I have no idea what you are talking about!"

They laughed and apologized; at which point, Bennie deferred to the pastor, who explained. "Several of us started having coffee with

Jones every morning a couple of weeks ago. At first it was just Keely, Oliver on Saturdays, Jones, and me. I've been every morning since—except Sunday, of course."

"Of course," I said and waited for more.

"Bennie goes too," the pastor said and looked at our friend, who nodded enthusiastically. "We just drink coffee and talk for an hour or so. There's a bunch of us now."

I smiled, never surprised that people sought the old man for conversation. "How many's 'a bunch'?" I asked.

"Eight or nine."

"Really? Wow. Where does everyone sit? Or do you just meet outside?"

Burke looked at me as if I were asking a question to which the answer should be obvious. "We just sit around the table." As an afterthought, he added, "You want to come tomorrow?"

"Absolutely," I said, "if it's okay." They assured me that it would be. It did not occur to me then that I had moved right past the fact that my old friend had gotten a table. After all, that didn't seem too out of the ordinary. I was trying to get my head around exactly where, in that packed jumble of a store, he might have jammed one—much less a table big enough for "a bunch" of folks to sit around!

I remembered something and turned to Bennie. "A minute ago you said, 'Coffee at the Peace Table.' Why do you call it that?"

Both men grinned, but this time Bennie took the lead. "Simple enough, really," he said. "Yesterday morning, when Jones kicked Blair Houston Monroe out of our group—"

I held my hands out to stop the conversation. "Wait, wait, wait," I said. "Blair Houston Monroe was a part of your group? And Jones kicked her out?"

"He kicked her out of the whole store!" Pastor Ruark said.

"Well, yeah, he did," Bennie conceded. "But within fifteen minutes of Monroe being gone, somebody said something about how peaceful it was. I forget how the conversation went after that, but Jack Bailey was the first to call it 'The Peace Table.'"

At 6:30 the next morning, I left the house. I wanted to be early and see Jones alone before the others arrived. I had this one day at home before being gone again for three weeks with my family. I was looking forward to this morning and my first "coffee conversation" at the Peace Table. In addition, I was fully briefed on all things Blair Houston...or as even my boys were now calling the woman: Psycho Monroe.

As I drove from my home to The Wharf, I listened to "Rick and Bubba" on the radio and realized that Blair Houston's beloved Star of Texas having been stolen was still news from Nashville to the Gulf Coast and from Tallahassee to New Orleans—north to south, east to west.

Blair Houston was obviously making a big deal out of it being gone, but frankly, I didn't care.

Furthermore, while I am aware that the lack of sympathy to which I just admitted might be seen as a flaw in my own character, I had a tough time feeling sorry for her. *Here*, I thought, *is a mean woman with a jillion dollars. She lost a piece of scrap iron that didn't amount to much more than a big Christmas decoration anyway.* It was not, I concluded, a sign of the apocalypse.

Far more interesting to me, I must admit, was Blair Houston Monroe's public ejection from Jones's Five & Dime. For the record, here's what happened:

Including Jones, there had been fourteen people tightly packed around the table. While most had been part of the group since the meetings had begun, more or less, yesterday morning was only the second time Blair Houston had been in attendance. My sister, Kristi, and her husband (my brother-in-law), Steve, had been seated to her right, with Keely to Monroe's immediate left, Dr. Charlie Cooper to the left of Keely, and Melanie Martin to the left of him.

Blair Houston Monroe faced the front door with her back square to the center of the store's middle aisle. Directly across the table from her, Jones faced Monroe with his back to the front door.

Allow me to interject here that I have now heard the exact story that follows from four different people—one of whom is my sister—and all tell the same tale. The conversation that day was not unusual—at least, had I been there, it would not have seemed unusual to me. Being a longtime friend of the old man, I had been privy to this type of oddly disbursed information for years.

It all revolved around the idea that one needs to think *beyond* the box—not merely outside it—because, as Jones puts it, "You can't always believe everything you think." Evidently, his examples that day were pretty funny.

"Why would people believe a rabbit's foot to be lucky?" he asked before answering his own question. "It wasn't so lucky for the rabbit."

The old man also stated, "You don't need a parachute to skydive." He grinned at the puzzled expressions and explained, "You only need a parachute to skydive twice."

There was almost an hour of this kind of banter, and, again, it was designed to encourage those present to think in expanded directions.

As I heard it told, Blair Houston's behavior the second morning she attended was just as off-putting as it had been on the first. She became angry when Jones requested she remove her hat—and he had to ask her to do it both days—but as my sister pointed out, the feathers were hitting people in the face!

Making everyone as uncomfortable as possible, she not only *never* cracked a smile but continually attempted to hijack the meeting by changing whatever subject was being discussed at the time. Blair Houston was a fountain of complaint, disagreement, and interruption. All this in addition to misquoting Scripture. "And every time she did *that . . .*" Kristi said, "Jones just stared at her."

"This was the best," my brother-in-law said. "I can't even remember what we were talking about at that moment, but Blair Houston came up with something way off-topic, totally out of context. I suppose she was attempting to appear intelligent, but, specifically, what she said was, 'In everything we do, we should always give 100 percent.'

"For a couple of seconds, no one said anything. Then Jones asked, 'One hundred percent, huh? Even when donating blood?'"

Steve finished by adding, "Everyone burst out laughing. I thought I was going to fall out of my chair!"

Apparently, Blair Houston didn't appreciate the old man's sense of humor, and I'm sure that the group's laughter rankled her as well. In fact, it probably lit a fuse . . . for there was an explosion about to occur that no one saw coming.

Having been off work the day before (doing chores for his *real* mother), Oliver entered the Five & Dime through the rear at almost 8:30. He'd heard the laughter from outside and was no doubt expecting the usual crowd of people to be gathered around the table. Easing through the narrow space of the crowded middle aisle, the teenager's eyes were on Jones as he approached. Absent the hat, Oliver hadn't recognized the person seated directly in front of him as he reached the group and stopped.

Blair Houston Monroe saw Jones glance over her head. When the old man smiled and nodded, she turned to see what had taken his attention. In that split second, she saw nothing but red, and like the snake she was, Blair Houston struck. There was no forethought in her lunge. No planning. Neither was there an element of guile. Before Oliver could move, the old woman had a fistful of his hair.

Though stories about the Old West have always varied in reference and scope, there is one fact upon which all novelists agree: no matter how great the reputation, there arrives a day in the life of every desperado when he is outdrawn by a faster gun.

Oliver was too surprised to make that particular connection as the action unfolded, but certainly the moment was a modern take on something Louis L'Amour or Zane Grey might have written. For when the Texas outlaw got the drop on "Ollie the Kid," she bushwhacked him, plain and simple.

Blair Houston had performed a full right turn, connecting with her trailing left hand and had the boy by the hair. Quicker than Ollie could yelp, she pivoted, coming back to add her right to the other side of his head and screamed in triumph. Perhaps it was the advantage of adrenaline over muscle, but in that moment the old woman was definitely stronger than she looked.

With equal parts glee and delight, Blair Houston's grip must have seemed otherworldly to the thirteen-year-old, for as the ambushed quarry, his struggles only served to energize the old predator.

The fight for survival is a narrative of the oldest sort, and while the casual observer might reckon millennia's victories and defeats to have been recorded in equal number, history shows us that losses gained a head start over wins from the beginning of time. They have become more prevalent during the passing of the centuries, and even today losses continue to outdistance wins, their far more desired counterpart.

While the casual observer believes the winner and loser of a struggle to be determined at the same moment, even manifesting itself at the same time, the truth of the matter is that failure—loss—almost always writes its name on the board before victory would consider doing so.

Victories are often gained by sheer perseverance. Defeats, on the other hand, are usually the first to "declare" for the simple reason that hope itself was abandoned before the possibility of a favorable result could be imagined.

Being older and far more experienced at using intimidation as a weapon, Blair Houston Monroe—as she always did—counted on the capitulation of her adversary to assure her victory. Therefore, the old crone never revealed a hint of weakness. Oliver's red hair sprang from the spaces between her fingers, and not a single strand of it slipped from her grasp—not the barest fraction of an inch—even as the panicked teenager pulled her out of the chair and onto the floor.

Of course, Oliver had hit the ground first. Attempting to backpedal away from the attack that had overwhelmed his senses, the boy had slipped, and in going down, took his worst nightmare with him. According to the witnesses, this was the moment Blair Houston began to yell, "Got 'im! Got 'im!" over and over again.

This also marks the point when the facts—as related to me in any case—got a bit fuzzy. My sister says that Keely was the first to jump on Blair Houston, but Keely says, "No, Melanie Martin got her first. I was on top of Melanie."

No matter who actually made the big hit, the witnesses seemed to believe an escalation in the brawl was inevitable until the old man intervened. No one seemed quite sure what he actually did, but, apparently, when Jones reached in and touched Blair Houston on the shoulder, she reacted as if she'd been tasered.

Not that she jerked around or anything like that, but everyone agreed that the old crone relaxed her hold on Ollie's hair and came out of the pile without resistance. Melanie and Keely got to their feet in as ladylike a fashion as could be expected, and everyone watched as Jones walked Blair Houston to the front door.

In the aftermath of Blair Houston Monroe's having momentarily lost her mind, the green and black feathered hat she had tucked under her chair might've been forgotten altogether. Jack Bailey, however, retrieved it from down the aisle where it had landed after being kicked during the scuffle.

Jack fluffed the feathers and after a brief conversation with Dr. Charlie Cooper, during which both men seriously considered not returning it, placed the hat beside the cash register to be dealt with at a later time.

While most of the group kept an eye on Jones as he escorted Blair Houston away, Dr. Cooper, with his arms crossed tightly across his chest, continued to steal glances at the hat. "I still say we could share it," he said to Jack. "I've never hunted ducks with a decoy on my head— but I'm telling you, that thing'd work."

When Jones moved Blair Houston toward the door, he did so with a guiding hand lightly touching the back of her arm. In light of what had just happened, one might have thought the old woman would have gone quietly, but if one *had* expected that, one would have been mistaken.

She was loudly quoting Bible verses she deemed appropriate for the situation. None of them was actually from the Bible, but that tiny fact had never bothered Blair Houston before, and it didn't bother her now. "Young men everywhere," she said with authority, "must show respect for the elderly as if doing so for the Lord Himself. Leviticus 19:32!"

"Drive out the troublemaker," she thundered, "for he is as a sticker bush in the bare feet of the Almighty. That . . . is from the book of Numbers, chapter 33, verse 55!"

Jones rolled his eyes.

At the door, the old man opened it wide with one hand while attempting to guide Blair Houston through the opening with his other, but she grabbed the door frame and turned back in the direction of the group. Their faces each bore the same expression. It was that look of horrified fascination—the absolute inability to look away—that is seen most often in the eyes of NASCAR fans or those who watch others ride bulls. It's not that they are hoping for disaster, but if one does occur, they sure don't want to miss it.

As Jones gently peeled the woman's fingers from the door's metal frame, she was in full cry, practically screaming, "The Lord rebukes those without compassion for the 'put-upon' and verily, they shall roasteth in the fires of the ungodly! Revelation 21:8."

Jack Bailey frowned. "Roasteth? Is that in the King James Version?"

"No," Melanie Martin snorted. "That's the Queen Monroe Translation . . . New Revised Crazy Edition."

The remark made everyone laugh, and though they continued to watch Jones say whatever he was saying to Blair Houston out on the sidewalk, the tension had been broken. In fact, if Keely hadn't asked her question, the group would have probably refilled their coffee cups and sat back down.

"Hey, guys . . ." the young woman said, "where's Ollie?"

Self-consciously, they glanced around, then back at each other. It was apparent that no one knew. Obviously, the teenager had slipped away during the chaos, but wherever he was, the boy was not in the store. Keely ran to the back door and called into the parking deck to no avail. Oliver was gone.

And less than twenty-four hours later, so was the Star of Texas from Blair Houston Monroe's front lawn.

Nineteen

Canal Road had been crowded, and it was almost 7 a.m. when I walked into the Five & Dime. Jones was leaning against the counter with a cup of coffee in each hand. "Welcome home and good morning," he said and handed one to me.

"Hey, good morning to you. I'm glad to *be* home." I looked into the cup in my hand.

"Don't worry," the old man said, then laughed. "It's your little-kid coffee."

I took a cautious sip. It was my coffee. I mean, it was *his* coffee—Just Jones Java—but had been prepared just like I like it. "Thanks very much," I said and took a full swallow. Watching him closely, I added, "It was nice of you to have this hot and ready . . . right when I walked in."

"Glad to do it," he responded.

I nodded and continued to look right at him. "How did you know I would be here early?"

He smiled. "I didn't until I saw you park your truck. Then I fixed your coffee."

"Oh," I said, slightly deflated and tried to change the subject.

"Hey . . . I heard you kicked Blair Houston Monroe out of the store. You're lucky she didn't beat you up."

Jones laughed. "You're probably right. I didn't really kick her out, though. It was more of a rushed escort." He motioned to the feathers rising from behind the cash register. "It all happened so fast that she left her hat."

"You ought to give it to Oliver," I said. "Kind of a concession prize. I hear he lost that fight."

The old man scrunched up his face. "Well, the fight part was one-sided. She scared him."

"I don't doubt it," I remarked. "She scares me. Did you tell her not to come back?"

"No," Jones said, surprising me. "I just talked to her for a few minutes to calm her down. And I complimented her on the extraordinary ability she possesses to memorize verses of Scripture."

"Seriously?"

He nodded. "I did. I told her it was an honor to know someone with as great an understanding of the Bible as she obviously has. She was very appreciative of my words."

"I'll bet," I said dryly. "Did you at least tell her she was no longer welcome?"

"Nooo," he said. "Quite the contrary, actually. It's against my nature to take away a person's hope. Therefore, I simply defined the criteria for her return. I gave her a small assignment and told her that when she had completed it, she would be welcomed back with open arms."

My jaw had slackened at that news and I was slowly shaking my head. "Really? Why did you . . . ? Jones . . . I think people are going to be disappointed in you for letting her back into the group after what happened."

"I think everyone will be fine."

"Well," I said, still strongly in disagreement, "what does she have to do?"

Smiling slightly, he said, "I asked her to memorize chapters one, two, and three of the book of Hezekiah in the Bible. It should be no problem for a scholar like her."

I looked at him quizzically. "You know," I began, "I don't think there *is* a book of Hezekiah in the Bible."

"Is there not?" the old man said airily. "Well, I guess she'll have a tougher time than I thought."

I was laughing when Jones moved to put his coffee cup down. Inadvertently, he had been blocking my view of the center aisle and all of a sudden, I saw it. "Oh my gosh," I exclaimed and headed toward the middle of the store. "So this is the Peace Table!"

He chuckled as he came up behind me. "I forgot you hadn't seen it. And, yes, sir, that's what everybody is calling it. There've been a lot of conversations around it already. Conversations lead to understanding and peace. Anyway, that's what the table is for. I guess it's a good name."

"Kind of an odd shape," I commented, and he agreed. "Beautiful tablecloth."

"Thank you."

"Why do you have a tablecloth?"

"Why not?" he said and shrugged.

"I don't know. Just seems like it would get dirty."

"It *does* get dirty," came a voice approaching from the back. "That's what tablecloths are for." Keely hugged Jones and shook my hand. "They are cloths that protect the table." She pointed out coffee rings and spills all over it, adding, "This one is doing a great job."

Jones and I laughed. Looking at the old man, Keely said, "It really does need to be cleaned. After the coffee group leaves . . . okay if I take it to the dry cleaners?"

It may have been me, but I thought the old man hesitated at the question. If he did, it was only a beat. "Sure," he said. "That would be nice."

I couldn't stand it anymore and ducked my head to peer underneath the tablecloth. My grin was ear to ear when I glanced at the old man. He returned my smile but said nothing. Just as I'd heard, the table's large surface rested evenly on books.

On my hands and knees, I tested the nearest "leg" with my fingers. Yes, the table legs were constructed entirely of hardcover books. Knowing there was still a bit of time before the rest of the folks showed up, I crawled all the way under for a closer look. What titles would have been chosen to support *this* table?

I inspected every inch of "table leg" and was excited to see books that were already favorites and some with which I was not yet familiar. *The Old Man and the Boy* by Robert Ruark was the first of my "personal top ten" that I spotted. Og Mandino's *The Greatest Salesman in the World* was there. *Something Beautiful* by Gloria Gaither. Jerry Jenkins had books in several places.

As I moved to my right, *To Kill A Mockingbird* by Harper Lee lay on top of Jack London's *Call of the Wild*. There was the funniest book I'd ever read, *Forrest Gump* by Winston Groom. Michael Perry was represented by at least two of his best, *Population: 485* and *Coop. A Cowboy Devotional* by the Harris Family was there. I loved that book.

"What are you seeing that you like?" Jones asked from somewhere above me.

"Well," I answered, "I don't recognize them all, but I haven't seen one I don't like. Hey, here's *Up From Slavery* by Booker T. Washington. I thought this was incredible. The content is amazingly modern to have been written more than a hundred years ago. Have you read it?"

"I have. I've read them all."

Of course, I thought and continued looking. There were biographies: Churchill, Lincoln, George Washington Carver, Eisenhower,

Truman, Bear Bryant, and John Wooden. I saw Golda Meir, Harriet Tubman, Margaret Thatcher, Joan of Arc, and Marie Curie.

As a Man Thinketh, the James Allen classic, was set on top of *All Creatures Great and Small*, the first James Herriot book I read when I was fifteen and again several times since. I spotted several titles each from authors Mark Twain, Stephen Ambrose, Zig Ziglar, and David McCullough. Dave Ramsey's *The Total Money Makeover* was another great one I recognized. *Stars on Alabama* by Sean Dietrich was also there.

"Do you see yours?" Keely had leaned over a bit under the table in order to see me.

"My what?"

"Your books," she answered, pointing to the other table leg.

"Really?" I said. "Where?"

"Left side, halfway up," she said.

I followed her direction and saw *The Traveler's Gift*, *The Butterfly Effect*, and *The Lost Choice* right where she'd indicated. Even though I was sure Jones had only included some of my books because we were friends . . . it was still pretty awesome.

"I really liked *The Bottom of the Pool*," Keely said. "It was the first one of yours I read. But I have to say, this one is my favorite." With a pointed finger, she touched a book under the other side of the table.

"I have another one in here?" I looked and was amazed. It was *The Heart Mender*. "I'm really glad you like *that* one," I said. "Of the twenty-something books I've written, *The Heart Mender* is actually *my* favorite."

Keely's eyebrows lifted. "That says something. That it's your favorite, I mean."

"I guess," I said and crawled out from under the table. I'd noticed a lot of legs gathering around and supposed whatever happened every morning around this table was about to start.

As I stood, Keely refilled my cup of Just Jones Java. I said hello to several of the folks I knew. My sister and Steve had been chatting with Bennie and when she turned around, I was standing next to her. "Where did you come from?" she asked, looking around as if I'd magically appeared.w

"I was under the table," I said.

"Oh," she replied and didn't even blink. Having been my sister for all but the first five years of my life, Kristi ceased being fazed by anything I do a long, long time ago. I could have told her I'd just returned from the moon and gotten the same reaction.

There were beach chairs or stools scattered around, and by the time everyone was seated, the conversation was already underway. As the hour unfolded, I became aware that this was different from anything I'd experienced with Jones in the past. Not that there was anything wrong with it, but having gotten used to digging into a single topic with the old man, I was distracted by this group that seemed all over the place.

They had a lot of questions, and Jones answered all of them. As I mentioned, I had a hard time following all the back and forth, but perhaps it was because the table so intrigued me. When I'd been under it, I was focused on the books and had not even looked at the underside of the table. While all the talking was going on, though, I slid my hand along the underside several times.

I zoned in and out of the conversation, once hearing Jones comment, "When a society allows feelings to determine its truth, trouble is on the immediate horizon."

My gaze remained fixed on the old man as my hand felt around under the table. It was rough in patches though most of it was smooth. I supposed it was wood, but if it was, it was really hard wood. I tried to gouge out a little piece with my fingernail but couldn't.

About that time, Jones advised someone by saying, "Never argue with an idiot. He'll only beat you with his experience." It was a funny line, and everyone laughed, but I hadn't heard what led to the remark. I was still trying to figure out the table.

Under the cloth, if the table *was* wood, it was certainly a big blob of wood. *Very strange shape*, I thought as I studied the lack of predictable curve along the entire table's edge. Jones was speaking again, and I tried hard to pay attention.

"That's just life," he said. "Along the way, there are times when everyone finds themselves in hot water. But you don't have to let hot water define you. Instead, make something of the experience. During times of hot water . . . be coffee."

I glanced at the faces around the table and almost laughed out loud as the old man calmly took a sip from his cup. They were confused. Of course, I didn't know what he was talking about either, but I also knew he wasn't finished.

"If you're in hot water, don't be a carrot. Hot water will change a carrot forever. Carrots in hot water get soft." Jones sipped his coffee again.

"You don't want to be like an egg either," he said. "An egg in hot water will turn hard inside . . . and later, the egg will become cold."

Reaching into the pocket of his jeans, the old man brought out a handful of his coffee beans and gently spread them across the table. Then he held up his cup as if giving a toast and said, "The next time you find yourself in hot water, be coffee. When coffee gets in hot water, instead of being ruined, coffee finds purpose. Coffee changes the water itself. Only in hot water does coffee realize its potential."

When the hour was up, Jones said good-bye and promised to answer more questions next time. *That will be good*, I thought. *And I do have a question. I want to know how you got this table through that door.* But because I knew I'd be given some logical explanation for a situation that defied logic, I didn't ask.

As the group said their good-byes and promised to be back tomorrow, the Five & Dime emptied out. I helped Keely collect the coffee cups, which went into a soapy sink in the tiny room. I was briefly checking a text on my phone when I heard Keely say, "I'll go ahead and take this, okay?"

Looking up, I saw that she was indicating the stained tablecloth. Jones turned his eyes briefly to me before nodding a silent yes to Keely. Without any more discussion than that, the young woman took hold of one end of the cloth and began to peel it away from the table's edge. It didn't come away easily, but Keely had expected that.

The tablecloth was a custom piece. Obviously created specifically for this table, it had been sewn to fit tightly, the seam running along each curve with perfect precision. The covering simply "held on" to every angle. I moved beside her, and by working it over the edge together, a wider area was loosened, and we soon had it ready to be removed.

"Thanks very much," Keely said brightly as I stepped back. She held onto the now unsecured piece of the cloth and walked around the end of the table with it, pulling the entire covering off in one move. And froze.

Keely did not move. Of course, neither did I for several long seconds. Then both of us took a step toward the table. I glanced at Keely, took a longer look at Jones, who was watching me, but my attention went right back to the table.

"Oh my gosh," Keely gasped.

Reaching out to touch its surface, I decided against it and drew back. I had never seen a table like this. I reached out again, very tentatively, hovering my hand just above the table's surface.

Jones had gotten another cup of coffee when the gathering had ended, and he took a sip of it now. "What do you think?" he asked.

"I've never seen anything like it," I replied.

Keely stood in shock, finally shaking her head as if to clear it and said, "It's just incredible."

"Well, touch it then," Jones said. "It's not like you'll hurt it. Heck, I doubt the three of us could even knock it over."

More than seven feet long and almost five feet across, the table-top was a single slab of natural wood that had been hewn from the middle of a massive tree. As I leaned over it to get a better view of the entire surface, my eyes confirmed that the top was indeed fashioned from one center slice, for there was bark—known as a live edge—lining both sides of the thick slab. Reverently, Keely placed her hands on the table's surface, and I thought, *Humanity cannot create art to equal this.*

Moving slightly, I saw that the table was a different masterpiece from every angle. Bearing the colors of cinnamon and honey, unbroken tributaries of the tightly spaced grain folded and swirled, tunneling the dense wood while darker spalting etched its way through shades of umber. It was as if one sunrise after another had been captured by the tree for centuries, each having left an essence to be revealed only when the giant fulfilled its final purpose.

Running my finger along a deep fissure, I assumed it had long ago worked from the bark edge to a place only six inches from the table's center. I saw that where the fissure began, it was an inch wide, but gradually narrowed to a tiny crack at its end. Suddenly, I realized the opening had *not* begun from the outside edge of the tree. The fracture started long ago from what was now the narrowest part of the crack, on the tree's inside.

This was not a split in the wood that had been caused by some mistake when the table had been built. Rather, because each side of the crevice was lined with bark, it was obvious it had existed—growing ever wider—for hundreds of years. Astonishingly, though it had taken generations to create, the fissure was not a natural occurrence.

As Keely looked closer at what had captured my attention, I began to wrap my mind around what I was seeing and arrived at another conclusion: while the crevice might have begun naturally, it had been *continued* in a decidedly unnatural way.

It was also interesting to note that though one might judge the fissure to have begun deep inside the tree, what is considered "deep inside" today, was in fact *the outside edge of the tree* several hundred years ago when the crevice first began to form.

"Do you see how the crevice was continued?" Jones asked softly.

So stunned were we by what we were seeing, neither Keely nor I had noticed the old man was now standing beside us. For a long moment, neither of us answered. We just stared. But I wasn't looking at the fissure, I was looking into it. At its smallest point, there was a white arrowhead with a stain of some kind on the side. Behind it, with its narrowest edge resting alongside the wide end of the first one, was a second.

I placed the forefinger of my right hand on the first arrowhead, then the second, and the third. Slowly, I moved along the length of the crevice to a place at the tabletop's outside edge. There, it appeared that when the tree had been standing, the crevice had been continued for a couple of centuries or more by one arrowhead after another. The tree had almost grown together behind the last arrowhead, virtually hiding the fissure from the outside world until the giant tree finally revealed its treasure.

I turned my eyes to Jones but quickly focused again into the jagged cleft. "I count thirty-nine," I said. "This is impossible."

"Mmm . . . not really," Jones said, returning to his chair. "I mean, I see how you might think so. Sometimes a thing can *seem* impossible. Until it is actually done."

Twenty

Another week had passed, school was already out, and summer on the Gulf Coast had begun in earnest. Keely was working virtually every moment she was not asleep but had never been happier. She talked often with the old man and found herself using what she learned in other places.

At the gym, the young woman regularly connected in conversation with people she found she could actually help. Some, she suspected, despite sometimes repeated attempts to change their lives, struggled to escape the worthlessness they'd felt for so long. "Too often," she told Jones over coffee one morning, "they are delving into their past hoping old answers will create a new future."

"That's a good way of describing what a lot of people do," the old man said. "How do you know that's what they are doing?"

"Because that's what I did," Keely replied. She sipped her coffee and murmured, "And sometimes still do, I guess."

Jones patted her arm. "I'm proud of who you are becoming," he said. "Relationships are still one of the most reliable ways to predict the direction in which a life is moving."

Keely thought about that before finally saying, "I'm really kind of talking about me . . . and struggling with myself . . . like the person I used to be versus the person I'm trying to be."

"I know," Jones replied gently.

Keely paused again. Hesitantly pushing forward, she probed, "But you said that relationships are a predictor of life's direction. And at this time in my life, you are my longest-term friend."

"Consider what you said a couple of minutes ago. How did you put it?" Jones asked. Not waiting for an answer, he continued. "You said there was a struggle between the person you used to be and the person you are trying to be."

Keely nodded and the old man went on. "That's two people: the old Keely and the new one. The new Keely does not need advice from the Keely who caused so much trouble. The Keely you are becoming should not seek approval from the old Keely. Do you understand?"

"I do," she said. "That makes a lot of sense. Thank you."

"Absotively," he said with a grin. "The last thing you need right now is a codependent relationship with your old self."

Keely laughed and thought about how much she had already changed in just a few weeks. She had decided that so much of what she did or did not do these days was because of Jones. The old man had a way of explaining the thinking (or lack of it) behind some of the things she used to do every day. Perspective, he called it.

One of the biggest life-changing lessons came the day she asked about what he'd said in court to the judge. "You said to her," Keely recounted, "that as the owner of a business, you did not have a job to give, but that you had results you required. What did that mean?"

Jones had smiled, crossed his arms, and leaned back in his chair. As he made himself comfortable, he said, "First, the job thing . . . I told the judge that I did not have a job to give because I didn't, I don't, and I won't."

Keely frowned. "What do you call what I do here?"

"Well, I'll admit that most people call it a 'job,' but that's just a word chosen by someone long ago—a word that today we associate with going to work. But it's only a word . . . a sound you make with your mouth. If whoever it was had chosen a *different* word, we would call it something different. It could have just as easily been named 'broccoli.'"

"I'm going to my broccoli?" Keely said skeptically. "When is your next broccoli interview?"

Jones laughed. "Very good, but it's true. We could have used any word because nothing changes the fact that the concept of a well-paying job is a myth."

The young woman remained silent as she struggled to understand.

"Think of it like this," the old man began. "Let's say a business owner invests his or her money in a new business. Part of that investment money is used to hire people who will hopefully be smart enough to figure out ways to grow that business."

"Smart enough?" Keely asked. "They just work there. It's the owner's place to worry about growing the business, isn't it?"

"It's everybody's place. Bottom line, if the owner's business does not grow, the owner will discontinue the investment.

"What I am saying is that a business owner does not have a job to give, he has results that must be accomplished. If a working person understands that and produces great results, not only is the owner's business safe, but the working person focused on producing results will be given greater opportunities.

"On the other hand, if the person who is hired does *not* produce results, the business does not produce profits. A business that does not produce profits is soon *out* of business. And when the business closes down, the person who did not produce results . . ."

"No longer has what they called their job," Keely said, finishing for him. "I never thought of it like that."

"Most people don't," Jones said. "It's a basic economic truth. The owner, the manager, and the employee are only compensated when there is a profit. In reality, everybody is on one payroll. Everybody on *one* payroll is in *one* boat. And the absolute fact that so many people seem to forget is that it's impossible to sink half a boat!

"You can't sink the officers' quarters and watch the crew continue to sail happily along. Neither can you sink the crew and see the officers whooping it up. They all go down, or they all stay up. They have a common interest that is bigger than anything that divides them. That common interest is to keep the ship afloat."

Keely nodded. "That makes perfect sense."

"One more thing . . ." the old man said.

"Okay." Keely waited as Jones closed one eye and cocked his head.

Watching her closely, he asked, "Keely, what would you expect me to do if I found out you or Oliver had been stealing from me?"

The young woman's eyes grew wide, and she felt a jolt of fear course through her. "Jones . . . I have never . . . I mean, I swear I have not . . . oh no . . . has Ollie—"

The old man touched her forearm, and she fell silent, but it was clear that Keely was scared.

Jones spoke, "Stealing from an employer is something that goes on every day. When the margin between up and down is so thin, a thieving employee can sink the boat for everyone."

Again, the young woman protested. "Jones, I hope you believe me. I have *not* stolen anything from this store."

"Keely," Jones said sadly, "I have seen you do it myself."

She felt the blood leave her face but couldn't talk. Her mouth was open, and she just shook her head. Finally, she was able to speak. "No," was the only thing she could say.

"Everything is going to be fine, Keely," Jones said. "I'm not angry with you, but there is a great future ahead of you if you can understand some things that most people do not. Okay?"

Keely nodded.

"Here's a big one: You are paid an hourly wage to work here. That means that I, as the owner, invest my money to buy the hours of time you are in the store. You, as the employee who wants to stay employed, work to make the hours I bought as valuable as you can.

"When you work those hours, if there is not a customer or specific task assigned, you want to look for something to do that will benefit this business. You are keeping the ship afloat, get it?"

"I do, but what about—"

Jones held up his hand. "It's very simple, really. The time you spend on your cell phone—texting a friend, watching a funny video, searching an interesting topic—does not benefit the business. You are being paid hourly to work. When a person works fifty minutes and is on their cell phone for ten minutes, but they accept pay for the full hour . . . that is stealing. As in 'Thou shalt not— '"

The old man paused, then added, "And this is not just an hourly wage example. It's the same thing for a salaried employee. Most folks wouldn't think of breaking into the business owner's home and taking a toolbox or a roast out of the freezer, but the end result is the same. Because whether you take a roast or take money that could have been used to buy a roast . . . stealing is stealing."

For a long moment, the young woman was quiet and still. She brushed her hair back with her fingers as she straightened herself in the chair. Looking at the old man, she spoke. "I don't even know what to say. You are right. That is absolutely right. I never thought of it that way, but it's the truth. I want to figure out a way to pay you back for the time I've . . . um . . . stolen. Ugh. I hate even saying it."

Jones smiled and waved her off. "Noooo. I'm good. We just start from here. I appreciate your willingness to think through things like this. I promise, you'll be a better person—a more valuable person—because of it."

Keely reached over and hugged the old man. "Thank you," she said, smiling as she sat back. Just as quickly, however, her smile faded as her mind picked up a thought she had been able to forget for a few minutes. "Jones, I'm really worried about Ollie—" she started, but the old man interrupted quickly.

He was gentle, but firm. "He's all right."

Keely searched the old man's face for any sign of deception, but of course there was none. "Have you seen him?"

"Let's just say we haven't talked," Jones answered, "but I'm keeping tabs on him."

Keely nodded her acceptance of the old man's answer but rose from the table quickly. She didn't want him to see doubt or fear in her eyes. The young woman trusted Jones, and she trusted his assessment of the situation. Nonetheless, she was afraid for the boy. She'd grown very fond of Ollie, and since the morning of the Blair Houston fiasco, he had not been back to the store.

Twenty-one

Visitors from all over the country were flooding into Orange Beach, and incredibly (to me, anyway) many of them were well versed in the details of what was now being called "The Case of the Missing Star."

Admittedly, some of the vacationers hit town with dollar signs in their eyes, which was no surprise. It was, after all, exactly the reaction Blair Houston had been counting on when she offered a $25,000 reward for the star's return to its rightful place in her front yard.

The amount of money offered was a pittance to Blair Houston, but to most everyone else, twenty-five grand was a fortune, and she expected the cash to prompt a *lot* of help from what she termed "the do-gooder crowd."

To those surprised and thrilled with her display of generosity, the locals urged patience in showering accolades anywhere near the woman. Jennifer Blanchard seemed awfully sure of herself when she said to my wife, "Oh, give me a break. I've known Blair Houston since I was a little girl. Trust me. Even if somebody finds that stupid star, she has already figured out how *not* to pay them!"

Jennifer was correct. She *had* already figured it out. If the star was recovered by law enforcement, she wouldn't have to pay because they can't accept rewards. It is also interesting to note the qualifier she had carefully woven into the reward offer. The star would have to be returned and reset in her front yard. It was a condition of payment fraught with hidden danger—one an ordinary person would never suspect. When the star was returned, the old woman planned to simply have the person arrested. Even if she could only make a Possession of Stolen Property charge stick, Blair Houston Monroe did not intend to pay anyone a dime—much less $25,000!

The Case of the Missing Star had become full-blown national news and not just because of the reward. No, there was another mitigating factor, and at least to the media, it was an even bigger deal than the money. With its own mobile command post, the FBI had arrived.

Special Agent Edie Jacobs from the Mobile, Alabama, Field Office had run the preliminary investigation. Long-standing procedure required a lengthy interview with the victim before the case could be categorized and assigned a strategy.

Blair Houston had pushed hard for a "hate crime" designation and almost got it. SA Jacobs conducted the victim interview personally and immediately forwarded the interview notes to *her* superior. "A hate crime in this case is not beyond the realm of possibility," Jacobs wrote. "I only spent ninety minutes with the woman, and I already hate her. There's no possibility I could be the only one who does."

In the end, the case was investigated under the classification that had captured the Bureau's attention in the first place, Interstate Transportation of Stolen Property, which, considering the star's initial location and its proximity to state lines, seemed feasible. Had the star been driven three miles to the east, it would have been in Florida.

To the west, SA Jacobs noted for the media that if the star had been placed on board a vessel in The Wharf's marina and that vessel headed west along the Intracoastal Waterway, it could have made the Mississippi line in less than an hour.

The FBI concentrated their efforts by coordinating with the adjoining state's closest field offices and followed up on every tip that was called in. Unfortunately, none of those tips led to anything productive, and without a single clue to pursue, the mobile command post left town after three days.

The area's tourists, however, concentrated their recovery endeavors closer to hand. Where, everyone wondered, would a gang of thieves sell, hide, or dump an item like this? Local law enforcement worked the possible angle of the piece having been sold. They scoured antique stores and pawn shops while the vacationing sleuths donned snorkel gear or scuba tanks and dove beneath bridges and in golf course ponds.

Wooded areas were explored on foot, while the touristy, sightseeing helicopters searched Gulf State Park and the National Seashore. Someone printed "Save the Star" T-shirts and most of us bought more than one.

Honestly, there were so many theories floating around about what might have ultimately happened to the star, it was hard to line them up in your head. There were only a few possibilities that we heard more than once or twice. Most suggestions were discounted by the question, "Where would you hide something that big?"

Though no one publicly discussed it, most of us quietly agreed with Mike Martin's conclusion.

Mike is known as a quiet individual, though, in reality, most of us don't really know if that's true. Is he a man of few words because that's his nature, or is it because he is married to Melanie and doesn't often have the opportunity to say anything? In any case, when Mike *does* talk, we listen.

After coffee at the Five & Dime last week—it was the day after the

FBI had given up—Mike signaled for several of us to ease away from the group. Jack, Bennie, and I followed him down the sidewalk.

We had only walked a short distance when Mike turned, made sure we were out of earshot, and quietly said, "Hey, guys, I think I know where that star is."

He glanced around for eavesdroppers, prompting the three of us to assume a posture and attitude of nonchalance as we scanned the area for anyone suspicious. During those few seconds, I admit to wondering what I was suspicious about, not having any idea what Mike was about to tell us. Nevertheless, being unable to spot a single tourist pointing a microphone toward the four of us, I was relieved to determine we were in no imminent danger.

We moved even closer to Mike, tightening the confines of our information drop. Instinctively, we ducked a bit in order for Mike to whisper directly into our ears while at the same time maintaining a line of sight over our lowered heads in case danger approached.

As Mike began to talk, he lifted his right hand to cover his mouth, protecting his information from any roaming teams of lip readers who might be close by. *Excellent tradecraft*, I thought and looked at Mike with newfound respect. *It might be interesting to rethink Mike's background.*

There were only two professions that I could recall being on constant alert for the presence of evil lip readers, and as far as I knew, Mike Martin had never been an international spy or a head football coach.

"Somebody went south with that star," Mike said through his fingers and seemed somewhat smug as we lifted our faces. "It'll be producing in a couple of weeks," he added. Slowly, we nodded. Mike saw that we understood what he meant and that none of us disagreed.

Someone went *south* with it? If true, that answered the other question everyone was asking, which was, "What would you do with the thing if you had it? It's not like you could display it on your own lawn."

South. The solution Mike was offering certainly made sense. From the jetties at Perdido Pass, it is three nautical miles to a latitudinal line that roughly parallels the beach. From Florida to Mississippi, this three-mile ribbon contains the jurisdictional limit of Alabama state waters.

Nose a boat just *over* that line and you have entered federal waters. Also known as the Territorial Sea, federal waters *officially* end twelve nautical miles from the coastline. However, though considered the beginning of International Waters, that twelve-mile mark is also the beginning of an additional twelve-mile buffer. Recognized by international law, this twelve-mile area is known as the Contiguous Zone.

Obviously advancing jurisdiction from twelve to twenty-four miles, the Contiguous Zone allows any nation with a coastline to assert its authority related to customs, fiscal issues, immigration, and sanitary laws. The United States Coast Guard heavily patrols this area.

Closer to shore, one is more likely to see the smaller vessels of our conservation officers or marine police. They deal with emergencies, enforce laws, and are often seen near Alabama's many artificial reefs.

Artificial reefs can be purchased or homemade. After the reef is inspected for environmentally suitable materials, a permit is issued, and the owner has ten days from that time to deploy (sink) their reef in specifically designated reef zones. These reefs provide habitat for marine life and are especially attractive to red snapper and all species of grouper. The state of Alabama has the largest artificial reef program in the United States and the reefs are "gold mines" for fishermen and divers.

Like everywhere, however, even here, there are some who ignore the rules.

In Orange Beach, it has been quipped, there are only two reasons a boat captain might head into the gulf at night, alone, without a permit, and covertly dump something overboard: (1) to get rid of a body or (2) to create an illegal reef.

"For years," Mike said, "just every now and then, I've heard guys mention what a great reef that star would make. The concrete was already attached . . . the star part would sit high off the bottom—" He looked closely at each of us.

"I think someone finally did it," he said. "I think somebody sunk that thing past the Contiguous Zone—forty or fifty miles out. I'm telling you . . . that location will be some family's secret forever. Their grandkids will be catching snapper from it. The GPS numbers'll never be marked on a map, but the Monroe Star Reef is now the fisherman's version of the Lost City of Atlantis."

Not one of us disagreed. To a person, we thought Mike had nailed it. As the larger story unfolded, however, that very cool and interesting bit of thinking he had done to explain the mystery in a perfectly logical way . . . turned out not to matter. Not at all.

Not wishing to leave it there, I should probably highlight a particular fact that would not be obvious to a person who wasn't physically present in Orange Beach during this time.

I'll put it this way: After word about SA Edie Jacobs's written opinion of Blair Houston made the rounds with law enforcement . . . after word got out about how she had grabbed Ollie's hair . . . and after the tourists—many of whom had rented metal detectors, scuba tanks, boats, and helicopters—figured out what the locals thought about Blair Houston Monroe . . . ? Well, let's just say that nobody tried too hard to find that star.

And you know what? None of them ever *did* find it. Of course, that's not to say it wasn't found.

Several days later, Ken Grimes, the Orange Beach city manager, was headed to meet friends for a fishing trip. It was just about daylight, and he was in a hurry when he drove past Blair Houston's house and saw a sign in the yard. It was not as far from the road as the star had been but seemed out of place for a real estate sign.

Ken knew better than to hope Blair Houston was moving anyway, and even though he was already late to the boat ramp, the city manager did a U-turn on the empty street. He put the car in Park at the side of the road and, unable to read the sign from there, he got out and took a dozen or so steps into the yard.

As he approached, Ken saw there were only four words on the whole sign. He glanced at his watch, aware that he needed to get going. The sign was weird, though, and he didn't know what it meant. Until suddenly, he did.

The white cardboard sign had been hand-lettered with a red marker. Ken put his hands on his hips and looked past the sign and onto Blair Houston's huge expanse of lawn. He shook his head and thought, *There is no way. There's just no way.*

The fishing trip forgotten for now, Ken walked slowly toward the center of the yard, never taking his eyes off the massive hole in the ground. Halfway, he stopped, backed up a bit, and looked carefully at the position of the house as it related to the hole and a live oak on the other side of the street.

Ken continued his walk. His feet were moving slowly, but his brain was firing on all cylinders. Arriving beside the hole, he stopped and looked in, before lifting his gaze to the massive pile of sand, compost, and potting soil. Ken didn't know whether to laugh or cry, but he didn't really struggle with the choice. He began to giggle as he circled the hole, and by the time he'd gotten around it, he was laughing so hard he could barely breathe.

The city manager stood beside the pile and marveled at its size. Its peak was higher than he could reach, so he just started on the debris at face level. He had to lean in and held himself against the mountain of earth with his left hand while his right burrowed into the sandy soil and pulled it back out.

It took him less than a full minute to locate the star. He uncovered more of it and sat down on the star's concrete base, once again laughing hysterically. He thought he might frame the sign with its four words. LOOK UNDER THE DIRT!

The star had never been found because it had never been lost. In fact, it had never been moved. Blair Houston Monroe's Star of Texas was right where it had always been, but someone had dug a huge hole beside it and simply covered the star with the dirt. Seen with no trees close by and in the middle of a five-acre front yard, no one could tell the difference between where the star used to be and the current hole in the ground.

On his way back to his truck, Ken did take the sign. Blair Houston would find out later in the morning that her precious star was safe, but Ken thought it would probably be best if she did not see the actual sign. He figured the hand-lettered red ink might push her over the edge.

Red ink. Yep, Ken thought he had a pretty good idea what that was about.

Twenty-two

To those who pay close attention to the natural world, nothing compares to an early morning in the woods. Before dawn begins to mark the horizon, there is a fleeting window of wonder that can be experienced by a person who knows where—and when and how—to encounter a magic most people never suspect exists.

The night creatures have quietly returned to their tiny rock caves, their holes in the ground, or a hollow log. The birds, still asleep in their nests, have not yet begun to chatter. On a morning such as this, absent moonlight or the slightest breeze, darkness and silence often find each other and are ordained to mingle in a way that can be felt only by one who has learned to recognize its touch.

As the old man stepped carefully through a patch of woodland ferns, the damp, uncoiled fronds leaned over his flip-flops, brushing the sides of his feet with dew. He was headed for a particular live oak he had spotted several days earlier and was enjoying every step he took along his way.

It was a short walk and in less than five minutes, he'd arrived. Jones patted the old tree with his hand and smiled. Then he sat down and, facing east, leaned his back against the huge trunk. The old man inhaled deeply, with a slow and steady pace. Exhaling the same way, Jones added no sound to the quiet around him.

Carefully, the old man lifted his arms to the sky and rested his head on the tree. Eyes closed, he did not move for a minute or more, but he smiled when he felt velvet in the air just as he had expected. Slowly, in the same manner his arms had gone up, Jones lowered them and folded his hands into his lap.

Shifting slightly, the old man positioned his back into a more comfortable place. The slightest hint of light was beginning to show in the sky to the east. Jones knew he was where he was supposed to be. He also knew he had time to rest, and so, closing his eyes again, he did exactly that.

When the old man opened his eyes, he was greeted by full daylight. It was still early. He'd only slept an hour but felt refreshed. For anyone but Jones, his next move would have seemed strange. Instead of looking around—checking out his location in the light of day—the old man grabbed hold of one of the live oak's lower limbs and scrambled up onto it.

From the lower limb, Jones easily climbed several more until he was almost twenty feet off the ground. There, he swung his right leg over a big limb and straddled it. Again, his back was to the trunk and he was facing east.

Only then did he pause to take in his surroundings.

While the old man was totally "in the woods," he was still able to see the tops of several nearby houses. Jones was at one end of a long, undeveloped tract of land that runs from Gulf State Park in Gulf Shores all the way to Orange Beach and—believe it or not—directly through the middle of town.

From their earliest beginnings, coastal communities are planned and developed in a way that is almost directly opposite to how landlocked towns are created. Traditional communities typically begin with a building at a crossroads, near a rail stop, or even beside a mill. Other homes and businesses are then added and the whole town expands from that initial center point.

On the other hand, coastal communities are founded on the waterfront. At first, everything is on the water—homes and businesses. When all the waterfront lots have been developed, new lots become available across the street from the water. From that point, new development predictably slows to a crawl.

In 1937, when the Intracoastal Waterway was expanded to connect Perdido Bay in Florida to Mobile Bay in Alabama, it was excavated just north of Orange Beach and Gulf Shores.

With the Gulf of Mexico to the south and Perdido Bay bordering Orange Beach to the east, Mobile Bay cradles the western edge of Gulf Shores. To the north, however, the entire area is bounded by a straight line cut through the earth. One hundred feet wide, twelve feet deep and referred to by locals as "the canal," the Intracoastal Waterway effectively turned the two Alabama towns into one big island.

Through the years, as Gulf Shores and Orange Beach were developed, the "island" allowed a circle of homes and businesses to slowly surround less desirable land. That is why even today, there are deer, bears, wild hogs, alligators, bobcats, osprey, and bald eagles right in the middle of town.

As Jones checked out his surroundings, two deer—a doe and her yearling—browsed through a clearing to the right of the live oak in which he was seated. The old man remained perfectly still as an old gray squirrel—barking all the way—cautiously descended the tree to within feet of his head.

After deciding the intruder posed no danger, the squirrel circled to the other side of the tree and continued on to the ground. Once down, he bullied a pair of chipmunks away from his feeding area only to dive into hiding as a red-tailed hawk silently passed through the canopy of trees. In the hawk's wake, somewhere in the woods, only a blue jay screamed its defiance.

Glancing up, Jones saw a dead branch to his right. Only a couple of feet above his head, it had been broken in a storm the previous fall. The break had not been complete, and though suspended at a ninety-degree angle, the branch still clung tenaciously to the old oak, hanging straight down along the tree's trunk.

The old man saw that part of the branch had fallen into a cleft between two large limbs. That had eased the pressure on the break, allowing it to remain stuck in the tree. The position had also protected much of it from heavy winds. That, Jones knew, was why some of last fall's acorns remained on the branch. Without having to move more than his arms, Jones filled his pockets with the acorns and picked another handful besides.

Continuing to enjoy the solitude and the view, it wasn't long before Jones's gaze came to rest a few yards beyond where the squirrel had been feeding. Peering into a thicket of brushy scrub oak, the old man saw contours that were clearly out of place in this natural landscape.

From where he was perched, looking through the brush, Jones was unable to see any of the objects completely, but their common size, curved shapes, and single color indicated they were all the same. The old man counted about thirty, but wasn't certain the number was accurate. Thirty was pretty close though, at least that's what he figured.

The old man crossed his arms and pursed his lips. Obviously, it was illegal to use this area as a dump, but as he considered the situation, it did not appear that anything had actually been dumped. No, this was a hiding place. Loosely stacked in the thickest of the small oaks, Jones could now see brush and dead tree limbs had been pulled over and around the objects.

It wasn't that Jones did not know what he was seeing, for he did, but the amused expression in his blue eyes became more pronounced as he thought about how much time, energy, and pure muscle it had taken to create this stockpile. Dragging thirty tires through the woods? That was a lot of work.

Thirty tires, Jones thought and almost laughed out loud. He held himself in check, however, for he'd heard a noise behind him. Carefully, the old man peered around the tree, and, sure enough, there was Ollie, headed toward him with two more tires for his stash.

Ollie's route took him almost directly under Jones, who, unable to resist, dropped an acorn and hit the boy on the shoulder. The redhead's concentration was great, however. He didn't even swat at it.

Watching Ollie pass the tree, Jones saw that the boy had tied the two tires together and was rolling them along as one. The old man nodded. *Smart*, he thought, tossed another acorn, and missed. The kid was out of range.

After adding the tires and brushing them in with the others, Oliver paused to stretch and catch his breath. He counted the tires before stepping back and staring at the lot as if he were deep in thought. Suddenly, as if he had just remembered something, Oliver hurriedly checked his pockets, calming when he found a small tape measure in the back pocket of his jeans.

As if it were of critical importance, the teenager carefully measured the width of several tires. Finally satisfied, he placed the tape measure back into his pocket and turned to go. It wasn't a minute before he walked directly under the old man.

This time, Jones didn't miss. He couldn't have, for he dropped the rest of the acorns he held in his hand, and they showered Ollie's shoulders, head, and back.

"Hey!" the teenager said, lurching away from the tree. "What the . . ." he started, but by then had spotted the old man. Jones was trying to be quiet but laughing so hard he was holding onto the tree to avoid falling out.

Oliver placed his hands on his hips. "It wasn't *that* funny," he said grumpily.

"Well," Jones said, still giggling as he climbed down, "yeah, it was."

Ollie did not reply, but his hands were no longer on his hips. He had crossed his arms and was not smiling. When the old man made it to the ground, the boy asked, "What are you doing here?"

"Hmm . . . I could ask you the same thing," Jones said, squinting, "but I won't. We've missed you, Ollie. Keely is worried about you."

"Oh," was all the boy said in response, but visibly relaxed his anxious posture. "Well, just tell her I'm okay."

"I will," the old man said and casually began walking to the tires. The teenager's tension returned immediately but he followed Jones without speaking. Once there, the old man inspected the pile and seemed to come to a decision.

While Ollie watched, Jones pulled some brush from an area and placed a single tire at a forty-five-degree angle onto another stack of two. Quickly, the old man repeated the process and declared, "There! It isn't a recliner, but it's more comfortable than the ground. Have a seat."

Oliver did so, grinning despite his determination to remain stoic. The old man talked for a while, all of it about nothing in particular. He told Oliver about some customers they'd had, several funny things that had been said during the morning coffee, and mentioned Keely again, telling the boy how well she was doing.

Jones talked a long time, laughing often, making Ollie laugh, and eventually told the teenager that since he had not officially quit work, and because they wanted and needed him back, he would be expected in—and on time—the following morning.

Ollie also began to relax. The old man, he decided, was not going to ask him about the tires. He did, however, ask about Blair Houston Monroe.

Oliver's face turned almost as red as his hair at the mention of her name and he moved to stand up.

"Hang on," Jones said, gently blocking the teenager's escape with his arm.

"Jones," Oliver said, "I'm serious. I really don't—"

"I know," the old man interrupted. "I know you don't want to talk about it, but at some point, you're going to have to. It might as well be now and might as well be with me."

Oliver said nothing but slumped back in resignation. Neither said anything for a time. Finally, without looking at Jones, the teenager quietly asked a question. "Do you know what happened when I was nine?"

Jones matched the boy's volume. He spoke softly, but he watched him carefully as he did so. Not hesitating, the old man said, "I do, Ollie. And I'm so sorry."

Oliver bent over, put his face in his hands, and began to cry. He didn't reach out for the old man, however, and though Jones patted Oliver's arm a couple of times, neither did he attempt to hug the weeping boy. They were alone. They were together. It was enough.

When he had gained control, Oliver took several deep breaths before speaking again. "She came to the funeral. We didn't even know who she was. We hadn't lived here a month, but nobody else came so we were glad, I guess.

"I say 'nobody' ... I mean, a couple of my teachers from school did, and our next-door neighbors did. Pastor Ruark was there. At first, we were all just standing around. There weren't any flowers at all.

"I guess she saw that because she went outside and called somebody. Pretty soon, a van showed up, and they put like ... this blanket made of flowers on top of the casket. My mom cried and cried. We thought it was really nice . . . I mean . . . we thought it was a nice thing to do."

"Yeah, I'd have thought the same thing," Jones said without enthusiasm. Oliver was too lost in his own thoughts to have noticed, but there had been a calm dread in the old man's voice.

The teenager was silent for several minutes before continuing. "Anyway, I told you my mom couldn't stop crying, right?" Jones nodded. "Well, she couldn't. She said I should thank the lady in the hat for the flowers." Oliver shrugged at the memory. "Heck, we didn't even know her name."

"So you thanked her?"

"I did."

"What did you say?"

Oliver turned his tear-streaked face to look directly at Jones. "I said, 'Thank you for the flowers for my daddy.'" Oliver paused, his gaze hardening. "And she said, 'You're welcome. Just don't grow up to be like him.'"

The teenager's lip began to quiver, and he looked away. When he did, Jones briefly closed his eyes before continuing. "Did your mom hear her say that?" Ollie shook his head. "Did you ever tell your mom what she said?" Again, the boy shook his head, no.

"I was confused at first," Oliver remembered. "I thought she had known my father, so I asked what she meant. She told me that she bought flowers because there hadn't been any and chose yellow ones because at a funeral yellow flowers are a sign of love from friends." Ollie's face was dark as he swung his eyes to Jones. "Then she said that my dad obviously didn't have any."

The old man wanted to spit. There was a really bad taste in his mouth, but he knew it was about to get worse.

"Then she said . . ." Oliver's voice wavered. "And I'm like nine years old, right?" He cleared his throat. "Then she said, 'Your father killed himself because he was a coward, and now he's in hell because of it. So don't grow up to be like him.'"

Ollie's voice had grown louder and angrier as he finished his story and he'd practically shrieked the last line before bursting into a gut-wrenching flood of tears. "I hate her," he screamed. "I hate her!"

And the old man totally understood.

Later, after they'd walked the woods and talked for a couple more hours, Oliver remembered the tires and was glad Jones had not asked about them. The conversation about his dad, he assumed, had taken the old man's attention.

They had talked a long time and Jones promised their conversations would continue. Ollie asked if his dad had been a coward. Jones said no. Oliver asked if his father was in hell because he had committed suicide. Again, the old man's answer was an emphatic no.

At one point, Jones had stopped walking and faced the teenager. Placing a hand on each of the young man's shoulders, he said, "Look into my eyes, Ollie."

He did, and for the rest of his life, the teenager never forgot what he saw. The unusual but familiar blue was front and center, but Jones's eyes seemed filled with tears that refused to fall. Oliver saw anger in them, but the anger was tempered—perhaps even overwhelmed—by love. There was compassion, strength, sadness, and a certainty of hope—all joined into a gaze that pierced the teenager's soul.

"Ollie," Jones said, "what I am about to tell you is the truth, and it can never be taken from you.

"First, love is more powerful than hate."

"Not *this* hate," the boy declared. "Not the hate I have."

The old man nodded slightly. "I understand why you say that," he said, "and I don't blame you for feeling that way. I don't even expect you to *want* to feel differently. But I do want you to be aware that a life consumed by hate is a tough one to navigate.

"There comes a time for everyone, Ollie, when the choice between love and hate becomes clear. The choice—when it is offered—will be like the knife edge of a cliff—live or die—continue to *give* hate or decide to *accept* love."

Oliver thought for a bit before shaking his head. "I don't get it," he said.

Jones smiled softly. "That's okay. I'm confident that you will. When you see the kind of love that can deliver you from the destruction of hate . . . you'll get it."

Jones paused for a beat and seemed to change the subject. "Ollie, I also want you to understand and be confident in the fact that your father was *not* a coward. Actually, quite the opposite was true. Your dad was a brave man.

"Yes, in one weak moment, he made a disastrous choice, but a coward is not created by a single weak moment. If that were true, all people would be cowards of one sort or another. I declare your father a brave man because of the many years he struggled and won.

"There were many days—many moments—he *could* have been weak, but he chose to be strong. Do you see what I mean?"

"Like a boxer coming back after a loss?"

"Exactly. That is a perfect example. I knew a boxer who everyone still calls the greatest, and he lost five times. Now . . . he *won* fifty-six times. In other words, those five losses do not define his career. Neither does what your father did define his life."

Oliver nodded solemnly.

"Also," Jones added, "your dad is *not* in hell."

"How do you know?" the boy asked.

Jones smiled. "Because that's not how it works." The old man's eyes twinkled, and he cocked his head as he added, "You know, your mom doesn't even know this . . . but I actually met your dad a long time ago."

Oliver's jaw dropped. "What?"

Jones nodded. "I did. I'll tell you about it sometime, but when we met, he was not much older than you."

Oliver had no words, but Jones did and continued. "So . . . about the hell thing . . . you *have* heard there's an alternate destination?"

Oliver nodded.

"When people talk about someone who just died, have you heard it referred to as having been 'called home'?"

"I have," the boy said.

"Well, here's what you need to know," Jones said. "While your dad was not '*called* home,' he was '*welcomed* home.'

"Your dad is not in hell, Ollie. Your dad is home."

Twenty-three

At the Five & Dime, one afternoon while Jones was away, Oliver asked Keely to ring up an eight-foot length of heavy-duty synthetic chain. The thick, darkly colored links were packaged in a tightly wrapped plastic bag and cost—of course—only ten cents. When Keely asked Oliver what in the world he wanted with fake chain, he shrugged and told her that his mother had asked him to find it. "Maybe," he said, "she wants to hang some plants."

As Keely handed Oliver the bag, she read the bag's label and remarked, "What is she hanging . . . palm trees? Whatever this chain is made of, it has a breaking strength of two hundred pounds."

Oliver laughed. He liked Keely and was uncomfortable lying to her. He was also uncomfortable because his nose itched and he dared not scratch it.

The chain was a small but necessary part of a contraption Oliver had designed, and while its strength was important, the fact that the chain was synthetic was critical. For when the links came in contact with each other, they could barely be heard. The chain was silent.

Like all great inventions, the device Oliver had in mind was becoming a reality because he had imaginatively answered the crazy, seemingly impossible question he had asked himself not long before. He supposed his idea could be patented, but that would (1) be a waste of time because no one else would *ever* want to do what he was planning, and (2) if he applied for a patent, everyone would know who invented it, which would basically be an admission of guilt. In any case, the contrivance would be used only once, before being disassembled and destroyed. Oliver definitely did not want the credit!

The lightbulb had come on for the teenager as he was leaving work one day, when he saw hollow, galvanized steel wall studs in a Dumpster. In fireproof buildings like The Wharf, these "boards" are often used as framing material instead of wood. Shaped like 2x4s, they are not only lighter and less expensive than wood but are manufactured with predrilled holes to be more easily assembled with bolts or screws.

These sawed-off pieces had been discarded after the build-out process or interior construction of a new store. Ollie selected three lengths of the hollow steel and after putting his imagination to work for a few minutes, knew exactly what *else* he needed to pull off the biggest prank of his life.

The rest of the components for the mechanism he had in mind were inexpensive, and to prevent any possibility of someone figuring out his end game, Ollie made those purchases from other Orange Beach stores. In reality, the subterfuge was unnecessary, for even if the items had been assembled in front of them, a panel of engineers couldn't have guessed how the boy planned to use them.

From Sam's Stop N Shop, Ollie bought a one-hundred-fifty-foot bundle of quarter-inch anchor rope, six steel bolts, and two packages of Marine-Tex Gray, a bonding putty that hardens like steel. He put his newly acquired items in a backpack and headed for the woods, where the metal boards had already been stashed with the tires.

Several days later, he picked out an inexpensive block and tackle at the Paris family's Ace Hardware. While there, he added four spring-snap hooks—the kind most people used for hammocks—and a large roll of Gorilla brand duct tape.

Those items, too, went into Ollie's backpack, then to his hideaway in the woods. All the articles were laid end to end before the boy stepped back to survey the bits and pieces of a final product that remained, for the moment, only inside his very red head. Kneeling beside the metal boards, he reached for the nearest but stopped before touching it. Oliver remained still for several long seconds and listened.

He heard nothing beyond the wind and birds, but the teenager had an overwhelming sense of not being alone. As he strained to hear, Oliver began to smile. He knew who was watching and this time would catch the old man. "Jones?" he said. "Aren't you too old to be climbing trees?"

There was no answer. "Jones?" he said again, this time with a bit more volume, but just like before, the sound of the woods was his only reply.

Okay, Oliver thought with an even bigger smile, *this'll do it*. Leaping to his feet and turning in one motion, Ollie was up and running in a heartbeat. Headed directly toward the big live oak where he'd seen the old man that day, the boy's long legs needed fewer than a dozen strides to make it to the tree.

As he closed on the trunk at a dead run, Ollie didn't reduce speed. Instead, he launched himself into the air like a long jumper. Having timed his takeoff perfectly, the gangly teenager planted his right foot as high up the side of the tree as he could manage and used the rough bark for purchase.

With his legs bicycling, the boy's tennis-shoed feet scrambled against the trunk and propelled him up. Within seconds, Ollie had both feet firmly planted on the live oak's first big limb and both arms wrapped around the branch above it.

Jubilant, the teenager was barely out of breath, and he laughed loudly. "Gotcha!" he yelled and grinning from ear to ear, looked up to see . . . nothing. Oliver's smile slowly fell. "Jones?" he called and leaned around to search the other side of the tree. "Jones?" he called again, this time with a bit less enthusiasm. Leaning the other way, he looked carefully one more time, but the old man was simply not there.

That's strange, Oliver thought as he hopped down from the tree and returned to his work. Not only had he been certain Jones was close by and watching, the boy continued to have that feeling for the rest of the afternoon. Oliver didn't run back to the tree again, but he did glance around for the old man every time he took a break . . . just as he had since that day . . . every time he rolled another tire or two into the woods.

Early one morning before work, Oliver visited his hiding place. Beginning his construction, he laid the three metal studs into a triangle of sorts. Perhaps a better description might be that once placed into proper alignment, the three metal pieces—at least from one angle—looked a lot like a wide, capital "A."

The two longer pieces—both about three feet in length—were bolted and bonded together at one end to form a ninety-degree angle. The shorter piece was a bit less than two feet long and used as a brace. It was also bolted and bonded into place. The longer sides each extended fifteen inches beyond the brace.

When the Marine-Tex had hardened, Oliver tested the strength of the bond by placing one side of the triangle flat against a medium-sized tree and Gorilla-taping it to the trunk. To accomplish this, he wound several loops around the steel in three places—at the lower end where the length of the stud extended below the brace, directly on and around the brace, and at the top where it attached at a ninety-degree angle to the other longer piece.

The taping finished, Oliver pushed on the top board with his hands, and then he sat on it. The simple braced frame, Gorilla-taped to a tree, held his weight easily. Satisfied, the boy cut the tape and removed the frame. Headed back to the tires, Ollie put the frame over his head and carried it resting on his shoulder. The whole thing weighed less than five pounds.

Next, he unwound the rope, stretching all one hundred fifty feet of it in a straight line, making sure there were no knots and that none of it was kinked or twisted. After unwrapping the small block and tackle, he took it apart, discarding the relatively short length of rope that had been tied to the stationary pulley. As a replacement, Oliver fixed a snap-hook onto the one-hundred-fifty-foot rope and attached it to the bottom side of the stationary pulley.

From there, Oliver threaded the other end of the rope through the second pulley, then back up and over the wheel of the first. With a hacksaw smuggled from home, the boy quickly cut the synthetic chain in half. Now with two, thirty-six-inch sections, Ollie snap-hooked the end of one of the chains to the top of the stationary pulley and added a snap-hook to the other end of that length of chain.

To the second length of chain, Oliver added the last snap-hook, attaching it to the bottom of the free-riding pulley. After inspecting his work, Ollie very carefully coiled the rope and stowed his re-designed block and tackle under the tires beside the triangular brace.

The discarded rope, the used tape, the chain's plastic bag, and the cardboard packaging for the block and tackle were placed inside his backpack. Ollie would carry them out of the woods to be dumped in several different trash containers. The teenager looked around before leaving, making sure all his materials were well hidden. Confident all was in order, he counted his tires. *Getting close*, he thought.

There were forty-three.

When Blair Houston Monroe bought the ten-acre property years ago, it had a natural beauty. At least that's what the locals tell visitors to Orange Beach. It has been said that the locals *have* to tell them, for looking at the place now, "natural beauty" is a tough concept to imagine.

Before she built the garish mansion, the property had been a showplace of live oaks and towering white pines. No one seems certain about what happened to the trees, but different stories—persistent rumors, really—continue to be told today.

Some say that Blair Houston kept changing her mind about where she wanted the house placed on the acreage and that by the time she made her *sixth* final decision, the builder had cut trees for six different homesites, virtually eliminating them all.

Among elementary-school children, the most popular explanation for the lack of trees is that when "the witch" moved in, the bugs from *her* got on the tree and killed *them*. "Run when you see her," they tell each other. "She'll give bugs to you too."

More likely to be true—or at least the tale with actual corroborating witnesses—is that shortly after Blair Houston bought the place, the trees actually left Orange Beach on a truck.

The owner of Blalock Seafood and Specialty Market, Pete Blalock, was the town's mayor when Blair Houston made the land purchase, and he swears that within the week, she applied for a permit to cut down all the trees.

According to Pete, the city council was appalled that anyone would think of clearing what amounted to ten acres of old-growth forest. The permit was summarily denied. Blair Houston loudly cursed the council for their decision. Immediately after doing so, she sweetly quoted a verse from Genesis. (Pete said he tried to look up the verse later and couldn't find it.) Finally, she narrowed her eyes and with a snarl threatened to "cut 'em anyway!"

The city council scoffed and counter-threatened to fine her if she did. When Blair Houston asked how much the fine would be, Pete says he pulled a number out of the air and told her ten thousand dollars. "Right then and there," he says, "the old bat wrote a check for ten grand to the city of Orange Beach, threw it at me, and walked out."

The mayor and city council were certain she was bluffing, but the next morning, before anyone knew what was happening, "what was happening" had been done. Blair Houston Monroe had sold the trees to a lumber company, and before noon, loggers from a sawmill in Mobile had every one of them on the ground.

There are, of course, other yarns surrounding the vanishing trees, but the major point remains: whatever *did* happen, the trees are gone. Today, with frontage on one of the town's major roads, there is nothing but ten flat acres of Bermuda grass. Blair Houston's house faces that road but is bordered on the remaining three sides by the woods that stretch all the way to Gulf Shores.

Oddly enough, when the loggers finally hauled the last tree off Blair Houston's newly acquired property, there was one thing left standing. The previous owner had erected a tall wooden piling. A square-shaped basket structure had been attached to its top in order to make it attractive as a nesting site to ospreys, the fascinating birds of prey.

Much like a utility pole with a big crate on top, the piling had been rough-hewn and rose forty feet into the air. The nesting structure added another three feet to its height, and the ospreys loved it. Year after year, one pair or another raised their chicks atop the lofty piling. But when Blair Houston's house was completed, the lawn sodded, and the Star of Texas installed in the front yard, the old woman hired a crew of men with a bucket truck to knock the structure from the top of the pole.

The teardown happened during what passes for winter in

Orange Beach, and, thankfully, the ospreys weren't nesting at the time. Nevertheless, Orange Beach was scandalized. To most people, while it was not yet against federal law, what Blair Houston Monroe had done was unthinkable. It was more insult than injury, however, when she had the forty-foot piling painted, transforming it into a pole to fly the state flag of Texas.

Then, in an in-your-face type gesture, she made a daily production out of raising and lowering the flag. In addition to doing Blair Houston's yard work, Donnie Mason (who also answers to "Brick," a nickname he's had since grammar school) raises the flag at daylight and lowers it at dusk . . . 365 days a year. He is also responsible for making sure the speakers—the ones pointed toward the street—are always at a volume level just below distortion.

Immediately after the flag is raised and right before it is lowered, a recording of "The Eyes of Texas Are Upon Us" plays loud enough to vibrate the windows in a passing car. As ridiculous as the twice-daily scene is, there are often people who park their cars and wait for Donnie to stride from the mansion's garage. Five steps out and the crowd has spotted him. By steps number seven or eight, they are howling with laughter.

Apparently, Blair Houston insists that he march. The "flagpole" is about one hundred yards from the side of the house, and not only does the man march, his boss obviously ordered him to do so slowly, with knees lifting to waist height. Oh, and there is this: while the music plays, Donnie must stand at attention and salute.

When asked for recommendations about what to do in Orange Beach during the off-season, Melanie Martin once told a visitor, "Go to Blair Houston Monroe's house just before dark. Watching that stupid Brick Mason march and salute is the funniest thing I've ever seen."

Occasionally, one can spot children—at the ballpark, church, or on the school playground—entertaining their friends by marching slowly while holding a salute. Donnie sees them, too, and claims not to care. "Ms. Monroe pays me a hundred dollars a day for that," he told a neighbor. "I'd do it naked."

When her Star of Texas disappeared, Blair Houston became more protective of the Texas state flag. *Obsessed* was the word some used. She considered hiring security guards but worried that one of them might've been the culprit who stole the star, so she didn't. She asked Brick to guard the flag, but he saw dollar signs and wanted too much money. Blair Houston was not entirely impressed with his attitude lately, in any case. The man was becoming a sloppy marcher.

One afternoon, in a continuing quest to protect the flag, Blair Houston even spent a couple of hours on eBay bidding on bear traps, but they were all antiques and turned out to be much too expensive. Besides, she didn't want to put up with all the crying and screaming if she caught someone.

Beyond the obvious, there was another problem with protecting Blair Houston's precious flag. It flew on the opposite side of the house from her bedroom. While the star had been in the front yard, the flag was flown in the side yard. Blair Houston's bedroom is situated at the front of the house, and for years, it had been a simple thing to glance out the window and expect to see the Star of Texas.

For two weeks, however, her glances only served as a reminder that her precious star was gone. A hole in the ground makes for depressing scenery and this one certainly ramped up Blair Houston's anxiety about the flag.

She watched Brick raise it in the mornings, lower it in the evenings, and walked all the way through the house and out the garage a dozen times a day making sure it was still there. After the flag was lowered at dusk, Blair Houston took it from her marching yard man and locked it in her bedroom safe.

Thank God, she thought, *I don't have to worry about it at night.*

Twenty-four

Nighttime has always favored the teenager, a fact especially relevant during the summer. When school is out, the cover darkness provides is multiplied for the simple reason that teenagers can use it all. They are like vampires and werewolves in this way and rarely go to bed until daylight unless forced to do so.

Adults, of course, work during the day. This is true even during the summer. Every evening, at whatever time they choose, adults lock the doors, say, "Good night," and go to bed. Soon, the parental units are fast asleep, soothed by a subconscious that has subtly convinced them that because the doors are locked, no one can come in and no one will go out. This is not always an accurate assumption. Especially if there is a teenager in the house.

Oliver's mother worked hard to make ends meet. As a housekeeper for one of the local hotels, she cleaned rooms from midmorning until midafternoon. From there—six evenings a week—she'd wait tables for the dinner shift at Sea N Suds. The Gulf Shores restaurant is still the best in the area and always busy, so the tips are generous, and it's not a late-night kind of place, so the schedule was perfect for her.

That schedule was perfect for Oliver too. He put in odd hours at

Jones's Five & Dime, but because his mom worked constantly during the day and slept soundly at night, Ollie had access to something that has traditionally created trouble for thirteen-year-old boys. It's a concept known as "free time."

It was Thursday evening. Oliver's mom didn't get home until ten thirty and was exhausted. She fixed herself a sandwich, watched a little television with Oliver, and went to bed. About midnight, the boy checked on her. "Mom?" he said in a soft voice from the bedroom door. There was no answer. She was asleep.

Retreating to his own bedroom, the teenager changed into black jeans and a dark green T-shirt. He put on black socks, then his tennis shoes. Rummaging under the junk on the floor in his closet, Ollie retrieved a floppy black hat and a small vial of black and brown hunter's concealment makeup. Both went into his backpack.

Slipping out the back door, he was in the woods and jogging to his hiding place within seconds. When Oliver arrived and immediately began to sort his equipment, he checked the clock on his cell phone. It was 12:23 a.m.–technically Friday morning–and, so far, all was on time.

The teenager forced himself to remain calm as he loaded his backpack. The block and tackle with all the rope went in on top of the hat, the makeup shoved now into a jeans pocket.

Unbuckling his belt to the second loop, Oliver ran the belt through the roll of Gorilla tape. Testing this setup as a tape dispenser, he pulled several lengths. Smoothing the tough black tape onto different parts of his tennis shoes effectively masked the white accents. Hefting the backpack, Ollie snugged it on before lifting the triangular brace. Placing that over his head and shoulder as he had practiced, he began to walk toward his final staging area.

It had taken almost two hours the day before, but all the tires had been moved about one hundred yards to the east and rehidden.

Including eight more he had found in trash piles and Dumpsters, Oliver had a total stash of fifty-one tires. Because of where they were now concealed, the boy knew there was an increased chance they might be discovered, therefore, he knew that tonight, no matter the weather, the operation was a "go."

At the staging area, all seemed quiet and in order. The tires were stacked three at a time in two rows. Satisfied that he was alone, Oliver slowly removed the brace and rope from the backpack, setting all of it on separate stacks of tires. The clock on his phone registered 12:55.

Leaving everything as it was, Oliver moved away but in a different direction from which he had come. At first, he walked as fast as he dared in the dark. Unfortunately, however, the boy was in an area he didn't know as intimately and, by necessity, slowed his pace. There was only the sliver of a moon above. True, Oliver had hoped the night would be dark, but this was ridiculous. He'd been to the yard he was looking for only twice before and wasn't sure he could find anything without his phone's flashlight.

Thankfully, he didn't need it. When he found the back of the neighborhood, Oliver quickly located the Pierce backyard and went straight to the far corner. There, beside the bottom of a tall sweetgum tree, lay both sections of a portable tree climber, an odd-looking camouflage vest, and a seat-belt-style black strap.

The Pierce family spent a lot of time outdoors and were always welcoming and friendly with Ollie. Mr. Jimmy's son, Conrad, had been up in the sweetgum tree one day when Oliver spotted him through the woods. Conrad was shooting targets with his bow, but as he got a closer look, Ollie was more interested in the climber.

It was a simple design with a small platform for the feet and an even smaller one that supported one's forearms. Conrad showed him how it worked and let him try it out ... *after* putting Ollie in his safety vest and showing him how to climb with the vest attached to a safety belt. The belt was secured to the tree with a loop that would slide up or down depending upon the direction of the climber.

"Always use the safety gear," Conrad had said. "*Always*. No exceptions."

Ollie remembered that, so when he borrowed the two pieces of the climber, he also conscientiously borrowed the safety gear.

When Ollie got back to the tires, he used the concealment makeup to smear big swatches of brown and black all over his face. Carefully, he parted the leaves to get "eyes on target."

The huge house seemed far away, but the flagpole was *right there*—twenty-one steps away from where he sat. On the same night he'd stepped off the distance, he had also measured the base of the pole. It was forty-four inches around.

This was critical information. Conrad had shown him how to adjust the climber according to the diameter of the tree. Most often, climber adjustments are made on the fly. It's an exercise in trial and error with small holes, bolts, and wing nuts, but Ollie knew he'd be in the dark and pressed for time. Therefore, he measured the circumference of the flagpole, divided by pi (3.14), and got the diameter. Sitting on the tires, almost ready to go, Oliver set the climber for fourteen inches.

The teenager made certain the rope was straight and wound properly through the pulleys. Snapping the chain for the stationary pulley to the top of his steel brace, it was 1:38 when Oliver started up the flagpole with it on his shoulder.

His feet were secured to the platform and his arms held fast to the top half of the climber. He wore the safety vest and made certain it was locked with a carabiner to the safety belt around the pole.

At first, the boy practically flew, but the higher he got, the heavier the rope became. Finally, Oliver made it to the top. He pulled his phone partially from his pocket—1:47.

Ollie carefully laid the bracket across the hand climber and suddenly wished he'd thought to bring a bungee cord. The bracket balanced well, however, and so, with the chain and top pulley hung below the platform, he grabbed the chain, pulley, and rope, pulled up about ten feet of it, and tied the rope onto the bar of the platform.

It was a temporary measure that took the weight off all the hanging rope, giving Oliver freedom to secure the bracket onto the flagpole. Without the burden of the rope, the bracket was once again easy to handle.

Ollie held one of the bracket's long sides flat to the pole and moved it until the point of the ninety-degree angle was perfectly aligned with the pole's top edge. This allowed the other longer side of the bracket to extend straight out from the pole's flat top on the same level plane. The teenager wound the rest of the Gorilla tape around the bracket and pole. Ollie wasn't going to sit on it this time, but he knew the bracket was secure.

Untying the rope from the platform, the teenager allowed it to fall and was very quickly on the ground himself. On the way down, he had gotten hold of the chain connected to the bottom of the free riding pulley and taken it to the ground as well.

Stepping from the climbing platform, Oliver unhooked the safety harness. His vest was still on and the belt still connected to the pole. When he came back, he would reattach with the carabiner in seconds. For now, he jogged over to the tires. He would start with one and see how hard this was going to be.

Ollie ran the chain through the hole in the tire he'd selected and connected one of its links to the same snap holding the other end of the chain to the pulley.

The teenager grabbed the loose end of the rope, known as a haul line, and began to pull, walking toward the woods as he did so. Oliver had done the math and knew how a block and tackle was supposed to work, he just wanted to be sure it actually did.

As he had scavenged worn-out tires all over town during the weeks before this night, he had taken several in his house (while his mom was away) and weighed them on her bathroom scales. His tires ran between seventeen and twenty-one pounds. He didn't figure he needed to weigh each one, and since the block and tackle would cut the lifting effort at least in half, he was counting on being able to handle two at a time.

He kept a record of the width of every tire. It was how he knew how many tires he needed. The smallest of Ollie's tires were nine inches wide, the largest around eleven. Any he found wider than eleven, the boy passed by, knowing they would also be heavier.

As Oliver pulled the haul rope, it was shockingly easy to lift its load, and in a very short time, the tire was snugged up to the bracket. With two loops around a small tree at the edge of the woods, he jammed the end of the rope into a tight branch.

It was now 2:10. That had taken some time, but as long as the next part of his plan went well, he was still okay. Oliver rolled two tires to the base of the flagpole and left them there as he stepped onto the climbing platform and hooked onto the safety belt. The boy made it to the top of the pole in less than two minutes.

Come on, Ollie, he thought as he studied the tire. *Get this right.*

He did. By moving the climber around the pole to his right, the tire hung level with his waist and less than a foot from his body. Oliver moved the safety clip over his shoulder so that he could turn around, and with his back to the pole, placed both hands under the tire.

Oliver lifted the tire up and with it still connected to the chain, pushed the hole of the tire over the end of the bracket and eased it back toward the pole. When the tire encountered the bracket's brace, Ollie held it there with his right hand. With his left, the teenager reached up and pulled the other side down and over the top of the flagpole.

The tire was still chained, but now rested on the top part of the climber. From there, Ollie simply backed the climber to the ground and the tire—completely around the pole—slid with him. Once down, he unsnapped and removed the chain. By reattaching the climbers above it, Oliver's first tire was resting completely on the ground and he was ready to go again.

The block and tackle handled the lifting of two tires easily. Oliver's only concern was that the chain be long enough for him to handle the tires separately at the top. It was and he did.

A few minutes later and the teenager was aware that a good news/ bad news situation was in play. It was 2:30, and the good news was that he already had three tires over the pole and on the ground. The bad news, as he considered the time, was that he had *only* three tires on the ground.

When fifteen tires were stacked around the pole, Ollie's learning curve was such that he was getting faster. He was also getting tired. It was 3:32, and the boy began to worry he'd run out of time, but he had not figured on his climbing distance being reduced. Soon he realized that even though he was now climbing the growing stack of tires just to reattach the climber above them, the climb itself was becoming shorter and faster.

At 4:46, the teenager had two tires left in the woods but thought if he tried to haul them up, he might not get the bracket off. The stack was already touching the bottom of the bracket. With relief that he had a legitimate excuse *not* to climb the pole again, Oliver opened his pocketknife, sliced through the Gorilla tape, and cut the bracket loose.

He had removed the climbers from the pole with several tires to go and only had to move the safety belt around the entire stack as he descended. Oliver moved the bracket, rope, and pulleys into the woods and jammed them into his backpack. He hid the bracket and would return Conrad's climbers and safety gear before daylight.

It was 5:01. The sky would begin to lighten soon and Ollie wanted to be long gone by then. Exhausted and stumbling a bit, he jogged back out to his work of art. There were forty-nine tires stacked up the flagpole. Standing under them, Oliver touched the screen on his phone to take a selfie. Focusing on his face from below to be sure the tires above him were in the frame, he risked the flash, took the photo, and ran.

Jones was so close when Ollie went by that he'd briefly considered reaching out to grab him. The old man chuckled to think how the boy would have reacted. Stepping from the woods out into the open, he looked up at the tower of tires and gave a low whistle.

Moving purposefully, he walked back to his right, keeping to the edge of the woods. After about thirty yards, the old man stopped to kneel beside an old fence post. Jones stayed in that position for a minute or two before standing and heading back the other way.

The old man went past the flagpole and, at about twenty-five or thirty yards, knelt down again. This time, it was under a large wax myrtle that was leaning into the clearing that was Blair Houston's yard. Again, he stayed for a few moments, then walked back to where his young friend had run into the woods.

Jones picked up a tire and stepped out of the trees with it hanging from his shoulder. Slowly, as if he had all the time in the world, the old man walked around the flagpole as if inspecting it from every angle. Then as dawn began to break, with the tire still on his shoulder, the old man climbed the stack of tires to the very top.

Holding on with one hand, he used the other to sling the tire he'd carried up and over what remained visible of the pole. He paused as if enjoying the view. Jones looked toward the house, at the road, back toward the woods, climbed down, and was gone.

Twenty-five

We had just landed at the Pensacola Airport. That should give you an idea of how quickly the word was being spread, but since Polly, Austin, Adam, and I were all out of town together, that's probably as fast as we could have heard the news.

We had been on Delta, connected in Atlanta, and flew into Pensacola on the last flight of the evening. It was almost 11 p.m., we were tired, and we still had a forty-five-minute drive home. But when we heard the star had been found, how, and by whom, we were suddenly wide awake.

John Blanchard gave us the news. His wife, Jennifer, a friend of Polly's, was also on the flight. She and Polly are both on the board at Youth Reach, and we all walked together to baggage claim. John was there to pick her up and while we waited for the luggage, he told us the latest information.

We all thought it was hilarious, Austin and Adam especially so. Our sons—now 21 and 18—also held a great degree of admiration for whoever had pulled it off. When our laughter had died down some, John delivered his bombshell.

"As they say on television," he began, "but that's not all!" John had our attention and proceeded to tell us about the tires on Blair Houston Monroe's flagpole. Our questions were fast and furious. He didn't have the answers to all of them, but it was as if we could hardly picture what had been done.

"All the way up?"

"How many are there?"

"None of them cut? Each one had to come over from the top?"

"How is she going to get them off?"

The answer to "When did it happen?" was "Last night, for sure."

John told us that Blair Houston's yard had been full of people all day long. The Mobile and Pensacola television crews were there. "Even the tourists," he said, "came off the beach to have their pictures taken standing beside what everybody's calling 'The Monroe Tower.'"

"I'll bet Blair Houston was pitching a fit," Polly said. "First the star, now this, and the people all over her lawn . . ."

"Actually," John said, "she never came out of the house. People saw her standing in the window over the garage, but she stayed inside all day."

"That doesn't sound like Psycho Monroe to me," I said, earning laughter from the boys and a stern look from my wife.

"Oh, I forgot to tell you . . ." he said. "Get this: when the local newscasts aired this afternoon, all three announced that Ms. Monroe—that's what they called her—is holding a press conference tomorrow at noon beside her desecrated flagpole. Evidently, she called the stations to tell them that she's going to make some big announcement."

"That can't be good," I said with a sigh, and John agreed. We collected our luggage, but by the time we all said our good-byes, there was still not a one of us who had come up with a single legitimate guess as to what that announcement might be.

Pastor Ruark arrived earlier than usual, but he found Jones waiting for him, already seated at the Peace Table with two cups of coffee. As he took his first sips from the hot mug, Burke thought about how much he had come to appreciate the old man. Jones had helped him think through some confusing issues these past weeks.

Today he was nervous. The subject he wanted to discuss seemed sacrilegious somehow, and while he really wanted to hear what Jones had to say on the matter, the pastor did not want to offend him.

"Jones," he began, "several times now, in several different ways, I've heard you talk about impossibilities being possible." He paused, and Jones waited patiently for him to continue. When he did, his voice carried an edge of despair. "I'm just not sure I buy that anymore."

Jones smiled ruefully and responded, "That's a sad and danger-ous cliff to approach, you know? Whatever it is you *are* buying, don't spend your belief foolishly."

"I'm not sure what you mean," the pastor said.

"Impossibility is not overcome without denying power to the concept. In your life, what's possible is often determined by what you believe. On the other hand, what is *im*possible can *always* be deter-mined by what you believe.

"Belief is a currency of sorts. If you spend it foolishly by believing a thing is impossible, then to you it will be. But if you spend your cur-rency wisely—by believing a thing *is* possible and allowing that belief to fuel your thinking and work—then to you it will be."

Burke looked into Jones's eyes. He wanted to believe the old man; he really did. *But that's the problem, isn't it?* he thought. *I'm not sure what to believe anymore.*

Jones saw Burke swallow hard. With a friendly smile, he said, "Some folks declare, 'I'll believe it when I see it.' But the deal really works the other way around. Most times you won't see it until you manage to believe it."

As the pastor took that in, they saw several people from the group had gathered outside. As they stood, the old man added, "Here's a last thought before everyone comes in. You mentioned before that you didn't know if you were 'buying' what I said. No offense taken at all—I understand and appreciate your honesty—but I *do* want you to continue to think through it."

"Okay . . ." Burke said, "why's that?"

"Because whatever you *do* end up buying will go a long way toward determining your life's results." The pastor frowned, unsure of the old man's meaning. "Think about it," Jones continued. "If belief is your currency, and you refuse to spend it in the direction of what's possible, that means you spent your belief in the other direction . . . and wasted it.

"You've heard 'you get what you pay for.' If your belief is used confirming that what you desire is impossible, that means you paid everything expecting nothing, and for all that mental effort, you got nothing in return."

Burke nodded slowly, feeling as if he were beginning to understand. But it was the last thing the old man told him that he'd never forget. "Pastor," Jones said, "ultimately, everyone chooses what they believe. Don't spend all your currency in one store . . . only to find out later that all your miracles were on the shelf in another."

I walked into the store with several others when we saw Jones and the pastor stand up. It was the first time I'd seen the table since it had been unveiled three weeks earlier, and while the others might have gotten used to it, I was eager to have another look. Quickly claiming a chair beside the line of arrowheads, I went for a cup of the Just Jones Java and talked for a moment with the man himself.

"Good trip?" he asked.

"Yes, sir, it was. We're all glad to be home, though."

"You've been missed. These mornings at the Peace Table are getting a mite crowded."

"Thanks," I said. "I've missed being here. Yeah, this is growing—" As I'd started the sentence, I turned to glance around and was astonished. People had lined up outside just to get through the front door. I looked in the other direction and saw folks spreading down the aisles. Many had brought their own portable seats and were settling in places their view was blocked by shelves or stacks of merchandise, but they had come to hear.

My eyebrows up and with a smile, I said, "There must be fifty or sixty people here. Where are they going to sit next week?"

Jones didn't answer. Instead, he appeared to be deep in thought and continued to scan the store and sip coffee.

I tried again. "What do you think?"

Without looking at me, the old man quietly said, "There are seventy-one. You know how these things go . . . next week they'll have moved to another place."

I frowned as he turned toward the table, speaking to people as he made his way through the crowd. I was unsure about the old man's statement . . . and about the expression on his face as he said what he had. *Is he unhappy about something?* I wondered. *Not that he seems sad. But he doesn't appear to be overjoyed either.*

I sat down as Jones did. He was about to begin, and I was relieved to see that his smile—along with the twinkle in his eyes—had returned. Before he could speak, a woman beyond my line of sight called out, "Jones, you promised another day for our questions. Is today the day?"

"If that is what you'd like today to be," he said brightly, "I'm ready."

The Five & Dime erupted in applause. Jones grinned, but I must admit that it was not comfortable to me. For some reason, it struck me as if the intimate gathering of a few, where people felt safe sharing personal challenges or professional uncertainty, had ceased to exist.

Yes, I was aware that three weeks had passed since I'd last attended, but this was more "theater crowd" than "discussion group." I supposed the transition was inevitable. It wasn't like the old guy was going to turn anyone away. It's just that I'd always thought of Jones as that rare someone who used his heart and mind saving individuals—mostly from themselves—just as he had done for me.

"Then I'll ask the first question," the woman called again when the applause died down. Jones nodded for her to proceed. "Are you going to attend Blair Houston's press conference today at noon?"

Once more, the whole place erupted, this time with laughter. I watched the old man carefully. With a pleasant expression, he calmly waited until the room grew quiet. Keeping them on the edge of their seats, he appeared to consider the question before answering simply, "I do plan to be there, yes," and the store exploded again.

"Since this is question-and-answer day," Jones began, "why don't I ask a question?" As everyone settled in, the old man asked, "What has four letters, occasionally has twelve letters, always has six letters, but sometimes has nine."

We were in the beginning stages of brain cramp when Jones added, "True or false?"

People all over the room looked at each other in confusion. Perhaps we had heard incorrectly. "Would you repeat that, please?" asked Lacy Smith. Lacy, I saw, was a note taker. Jones repeated what he had said before, added the "true or false" bit at the end, and did it all with a slow and careful cadence. I watched Lacy write down every word.

We closed our eyes, we looked at the ceiling, we looked at the floor and at each other. No one had a clue. True or false? Finally, some brave soul in the back of the store challenged the old man. "There is no answer to that," he said. "You can't assign true or false to a question."

That makes sense, I thought and saw that others agreed. People were nodding at each other and beginning to smile. Everyone thought that, at last, they had cornered the old man. The smiles grew larger.

"Who says I was asking a question?" Jones replied.

The smiles vanished. Again, we were confused. "But you *were* asking a question," Lacy said. "See?" She held her notepad up for Jones. I could see it from where I was. She had dutifully transcribed what the old man had asked. The problem, apparently, was that he had not asked anything.

"Erase the question mark, young lady," he said. "Just use a period." When she had done so, he crossed his arms and with a sly grin asked, "Now . . . true or false?" Jones's Five & Dime was silent. To her credit, though she was not the only one following by notes, Lacy was the first one to get it.

"Oh my gosh! True!" she exclaimed. "That is so great!" Lacy's excitement quickly spread, first through the smaller group of people who had actually written down what Jones had said and, because of that, were able to understand the hidden riddle. The second wave of comprehension swept the store as those with notes showed them to the rest of us and explained what the old man had done.

As usual, I thought, *there were several lessons in that*. Of course, as Jones smiled at me from across the table, I knew . . . that *he* knew . . . that I *already* knew . . . those lessons.

1. Take notes.
2. Don't make the same assumptions everyone else is making.
3. Think beyond what seems obvious.

So if I knew those things, why was I not doing them? At that moment, watching the old man watch me with a bemused expression, I was embarrassed enough to admit to laziness. Jones, on the other hand, would have probably explained my lazy choices in a way that sounded less offensive. Certainly, I had heard him explain it before.

"The current of life never stops," he'd say. "One can *choose* to swim downstream. That's an easier trip, of course, and there's always lots of company, but sooner or later it's also where all the garbage collects.

"Upstream, on the other hand, is where the water is pure. The things that make life special and worthwhile are all upstream, and to get there, you must discipline yourself to swim against the current.

"Be most aware," Jones would say, "of the danger of treading water. Many people believe there are three choices: swimming upstream, swimming downstream, and holding in place by treading water.

"In reality, the choices are only two. One can struggle upstream or travel downstream, but when a person chooses to stop swimming midstream, there is no such thing as holding in place. Water—like a life without purpose—always flows downstream, and everything that does not struggle from its grasp goes downstream too."

Years ago, the old man told me, "I cannot do life for you. I can teach you, explain to you, and encourage you. I can get you close. I can show you the way. But I cannot do it." Then Jones added a tag line that made me laugh. "Yes, sir," he said, "I can lead a horse to water, but I can't make him think."

Twenty-six

Once again, I found myself concentrating on something other than the conversation. I wondered why Jones had seemed unhappy. I wondered if there was any more coffee. I looked at the arrowheads in the wood. My mind was everywhere, it seemed, except where it should have been, in the present.

I heard some of it, zoning in one time when I heard my name. "How did you and Andy Andrews become such close friends?" a lady asked.

"It was a very natural thing to happen," he answered. "We had mutual strangers in common." Of course, everyone laughed.

Someone else asked Jones to define *wisdom*, and though he had spoken to me about wisdom many times, I listened closely to what he said. By this time, I had gotten paper and borrowed a pen from Lacy. I wrote quickly but am confident that these were his exact words:

Wisdom is the deeper understanding of principles that have been proven through the ages yet still remain relevant to life in the here and now. A deeper understanding of a principle requires a constant search for additional meaning and a better way to explain how the power of the principle can be harnessed by others.

As wisdom is gained, change is required. To become wise, one must change, and it will be a never-ending process. The rules by which you work and live must change as well, for the rules by which you managed your life at one time were adopted as a result of the knowledge and understanding you possessed at that time.

The wisdom you have gained since has allowed you greater knowledge and understanding than you had at that time. Therefore, if you are still clinging to those same rules, they are obviously outdated.

The rule "do not talk to strangers" is perfect for a specific period of time in one's life. So, too, is "hold hands when crossing the street." There should, however, come a time when wisdom makes these rules obsolete.

There was a moment of reflection as people either wrote furiously or swore to themselves they would not forget what he had just said. In that pause, I raised my hand until I had the old man's attention. "Jones," I asked, "how did you get this table? Where did it come from? And this . . ." I ran my index finger up the line of arrowheads. "How was this done?"

There were sounds of excited agreement around the store. It appeared everyone wanted to know. Jones nodded slowly. At first, because he continued to look at me, I feared he had not wanted the question asked. As he began to talk, however, I chose to believe he had only been considering his answer.

"How did I come to be the caretaker of this table? It was a gift. I think of myself as its caretaker because of its age and increasing beauty. A work of art such as this cannot be owned, only cared for until another generation is allowed to protect and preserve it for the next. The table was, and continues to be, a gift."

I heard a couple of quick, deep breaths nearby—people were about to ask questions—but the old man held up a hand and continued to talk. "The answers to where this table originated and how the arrowheads ended up inside it? I suppose we can imagine an answer. After all, imagination is life's grand advantage. It places everything within the realm of possibility."

"Everything?" someone asked doubtfully.

"Of course." Jones grinned. "Even time travel. Properly harnessed, one's imagination is a key to the future because it can unlock the secrets of the past."

The old man lifted his arms straight out from his body. With his palms down, he leaned forward slightly as if testing the air above the table. Briefly, he closed his eyes. Upon opening them, Jones said, "Imagine with me now. In fact, imagine how wonderfully accurate your imagination has become. As a group, you named this slab of wood the Peace Table.

"It was a remarkable choice, really, for the table was created more than a thousand years ago, deep inside a tree known as Le-homahtvke Lakcvpe—the Peacemaker Oak. That tree was a massive live oak, surrounded by twelve other live oaks almost as big. It was under the branches of this center tree—the Peacemaker Oak—that large groups of people actually maintained peace for several centuries.

"Every clan of Muscogee—the people who later became the Creek Nation—held their most important council fires at the Peacemaker Oak. Every decade or so, when disagreements occurred and war seemed imminent, the chiefs would meet at the tree and talk peace until an agreement was reached. These special victories were memorialized by an arrowhead symbolically binding two opposing sides together."

Jones motioned to the line of arrowheads in the table. To be sure I understood, I said, "These arrowheads did *not* split the tree? No? Instead, they were used one at a time over the years to *close* the crack?"

"Yes," Jones said. "Exactly. At least, that's exactly what I imagine."

We laughed. "Furthermore," he added, "I imagine the Peacemaker Oak to still be alive today and as big as it ever was."

That statement stopped us cold. "If the table is a crossways slice from the Peacemaker Oak," Jack Bailey pointed out, "how is it possible that the tree could still be alive?"

"Good question," Jones replied. "Here's the story. . . . In 1540, the Peacemaker Oak was already hundreds of years old. The tree's topmost limbs were practically woven together with the highest limbs of the twelve surrounding oaks. From their earliest memories, the clans who lived in the area called it the Place of Coverings.

I mention 1540 because that's when Hernando de Soto and his Spanish explorers made their way through the southern part of this state. The Coverings was located on a bluff beside an ancient lake. The lake was, and still is, situated between two rivers, the Alabama and what is now known as the Tombigbee.

"The Spaniards were being silently followed by many clan warriors. Unfortunately, de Soto and his men chose the Coverings as an extended campsite. This infuriated the clans, and when some of the warriors were spotted, the explorers decided to fortify their location. There were already twelve giant live oaks in a circle. They needed only to fill the space between the twelve trunks in order to create effective protection.

"So they cut down the center tree. Chopping off all its limbs and branches into manageable pieces, de Soto's men dragged them into place—"

"They cut down the Peacemaker Oak?" Lacy said in disbelief.

"Yep," Jones answered. "The trunk lay where it fell. Several days later—it was October 18 of that year—the clans attacked. Almost all the warriors perished in the effort, and when the battle was over, de Soto and his men set fire to their fort . . . which, of course, killed the other twelve trees.

"When the Spaniards left, what remained of the clans arrived. These were the women, the children, the elderly, and a few surviving warriors. Because the ground was too hard to dig graves, boulders were piled over the dead warriors. Called cairns, these sites were created to entomb six to ten bodies at a time and took these wives, children, and parents more than a week to construct.

"These remnants of a formerly great people sadly made ready to leave their once sacred place. The last thing they did—and it took all of them working at once—was to roll the trunk of the Peacemaker Oak off the bluff and into the lake. There, it sank to the bottom in forty-seven feet of water.

"Several months later, part of the bluff collapsed in a springtime flood, burying the enormous tree trunk under tons of limestone and clay. There, deprived of oxygen, the body of the Peacemaker Oak was preserved, lying in suspended animation for almost five hundred years.

"A while back, it was brought to light in much the same manner as it had been hidden. The Tombigbee and Alabama flooded at the same time, sending water raging through the lake. The blistering current uncovered and dislodged the old tree, moving it more than a mile away and into the flooded forest. When the flood waters receded, the mountainous remains of the sacred tree lay on dry land.

"Months later, it was spotted and except for the bark having been scraped off in areas, the wood was dry and in good shape. It was taken to a mill and while processing the log for lumber, a single slab was sliced from the middle to create a table. As you can see, the saw's blade shaved along the line of arrowheads without nicking a single one."

"That's . . . impossible, right?" someone said, prompting an almost immediate reply from Jack Bailey.

"Sure," he said. "I'd have thought so. Until there it is, right before your very eyes."

Melanie Martin called from halfway up the center aisle, "Jones, we love the Peace Table, but I'm sad about the tree."

The old man smiled gently and said, "Don't be sad. I already told you, the Peacemaker Oak is alive today and bigger than it was before."

There were doubtful expressions on faces all over the store. "How is that possible?" a man asked.

Jones answered simply. "Everything is possible. In this case, though, the Peacemaker Oak was cut off at its base, but there remained a root system underground that was larger than the tree itself. Not only did frequent rains keep the roots from drying out, but the fallen warriors, whose rock-covered remains were located in several places directly above the root system, thus continued to feed their sacred tree.

"Then within a year, from the center of its former self, the Peacemaker Oak once again began to reach for the sky. At first, it was small . . . a sapling growing from a stump. Now it is massive and more beautiful than before."

"Where is it?" Melanie asked. "I'll go there this afternoon!" Everyone laughed, but I saw people looking at each other and figured if Jones actually gave away the tree's location, most of us would not be far behind her.

He did not reveal the whereabouts of the Peacemaker Oak, and none of us was surprised. We were thrilled, however, when Jones reached behind himself and retrieved a small burlap bag from a shelf. Opening it by untying the drawstrings, the old man said, "One apiece, please, there are just enough." As he poured the contents out onto the table, Jones added, "I picked them up one at a time, just for you."

I thought there would be a mad scramble, but there wasn't. Instead, a reverent hush fell over the group. It was almost strange. Without pushing or shoving, one person at a time approached. They hugged the old man and whispered their thanks before each in turn selected one from the scattering on the table.

In minutes, except for the old man, Keely, and me, the store was empty. As she and I picked up the last two left on the table, it occurred to me that Jones had been right again. There were just enough. Everyone now had an acorn from the Peacemaker Oak.

Twenty-seven

"Probably because I was thirteen."

One day, a couple or three decades from now, when Ollie is asked why in the world he did it, that'll most likely be his answer.

The kid is brilliant. On that point, everyone agrees. In the future, Dr. Sutherland or Professor Sutherland will be at lunch with friends. Perhaps he will be General Sutherland and playing golf with the other three-stars . . . or Academy Award–winner Ollie Sutherland. No matter. At some point, when the story gets out there, people will want to know.

"Why," they will ask, "after successfully pulling off the greatest prank in the history of prankdom and getting away clean . . . *why* would you take a photograph of yourself with the tire pole and e-mail it to Blair Houston Monroe?"

"Why did you do it?" is a great question. Because after it was done, not even Ollie knew the answer.

When he had first looked at the picture, he was somewhat surprised to see that his dark, commando-style hunter's makeup was almost completely gone. Wiping sweat from his face with a T-shirt every few minutes for several hours had removed most of it, and in the photo, Ollie did not look as cool as he had imagined. *The tires are kinda blurry*, he thought, *but when she gets this, she'll know what she's seeing.*

He had downloaded the photo from his cell phone to a "burner" he had purchased online for less than twenty dollars. It was a throwaway that came with its own number and e-mail account. Preloaded with fifteen minutes of use, it was the same model the CIA bought in bulk.

Burner phones are just an example of the inevitable end result when a manufacturer understands the concept of planned obsolescence. These units are built and purchased to be used once, maybe twice, then discarded. The phones—chiefly because of how they are employed—are untraceable. Of course, an untraceable asset loses much of its value when used to e-mail photographs of oneself.

Ollie had been standing outside Blair Houston's house yesterday, late morning. Vacationers milled around the yard as if it were a tour stop they were expected to visit while in the area. ("Did you see the tire pole while you were there?") Amused locals mixed in and out of the crowd.

Raleigh Woods had set up her Nikon D810 with a 200mm lens on a tripod and was doing portrait sessions for the tourists. Her company, Shots from the Woods, would e-mail the final product. Raleigh's younger sister, Rae, had set up a table nearby and was selling vintage clothes.

"Hi, Rae," Ollie said as he passed the table.

"Hey, Ollie," Rae responded and conspiratorially waved him over. He moved around two high school girls arguing over the only velvet, bell-bottomed jumpsuit Rae had on the table and met Rae on the side. She looked around carefully, leaned toward the boy and whispered, "I'm making a fortune here."

"Oh. Well. That's good," the boy replied, not sure why she thought he should know.

"Yeah," Rae whispered again, "this tire thing has really drawn the people. You know tourists, they just have to buy *something*." Ollie gave a polite chuckle. "Anyway," Rae continued, "it would be great if I could somehow get prior notice of something like this." She stared at the boy with wide eyes. "You know? Before it happens? So, like, I can be prepared?"

Ollie immediately began to move. "Okay," he said. "If I ever hear anything, I'll let you know. Good to see you!" He waved and was away. *That was weird*, he thought.

Camera crews from two television stations were set up on the lawn. The teenager gave them a wide berth but wondered who they were interviewing for this story.

Through conversations with several of the locals, Ollie learned that Rick and Bubba had talked about the tire pole on their syndicated radio show. Apparently, a listener had called in during the eight o'clock hour with the news. Bubba asked for a picture, and in minutes he was on the air, describing the photograph of the flagpole that had just come in on e-mail.

"Rick," he said in his inimitable voice, "this is a work of art, but if I am not mistaken, this is the *same* Blair Houston Monroe whose Star of Texas was stolen—*but not really stolen*—from her front yard. First, her star, now this. It has become spectacularly apparent that somebody has it in for this woman."

"First the star, now the tires on the flagpole," Rick responded. "Bubba . . . does anyone need to point out how much actual physical labor was involved to pull this off? I think you're right. Somebody *does* have it in for her. But I've got to say, it's been my experience that when a person gets *this* kind of attention, they've done something to deserve it!"

Local people also told Ollie that Blair Houston had been holed up in her house all morning. That was probably the news that sparked

Ollie's thirteen-year-old moment, for that was when he pulled out the burner phone from his pocket, attached the photo to Blair Houston's e-mail address, and pressed Send. *This'll get her out,* he thought.

But it didn't. More than an hour passed, and *still* she had not run screaming out of her front door, exploded through the roof, or jumped on her broom and flown around town looking for him. He was disappointed.

But as the afternoon wore on, the disappointment turned into uneasiness. There was no particular reason to be nervous, he thought, but the fact that Blair Houston had not reacted like she usually did gave him pause.

This was supposed to have been "the one." *This* was the prank that should have put her over the edge. By now, the men in white suits should have been loading her into the looney bin truck. But no. All was quiet. That, Ollie decided, was *not* good.

When he heard about Blair Houston's press conference and announcement to be made at noon the following day, the needle on Ollie's emotional index moved into the space marked "Worried."

For the rest of the evening, however, the boy reviewed the decisions he'd made and the plans he'd followed. Finding no holes in what he'd done, Ollie would manage to push the needle back to "Concerned" or even "Caution!" Before long, however, the next day's press conference would pop back into his mind, and the needle would move right back to "Worried."

Ollie didn't understand *why* he was worried. Even the e-mailed photo was no *real* concern. After all, it was only an image of him with a stack of tires.

I could say, "Who says they're my tires?" he thought. *Or I can say, "I was roaming around early, like, before daylight, and look—I got the first picture of what somebody did to your flagpole!"* The photo he'd sent was proof of nothing. Still, he was worried.

By the following morning, he had become more nervous but for no logical reason Ollie could identify. *Maybe "no reason" is the problem,* the boy mused. There were two pieces of information Jones had delivered during the previous weeks that came to him now.

The first was this: If all the evidence points to an obvious conclusion and yet the conclusion cannot be reached . . . if everything seems to have been done and yet the results refuse to come in . . . then a fact is missing from your equation. In other words, *there is something you do not know.*

It had sounded ominous when the old man said it, but now Ollie could somehow *feel* its meaning. It was the second thing Jones told him, however, that was pushing him over the edge. "Conventional wisdom," the old man began, "is sometimes neither conventional nor wise. That's why we must think through *even* the things we believe we know for sure."

The old man paused for a beat before adding, "Hey, Ollie . . . you know how folks say, 'What you don't know can't hurt you?'" The teenager nodded. "Yeah?" The old man nodded back. "Well, don't you believe it. What you don't know *can* hurt you. And, sometimes, it can hurt you badly."

Uh-oh . . . Ollie thought, and the needle pegged into "Panic." *There is something I don't know.*

Because we live in a beach town, I am quite used to seeing "banner planes" fly along the edge of the water, towing advertisements for local shops or restaurants. Therefore, when I arrived at Blair Houston's place for the press conference and saw more than two hundred people gathered, I was not surprised to see a banner plane circling the property.

I must say, however, that I laughed out loud when I read the long sign the Cessna was towing. The plane had been hired by a store on nearby Dauphin Island and the banner proclaimed: *Clint's Tires! We will do almost anything for your business!* I thought it was a stroke of genius.

I had to park what felt like a mile away, and when I finally walked onto the lawn, it was 11:51. I looked for Jones, but the place was a circus. The Woods sisters were there, I saw. Both entrepreneurs, they seemed to be tired, but happy, and had customers lined up.

There was a guy selling hot dogs and a lady with popcorn. The Orange Beach High School Band Boosters had a snow cone booth and appeared to be covered up with hot, thirsty people. I bought a bottled water from a church youth group and headed toward the flagpole. It was a typical hot summer day.

Approaching the tower of tires, I saw that a small stage with a podium had been set up at its base. Mounted on a scaffolding erected up and over the stage were five large televisions faced in different directions.

Three television stations had cameras in position and the on-air talent waited miserably for noon to arrive. Usually beautiful people, today their pancake makeup was melting from their faces in the heat of what I'm sure they thought of as their own shadeless patch of hell.

There were also a few radio stations represented, each doing their own "live remote." *It was days like this,* I thought, surveying the scene, *that a person is happy to have a face for radio.* The radio announcers, wearing shorts and T-shirts with visors and sunglasses, were comfortable despite the heat.

Still unable to find the old man, I glanced at my watch. It was 11:58. A moment later, someone yelled, "Here she comes!" and as if we were a single organism, every person in the crowd looked toward the house. Sure enough, with Brick Mason in front of her and two Orange

Beach police officers behind, Blair Houston Monroe strode down the front steps of her home wearing the biggest hat I'd ever seen.

The hat looked like an umbrella that had just hosted a duck fight. It was orange with orange feathers. To complete her ensemble, the woman of the hour was wearing an orange dress with brick-sized orange platform shoes. *Orange?* I thought. *Well . . . it is Orange Beach.* I shook my head, certain the town's founding fathers were turning over in their graves.

Brick walked with his chin up, and while I was disappointed that the man wasn't marching, it did seem like he'd been ordered to act as if he were proud.

I felt sorry for the police officers. They were stoic and professional but quite obviously embarrassed, and I didn't blame them. I was sure the mayor—or someone else to whom Blair Houston had contributed campaign funds—insisted she be escorted by the police.

Suddenly, I saw a bright redhead about fifteen yards to my right. It was Oliver Sutherland, and as I watched, the old man came into view as well. He had apparently seen the kid about the same time, but he was closer to Ollie than I was.

While the rest of the crowd had their gazes fixed upon Blair Houston and her approaching entourage, I continued to watch the old man and the boy to my right. Jones angled in behind Ollie and surprised him. I smiled when I saw the kid's reaction: he grinned and put a fierce hug on the old man.

Jones gave something to Ollie just then. Whatever it was, the old man didn't just hand it over. It was as if he made a presentation. I couldn't see from where I stood and had no idea what the item might be. I only saw a small, off-white cloth bag. Ollie held it up by a drawstring as he thanked the old man and hugged him again. Once more, I found myself smiling and nodding. Ollie carefully tucked the bag in his pocket as the crowd suddenly cheered. Blair Houston was taking the stage.

The cheer, with its accompanying applause, was short. Delivered almost entirely by tourists, the cheer ended abruptly when our summer visitors noticed the local people had not joined in the acclaim. In fact, many of us had our arms crossed. Yes, we were interested enough to be in attendance but suspicious about whatever announcement was about to be made.

Blair Houston held up her arms when the cheering began, but several seconds after it had stopped, she was still doing the palms-down motion, indicating her desire that all the adulation could stop. It had.

"Ladies and gentlemen of the press," she began, "fellow citizens . . . I would like to thank you all for being here. I would also like to take the opportunity to thank Mr. Brick Mason, my faithful manservant, for his years of loyal service."

There were audible snickers from the crowd. I looked at Brick and unexpectedly felt sorry for him. His head was down, his lips were moving, and I figured he was asking the ground to swallow him up. Or perhaps he was making the request on *her* behalf. Either way, Brick was aware that life as he had known it was over. He played church league softball with a lot of these guys. "Manservant" would not be forgotten, and he knew it.

"I would also like to thank the Orange Beach Police Department for their protection."

The police officers' posture was much like that of the manservant. Their attention seemed to be on the polish of their shoes. I heard a voice whisper, "Andy!" behind me and half turned. It was Melanie Martin. Continuing her entirely audible whisper, she said, "Protection? If that woman expects to be protected from everybody who hates her guts, she can move *on* from the Orange Beach Police. She needs the National Guard."

I couldn't help but laugh out loud, causing people to look my way and prompting me to think about embarrassment as a general concept and marvel at the amount spreading around this event. In fact, I suppose I thought about that for a couple of minutes, for when I zoned back in, Blair Houston was speaking angrily and gesturing with both hands.

With one, she indicated her Star of Texas, claiming it had been "defiled," while the other directed our attention to the tires that were, as she put it, "desecrating an old woman's flagpole."

Blair Houston had not needed to draw our attention to the tire pole, I thought. It was huge and right above her. Not only had we noticed it, a significant percentage of those gathered were hoping it might fall on her.

After a few more long, hot minutes of being told how much she had done for us over the years and detailing all she meant to the community only to be targeted by a felon with no regard for her social status, much less the law as it applied to people in her tax bracket, Blair Houston Monroe finally got to the point.

"As you all know," she began, "I have an announcement to make."

"Then please—for God's sake—make it!" someone yelled from behind me, eliciting laughter from the crowd. I studied the group and smiled. *This really is a circus atmosphere*, I thought. *People are having fun* . . . And they were. Some had big beach blankets spread out and were making sandwiches. Folks were laughing. It was like the improv group Second City had come to town and we were watching outdoor theater.

Only this was no joke. Not to Blair Houston Monroe. The more fun people had, the angrier she was becoming, and now she was worked up just in time for the big announcement. The cameras were rolling, the crowd grew quiet, and the old shrew pointed to the tires stacked behind her. Slowly, she growled, "I know who did this."

Uh-oh, I thought. *This is not going to be good*. I couldn't help but wonder how other people were reacting to what she had said. I cut my eyes to the left and right and saw that others were doing the same. No one moved. A woman near me had a slice of bread in one hand, and in the other she held a butter knife. She had stopped in midbreath and remained perfectly still, the knife balancing a huge glob of mayonnaise she'd just scooped from a jar.

"There are laws against trespassing," Blair Houston continued, "and against vandalism, and if this were Texas, there would be a law against dishonoring the displaying mechanism of our state flag!"

Immediately, there were a few boos. Some profanities were mixed among them, but all of that was drowned out by cries of "Roll Tide!" and "War Eagle!"

I turned to see Melanie Martin with her hand over her mouth. She was pretending to cough while adding to the noise. I distinctly heard her yelling "Roll Tide" *and* "War Eagle." When she made eye contact with me, not only did Melanie continue, she waggled her eyebrows at me. I couldn't help but laugh.

In Alabama, we take college football very seriously. Melanie didn't care about that, though. She just saw the opportunity to stick it to Blair Houston Monroe and took it.

If I'd known what was about to happen, I'd have joined her.

Twenty-eight

Harassment is also a crime!" Blair Houston yelled in an attempt to silence the gathering.

They weren't listening, choosing instead the opportunity to share their commitment to the University of Alabama or Auburn by chanting back and forth to each other. "Roll Tide!" half the crowd would roar. "War Eagle!" the other half would answer.

"Harassment! Trespassing! Criminal mischief! Vandalism!" the old harpy screamed from stage while the camera crews gleefully confirmed their units were recording.

"Roll Tide!"

"War Eagle!"

Back and forth it went until people realized Blair Houston was about to have a "come apart" and settled down.

To be clear, the crowd did not stop their chanting out of any sense of concern for the woman. Certainly, the teamwork these opposing sides demonstrated and the quietude they achieved within a matter of seconds had nothing to do with any respect they might have suddenly found for her.

Instead, their almost immediate group decision was prompted

by their almost simultaneous observation that Blair Houston Monroe was almost "off the rails," and in conversations later about what had occurred, almost all of them agreed that almost none of them had ever seen a crazy woman almost melt down in front of that many people.

Simply put, because Blair Houston was more interesting to them than they were to themselves, the audience redirected its attention and settled in for the show.

Her eyes narrowed under the brim of the huge hat. The outrageously long, feathered plumes pointed in all directions and seemed to jerk and quiver every time she moved. This look, coupled with the predatory vibe she possessed, seemed to demonstrate with a great deal of imaginary accuracy what an ostrich with rabies might look like.

She placed one elbow on the podium. Facing the side of the stage with her body, Blair Houston turned her head to the left, her face still aiming to the front. With her body posture, it occurred to me that she intended the audience hear her every word while, at the same time, showing them as much contempt as possible.

Aware that her public was now completely focused, Blair Houston waved a dismissive gesture at the police officers without looking in their direction. "These people are sworn to uphold the law," she said, slowing the pacing of her delivery. "There have been laws broken here. I know who is responsible, and I want the satisfaction of justice . . . right now."

She straightened to her full height, and again without a glance or a nod to the officers, gave them an order. "Arrest that boy!" she screamed and pointed at Oliver Sutherland.

There were several cries of protest and a few more of disgust. The police officers, while now appearing to have gained a modicum of interest in the proceedings, remained calm, cool, and anchored in place. As soon as she had pointed, however, Ollie broke as if to run, but Jones grabbed him so quickly, he couldn't get away. Not that he tried.

The old man whispered something to him, and there was no struggle at all. Blair Houston was infuriated by the officers' failure to obey her and, predictably, was now yelling at them about how she paid their salary, how she would have their jobs, and whether or not they knew who she was.

Finally, she turned back to the crowd and again pointed at Oliver. "That boy is a menace to this town," she said loudly. "That boy"—she jabbed her finger at Ollie—"did this!" She poked her jabbing finger into the air indicating the tire pole. "And I can prove it!"

At that, the officers glanced up. From where I stood, Ollie looked ready to bolt again, but Jones gave him a couple of pats on the shoulder, and he stayed put.

"I have purposefully remained inside my home since this tragedy was visited upon me," Blair Houston said. "This press conference is the first time I have ventured out. Safety was part of it, of course, but the main reason I sequestered myself away from this crime scene was to avoid charges of tampering with evidence."

Many people shook their heads at each other. A few rolled their eyes. What was she talking about?

"As I said, I have proof that—"

"Hey!" a man interrupted from somewhere in the back. "It's hot out here. If you have proof, get to it!"

I could tell Blair Houston had been startled, but she didn't scare easily and remained cool. "Very well," she said. "Officers?" This time, she looked at them. They looked at her. "If one of you would please walk along the edge of my property in that direction, you will come to an old fence post. Please?" She gestured in that direction.

"And you?" she addressed the other officer. "If you would humor an old woman, please walk the edge of my property that way." She had indicated the opposite direction. "See the wax myrtle? It's the bushy tree hanging over the yard?" We all looked. We all saw it. "When you get to the wax myrtle, please stop there."

Everyone's eyes were on the police officers now. They had not moved. "Please?" Blair Houston asked again. They looked at each other, shrugged, and separated, one headed to the fence post, the other to the wax myrtle.

As we looked on, Blair Houston continued to talk to the officers and, I suppose, to us. "After the incident involving my star," she began, "I realized I was under attack. It was then that I secured the very best hidden cameras available and had them professionally placed around my property. Two of them were focused on my flagpole."

I looked at Ollie and saw him droop. The old man had his hands in his pockets.

Blair Houston spoke loudly to the officers. "Look at the base of the fence post and near the bottom of the tree. Please remove the cameras and bring them to the podium."

As they each unfastened small, darkly colored boxes, the old woman turned and addressed the crowd again.

"These cameras are the finest available," she said. "Made by Reconyx, they are the model XR6 UltraFire Covert. They are battery-powered, fully mobile, and record 1080P HD video at 30 frames per second, including 24-bit digitally enhanced stereo audio with wind noise reduction."

As she chattered on, sounding like a product rep for the camera company, the police officers were returning to the stage but ever so slowly as they inspected the cameras, both obviously interested in the technology. I looked across the crowd and locked eyes with Kevin Perkins. Practically my brother, Kevin and I have known each other long enough to finish each other's sentences. I knew—and Kevin knew—that we were both thinking the same thing: *Reconyx. Wow.*

The officers had almost reached the podium. Blair Houston was continuing to talk. "The Reconyx UltraFire Covert also captures still images with 8-megapixel resolution. A 2.4-inch color display allows playback of images and videos with sound directly on the camera. In other words," she said, "these police officers and I would ordinarily view what is captured right here, right now, on the camera's own screen." Folks were glancing at each other with raised eyebrows.

"However," she went on, "with micro HDMI and USB output connections, we will be able to plug in to the high definition screens arrayed here above the stage. Together, we will all see what has been captured on camera for the first time, right here, right now."

I looked again at Jones and Ollie. Neither had moved, but I could tell the old man was talking quietly to the boy, who was looking toward the woods. The police were back up on the stage, each still holding a camera, but now glued to what Blair Houston was saying. I caught another glance from Kevin, and he slowly shook his head. *Yeah*, I thought. *Me either.*

I did not have a good feeling about this.

Blair Houston asked the officers to give the cameras to the television crew who would connect it for us all to see. To us, she explained that she had never touched the cameras and would not now. The absence of her fingerprints, she said, would prove she had not altered what was about to be witnessed, and the cameras, we learned, would remain in police custody until the trial.

Trial? People all around were glancing at familiar faces where they could find them and frowning. I think most of us were recalibrating the level of consequence we had subconsciously assigned this event before we had arrived. While we waited for the cameras to be connected, the old woman continued to extol the virtues of Reconyx.

"High-sensitivity sensors coupled with the latest-generation infrared illuminators provide exceptionally clear nighttime images, even at extended ranges of up to eighty feet. And all these cameras are proudly made in the USA!"

She is nuts, I thought, *but she knows a lot about game cameras.*

Apparently, Psycho Monroe had somehow found out what outdoor people had known for some time: in the open air, whether for wildlife or security, Reconyx has no peer. Rain, heat, freezing temperatures? No matter the conditions, these cameras deliver crystal-clear images and stunningly crisp video, even during the darkest of nights.

Again, people who have a passion for wildlife and the outdoors— and there were a lot of us present—were already aware that Reconyx was the gold standard in trail cameras. Those of us who were also familiar with Oliver Sutherland couldn't help but connect the dots, fast revealing a picture that none of us wanted to see. This time, we figured, the kid had gotten in over his head.

Given the thumbs-up by whoever had connected the cameras to the screens, Blair Houston made one last declaration, and its vindictiveness stunned us all.

"Oliver Sutherland," she said, staring directly at the boy, "I am well aware of your status as a minor, and while you and your protectors might believe your age will protect you from punishment, I intend to spare no expense or waste any influence I have to make certain you pay for your crimes.

"While you *are* underage and not technically accountable for your actions, your remaining parent is the responsible party. This afternoon, I will use the evidence we are about to see to file a formal complaint against your mother. She will be found unfit, and you will be taken from her and become a ward of the state."

Ollie burst into tears, and many of those who saw his agony began to surge forward. It had been an incredibly cruel thing to say, and at that moment I thought the crowd might lynch her. Jones placed his arm around the teenager's shoulders, but the old man's eyes stayed on Blair Houston Monroe. She stood alone at the podium, the police officers having backed as far away from her as they could get.

There were angry shouts as people milled around the edge of the stage. I didn't think anyone would actually attempt to harm her, but it was obvious that no one was about to let her off the stage. Then the videos began to play, and everything stopped.

The images coming to life onscreen conflicted so completely with our expectations—especially those of Blair Houston Monroe—that, at first, it was as if a cloud of incomprehension had settled on the whole throng at once. What we were seeing simply did not register. Most of us moved to the right or the left, assuming our perception was being confused by the sun's glare on the screens. That wasn't it.

In the *next* instant, we moved from a state of "that is not Ollie" to an awareness of just who the figure onscreen actually was. We stared open mouthed. It was Jones.

I moved toward the stage, glancing from screen to screen, confirming the same scenes were on each one. Momentarily, I looked away, removed my sunglasses, and tried again with the same result. Same scenes, same guy. It was Jones.

Blair Houston Monroe was doing her version of what I had just done, but because she was so close to the screens, she walked quickly back and forth between them. *Yes*, I could have told her, *they are all the same.*

In thirty-second increments, the videos showed the old man at varying locations in the yard. But it was definitely Jones, and there was no doubt that the circular-shaped object on his shoulder was a tire. In fact, the images were so crisp and clear, the tire's tread pattern was visible. The still images were repeats of the video: the old man walking around with a tire over his shoulder, the tire pole in the background.

With Blair Houston screeching at him to "find the video of that red-headed kid," the technician who had hooked up the camera ran the video back and forth at high speed and shrugged at her. There was no one else on the recording.

She screeched at him again, and he attached leads to the second camera. Once done, the screens merely allowed everyone to see the same action from a different angle.

Blair Houston began looking in Jones's direction as if he had robbed her. She was coming unglued. Ollie sat cross-legged on the ground with his face in his hands while the old man stood beside him, his own hands clasped behind his back. He was watching Blair Houston, and I thought I detected the hint of a smile.

All assembled had grown quiet. The locals knew Jones and by this time had pointed out the old man to the tourists. "You," Blair Houston bellowed at him, "did *not* do this!"

Jones's smile grew by a fraction as he furrowed his brow, cocking his head as if to say, *I didn't?* and shrugged an *I don't know what to tell ya.*

She turned to the police officers and said, "The boy did this. Arrest that boy!" When she saw they were not about to do *that*, she ordered, "Well, arrest somebody!" and pointed at the old man. "Arrest him! Arrest Jones!"

The old man had known it was coming. He had known what she would do. Ollie, on the other hand, was confused and frightened. When the video had begun, Ollie did not understand what had happened. "But you weren't there!" he protested to his old friend.

"Videos don't lie," Jones replied quietly. The boy stared at him, having no clue what to say. The old man chuckled to himself before whispering in Ollie's ear. "They don't always tell the whole truth, but videos don't lie."

"Jones! No." Big tears welled up in his eyes again. "I can't let you—"

"Ollie," the old man interrupted and held him at arm's length.

"Ollie . . . I have already done it. It is finished. I want you to embrace this gift."

The boy shook his head, not comprehending what the old man had done, why he had done it, or what he was saying now. "Ollie," Jones continued, "do you remember the day you threw the flowers away?"

The boy nodded solemnly.

"That day, I told you that love is more powerful than hate. You know, that woman up there is consumed by hate." He had gestured to the stage, where Blair Houston was having a fit because the officers were not moving on Jones.

Except for Blair Houston and her histrionics, the whole place had become rather still. We couldn't hear what was being said, but it seemed all of us were watching closely as the old man talked to Ollie.

"Remember?" Jones continued. "I said that there comes a time for everyone, when the choice between love and hate becomes clear. I told you that the choice—when it is offered—will be like the knife edge of a cliff. And with that choice, you really begin to *live*"—Jones paused and cut his eyes toward Blair Houston—"or you become like her."

"I don't ever want to be like her," Ollie said.

"I know you don't," Jones responded gently, "but trust me, she was about to push you into that camp."

"What do you mean?"

"Son," Jones said, "she really did intend to separate you from your mother. I have removed that opportunity from her. Now, only you and I *know* that, so there are no more conversations about the subject needed."

"But, Jones," Ollie said, choking up, "I don't want you to take the blame for what I've done."

"I am doing this willingly, Ollie," Jones explained. "I'm doing it because I love you. The choice you make now is whether you will continue to produce hate or decide to *accept* love. It's a 'one or the other' proposition. By accepting the love I am offering you, the tires—and all the other things you've pulled around here—are off the books."

"Does that mean—"

"That means I'm taking it all. The blame, the guilt, the fear . . . I have it. You are starting fresh." Jones winked at the boy, then hugged him. "Take care of your mother, Ollie. No more of this," he said with a quick jerk of his head toward the tower of tires. Then the old man smiled and hugged the boy again.

When Ollie finally released his grip on the old man, he stepped back and asked, "Jones . . . when can we talk? I mean, just us, with no one around?"

"Anytime!" The old man laughed as he walked around him and toward the stage. Over his shoulder he called, "Don't worry, Ollie. I'll be around. I always am!"

At the edge of the stage, Jones stopped and extended his arms. Holding his wrists close together, he smiled at the officers, who looked terribly unsure at the moment. Brick Mason, to his credit, was holding Blair Houston on the other side of the stage. This, despite her screaming, "You are fired!" over and over again.

"Come on, fellas," Jones urged with a smile. "It's okay. Cuff me and take me in. I wouldn't mind the air-conditioning."

Still, the officers didn't move, and it didn't look like they were going to. Both had been to Jones's Five & Dime for coffee at the Peace Table. Clearly they did not want to arrest him, but when Jones glanced over at Blair Houston and said, "It'll get you away from her," the old man was handcuffed and on his way to jail in record time.

I hurried to my truck but had parked so far away that by the time it was cranked and moving, it was too late to follow the police car. I saw it leave, though. And I heard it too.

Arriving at the Orange Beach Justice Center too late to see the old man before he was taken inside, I was just in time to greet the arresting officers as they exited the building. Knowing both, I had seen Jones insist on being handcuffed and didn't blame them for that, but I was not happy they had used their lights and siren all the way to the jail. I told them so too.

"Hey, Andy, come on," they said. "You know him . . . he *made* us run the lights and siren. He loved it!"

"Yeah," I admitted. "That sounds just like him," and I apologized.

For whatever reason, I was not allowed to see Jones until the next day and was told I could get in at nine (which sounded familiar). I was prompt and drank coffee with four police officers, two city council members, and Ken Grimes, the city manager. We all sat in the cell with Jones in chairs that had been borrowed from offices. I couldn't help but notice the heavy door was wide open, held fast courtesy of a yellow bungee cord.

I stayed until that evening and not only got to spend time with the old man but enjoyed listening to the conversations he had with the other officers and city officials who were in and out of the cell all day.

Keely showed up around noon with salads from Cosmo's, and the three of us were alone for lunch.

Later, as she got ready to leave, Keely hugged the old man and cried. "You saved my life," she said. "I will never be able to repay you, but I will *never* forget what I've learned." The old man just beamed.

"Jones," Keely said, "are you sure you can handle the store? I'll say no to everything and stay as long as you need me . . ."

"The store will be fine, and I will be fine," the old man said. "Go. It's time. You know you are loved, and I'm very proud of you." They hugged again. She said good-bye to me and walked out of the cell, her footsteps echoing down the hall.

"What was that about?" I asked.

"Living a victorious life," he replied, and I didn't ask any more questions. I'd been around him long enough. Even without the details, I knew what he meant.

When the phone rang, I turned the clock on the bedside table toward me. It read 3:27 a.m. I was wondering why the time seemed familiar as I answered. "Hello," I croaked and cleared my throat.

"Andy?"

"Yes . . . ?"

"Hey, this is Ken Grimes."

"Oh, hi, Ken."

"Yeah, hi," he said. "I'm sorry to be calling this late, but ahh . . . well, they just called me from the jail . . . ?"

"Okay?" I was waking up quickly. "Is something wrong?"

"Yeah, maybe, but probably not."

I paused before asking, "What does that mean?" He was silent a beat too long. "Ken!" I said. "What's going on?"

"Jones is gone."

I said nothing.

Ken waited before finally asking, "Are you there?"

"Yep."

"Did you hear me? Jones is gone."

"I heard you," I said and sighed. "Is this a problem for you guys? Or is it going to be?"

"No," Ken said, surprising me. "Not now, and not next week. The cell door was open and stayed open because Jones was never charged with anything. As far as anyone knows, he never went close enough to Blair Houston's house to be charged with criminal trespass. And as the chief said, there's no city statute against walking around at night with a tire on your shoulder."

I was relieved. "Okay, then. Thanks very much for letting me know."

"No problem," Ken said. "Hey, will the old guy be all right?"

"Without a doubt," I assured him. "This is not totally unexpected. He'll be fine."

"Okay, then. Well . . . where do you think he's headed?"

"I don't know," I said, "but you can bet he'll be around."

"Really?" Ken asked. It was a one-word question that allowed me to end our call with the one thing about Jones that I knew for sure.

"Oh yeah, really," I assured him. "He *will* be around. He always is."

Twenty-nine

Predictably, I couldn't go back to sleep. Finally, I got dressed, woke Polly to tell her I was going to drive around for a while, and slipped out of the house. Through dawn and on into full daylight, I looked everywhere I imagined he might be, but never spotted the old man.

Finally, headed south on the Beach Express, I crossed the Canal Bridge and saw The Wharf spread out below me. It was early on a Sunday morning, and the huge complex was as empty as I'd expected.

Circling around, I drove through the main entrance and parked on the side of Main Street opposite the store. Exiting the truck, I headed across. My intention was to see if the old man had spent the night in the store, but when I reached the median, I glanced up at the second floor and stopped. I was confused.

I looked around, attempting to relocate myself. From where I stood, I peered up again but could not spot the sign for Jones's Five & Dime. Was I in the right place? Because of the empty parking spaces, had I gone down too far? Not far enough?

I moved back and to my right. Standing in the middle of Main Street, I looked to the marlin sculptures and from there, carefully counted the palm trees back to where I was standing. Eight. I looked up to the second floor again. I was in the right place. The sign was gone.

I ran, taking the steps two at a time. The door was unlocked, of course, and I stepped into the air-conditioning while attempting to catch my breath. I stood there as my heart rate slowed. After a moment, my breathing had eased back as well, but my brain was still trying to catch up to what my eyes were taking in.

"Jones?" I called. There was no answer, and I didn't try again because I knew he wasn't there. There was no clanging when I'd come through the door. The cowbell was gone. And so was every last piece of merchandise in the store.

The place had been swept clean. The walls looked as if they'd been painted, the windows polished, but the merchandise was gone. And the rows of shelves? It wasn't that they were empty . . . they were gone.

Still not having moved, my eyes roamed left, right, to the back. Then I did it again, just to confirm what I had seen. I sighed and stepped forward. There was nothing left in the entire place. Nothing . . . except the Peace Table.

The table—and the books that made up its legs—had not been moved. I stepped up to it and stood where I had been sitting only . . . a couple of days ago? *Good grief*, I thought. It felt as if a month had passed.

I looked at the arrowheads as I slowly circled the table, stopping when I reached the place Jones usually sat. I was still for several minutes, simply looking into the swirling grain of the wood. There, colors I'd never even seen in dreams dissolved into each other.

I thought of Jones and that night so long ago when he'd found me living under a pier. I remembered watching him teach a parenting class and how he'd built a treehouse for my boys. I could recall every hour I had listened to the old man talk as he invested in me.

At that particular moment, I remembered a specific line he repeated often. "Anybody can see the surface," he'd say, "but a wise person searches deeply. Focus your vision *below* the surface. Only then will secrets be revealed to you."

With those words echoing in my head and mesmerized by the billowing colors, I tried to do as he had instructed, this time with a table. I located two opposing grains of the wood that despite their curving swirls ran a tight parallel through the table's heart.

Now, I am aware that it was probably my imagination, but as I focused my gaze deep between those two parallel grains, I saw a man and a boy in a canoe. Both had long black hair, and their skin was the color of faded copper. They were clothed in natural furs and laughed as they paddled.

I saw them glide the canoe onto a bank where they were greeted by a beautiful woman and a lovely young girl. Others of the same people joined them at the river's edge until their numbers were overwhelming.

As my vision grew cloudy, an old man walked from their midst. His skin was the color of the people crowded around him, but everything else was Jones. The image slowly faded, but just before it vanished completely, the old man turned to look at me. First he smiled, then he winked . . . and was gone.

"You okay?"

At the sound of Jim Bibby's voice, I jumped so hard I almost fell down.

"Jim!" I said, holding my chest. "You almost scared me to death!"

"I'm sorry," he said and laughed. "I thought surely you heard me come in . . ."

"No, I didn't," I said and attempted to laugh with him.

"I just saw your truck out there and figured you were up here. What are you going to do with the place?"

I frowned. "What am I going to do? With *what* place?"

"This place," he said. "Here."

"I don't even know what you're talking about. When did you clear this out?" I asked. "Did Jones not pay the lease?"

Jim put his hands on his hips and gave me a sidelong glance. "Yeah, he paid the lease," he said. "For five years. And he listed you as the beneficiary of its remainder."

I didn't know what to say and for once, in a move totally unlike me, said nothing.

"I thought you were ready to do something with it," Jim said as he began to move around. "You sure got all that merchandise out of here quickly."

"I didn't move that stuff," I said. "I thought *you* did. Your guys moved it all *in*, right?"

Jim was already shaking his head. "No. Not us. Jones *asked* me to move it in, but we don't do that, and I told him so. Then he asked me to move the table in, and I told him again, we don't do that. So if *you* didn't do it, he just hired somebody else. But we never touched any of it."

I didn't mention it but *did* remember that every time I'd questioned Jones about this very topic, he would say that he had *asked* Jim Bibby to do it. The old man never actually said Jim *did* anything.

We talked a bit more before Jim had to leave, but as he walked out the door, he made it clear that the space was now my responsibility. "Hey, figure it out," he said. "I have to put the utilities in your name tomorrow."

Epilogue

Autumn has arrived now. The moist, steamy air has moved south for the winter and the sand dunes are coming into bloom. It's a beautiful time of the year; an opportunity for the local people to take a breath before the Shrimp Festival in Gulf Shores.

The Shrimp Festival is always held the second weekend in October, but for now, with the crowds still a couple of weeks out, Orange Beach and Gulf Shores are both pretty quiet. The summer tourists are gone and the snowbirds—our name for the winter visitors—have not yet arrived.

The coffee conversations are still happening, but only once a week now and hosted by Pastor Ruark at the church. They say he's a new man and doing a great job as host and leader. I hear his advice is wise, his stories funny, and his coffee incredibly mediocre.

Blair Houston Monroe finally hired someone with a bucket truck to remove the tires from her flagpole. Brick (her manservant) had attempted without success to cut them off with an array of power tools. As an aside, it is shocking how much damage a steel-belted radial can do to a chainsaw.

Even though I didn't know either of them well, I think of Oliver

Sutherland and Keely Higgins quite often. Both have managed to keep in touch with me, mostly to ask if I've seen Jones, but that's fine. I understand.

Ollie and his mom moved to the other side of the state–Dothan, Alabama–before school started. Mrs. Sutherland was offered a great position at Bob Woodall Air Care Systems and for several reasons, she thought it best to start fresh in a new town.

Ollie came by to see me before they left. He asked if I thought Jones would know they had moved. I assured him that yes, Jones would know and be nearby, no matter what. I remembered to ask Ollie what Jones had given him that day in Blair Houston's yard and he pulled it out of his pocket.

It was the small, off-white drawstring bag I had seen that day. He opened it and showed me a huge acorn. I had one, too, of course, but when Ollie turned the acorn around in his hand, I saw it had been marked. Burned into its side, in tiny block letters–THE PEACEMAKER OAK.

"He wrote me a poem too," Ollie said, digging into the bag and fishing out a rolled-up piece of paper. He opened it and held it up for me to read. In the old man's handwritten scrawl, the note said:

> When you are discouraged,
> When you're feeling sad and blue,
> Remember that the mighty oak,
> Was once a nut like you!
> Love, Jones

Keely is living in–of all places–Clanson, Florida.

It seems that Judge Gritney kept a closer eye on her than anyone knew. The timing still seems odd to me, but, apparently, the judge offered Keely a clerking position on the afternoon before the day of

Blair Houston's big show. The offer came with a unique opportunity. If Keely does well, she will be awarded the scholarship to law school that is named for the judge's daughter.

"She is doing very well," Judge Gritney told me recently.

I had called her to ask if Polly and I could help Keely in some way. "No," the judge said. "Thank you, but Keely is thriving." Then she said, "Well, she is thriving in every way but one."

"What is that?" I asked, suddenly concerned.

"I have grown to love and appreciate Keely," the judge said, "but I have become concerned about her penchant for wild exaggeration. Especially when she talks about the old man who owned the dime store."

"Oh?" was all I said.

"Yes, and while I am aware that she is grateful to him for helping her, some of the stories about the things he did while she was in Orange Beach are just ridiculous."

"Yes, ma'am," I said and tried not to laugh.

With five years left on that paid lease, The Wharf actually put my name above the doors in big block letters. At first, I was horrified and asked Jim to *please* have it taken down. He laughed his response and told me the three-foot-tall letters were another thing the old man had paid for and that he'd be glad to take it all down if he got a written authorization from Jones.

I griped a little more and Jim said, "Quit telling me you don't need the place, and figure out what to do with it." It turned out to be great advice.

We could not move the Peace Table; therefore, we had a beautiful glass enclosure constructed around it—a sound chamber.

I record audiobooks there, do interviews for *The Professional Noticer* podcast, and do my live show on all social media platforms called the *Andy Andrews Blue Plate Special–Lunchtime, Learning, and*

Laughter. We call it Wisdom Harbour Studios & General Store. It's on the second level, eight palms down from the marlin sculptures, on the west side of The Wharf—all in the location formerly known as Jones's Five & Dime.

When the remodel started, we found some unexpected surprises in the tiny closet. There was a huge sack of Just Jones Java coffee beans, an almost-as-large bag of acorns from the Peacemaker Oak, and the hat Blair Houston Monroe left in the Five & Dime the day Jones kicked her out.

There is a large open space now for people to come in, visit, and watch as we record. My books are scattered around, and I sign them all. Jones's suitcase—the one he left in town years ago—is on display. And, of course, Blair Houston's hat hangs where visitors can put it on their heads and have a photo taken.

A lot of folks just like to linger around the glass sound booth whether I'm there or not. From many angles, there is a great view of the Peace Table.

I totally understand the attraction. After all, I am still not immune to its presence. Many times, when the store is empty and the people who work with me have gone home . . . when I'm alone inside the glass booth and no one is watching . . . I will look into the table.

I'm aware that it's probably my imagination, but as I gaze into those colors, deep between the opposing grains of the wood, an old man often comes into view. Honestly, the color of his skin varies from one sighting to another, but everything else is just Jones.

However he appears, the image always fades eventually. But every time I see him, just before he disappears, the old man turns to look at me.

He smiles . . . he winks . . . and he's gone.

About the Author

Hailed by a *New York Times* reporter as "someone who has quietly become one of the most influential people in America," Andy Andrews is a bestselling novelist, speaker, and consultant for some of the world's most successful teams, largest corporations, and fastest-growing organizations. Listeners in more than one hundred countries have subscribed to his weekly podcast, *The Professional Noticer*, on AndyAndrews.com/podcast and other sites that offer podcast subscriptions. He also live streams the *Andy Andrews Blue Plate Special–Lunchtime, Learning, and Laughter* on all social media platforms.

Andy is also the creator of WisdomHarbour.com–a portal that has become one of the most shared websites of the decade. He has spoken at the request of four United States presidents and works closely with America's Special Operations Command.

Zig Ziglar said, "Andy Andrews is the best speaker I have ever seen."

Andy is the author of the *New York Times* bestsellers *The Noticer, How Do You Kill 11 Million People?*, and the modern classic *The Traveler's Gift*–which has sold millions of copies worldwide.

He lives in Orange Beach, Alabama, with his wife, Polly, and their two sons.